Praise for *Two Cheers for Politics*

"*Two Cheers for Politics* is a powerful antidote to the despair that characterizes discussions of democracy in our times, combining clear-eyed analysis of the challenges democracies face with a refreshing historical diagnosis of how we got to this point—and how we might move beyond it. Jedediah Purdy's eloquent book restores moral dignity and political plausibility to the idea of democracy."

—Pratap Bhanu Mehta, Princeton University

"In this imaginative history of ideas, Purdy provides a provocative account of democracy—what it is, what it has been, and what it might be if only we believed in it. This is a bracing critique of politics as usual and an important defense of democratic life."

—Katrina Forrester, Harvard University

"What a demanding, profound, and timely book! I started Purdy's excavation of anti-political beliefs with a confidence that I both knew and scorned his targets, and found instead an intimate portrait of my own fears and a fascinating genealogy of the antidemocratic frameworks that pass as democratic. *Two Cheers for Politics* reads easily over rough terrain—dare we take power for a chaotic we, dare we trust in the incompleteness of shared sovereignty? I strongly recommend this brilliant fabric of our past and possible futures woven together."

—Zephyr Teachout, professor of law, Fordham University

"Purdy's sweeping review of the historical and philosophical underpinnings of democracy reminds us that the problems we face are not new. Concentrated economic interests often try to narrow the scope of what we can achieve through collective political action, but we have the potential to shake loose the cobwebs of our Constitution and give life to a multiracial democracy. Too many have shed blood for the right to vote for us to pretend now that politics don't matter."

—Rev. Dr. William J. Barber II, author of
We Are Called to Be a Movement

"Purdy brilliantly argues that we need politics, and that our politics needs to be democratic. Democracy means voting rights, but also much more: an economy that empowers citizens and a culture where what joins us together matters more than what divides us. The alternative is an apathy and anti-politics which will make justice impossible. We need to defend our democracy and also to build it up and deepen it."

—Ro Khanna, member of Congress and
author of *Dignity in a Digital Age*

"An essayist and moralist for our generation, long known for capturing the incongruity between our arrangements and our aspirations with great eloquence, Purdy has become the advocate for redeeming democracy from its limitations that we need right now. Addressing how constitutional law and economic hierarchy leave Americans tempted to despair, Purdy avoids blind alleys in search of exits from political impasse, with self-rule by equal citizens a credible—indeed, our only—hope."

—Samuel Moyn, Yale University

TWO CHEERS FOR POLITICS

TWO CHEERS FOR POLITICS

WHY DEMOCRACY IS FLAWED, FRIGHTENING—AND OUR BEST HOPE

JEDEDIAH PURDY

BASIC BOOKS
New York

Basic Books
Hachette Book Group
1290 Avenue of the Americas, New York, NY 10104
www.basicbooks.com

Printed in the United States of America

First Edition: August 2022

Published by Basic Books, an imprint of Perseus Books, LLC, a subsidiary of
Hachette Book Group, Inc. The Basic Books name and logo is a trademark
of the Hachette Book Group.

The Hachette Speakers Bureau provides a wide range of authors for speaking
events. To find out more, go to www.hachettespeakersbureau.com or call
(866) 376-6591.

The publisher is not responsible for websites (or their content) that are not
owned by the publisher.

Print book interior design by Jeff Williams

Library of Congress Cataloging-in-Publication Data

Names: Purdy, Jedediah, 1974– author.
Title: Two cheers for politics : why democracy is flawed-and our best hope /
    Jedediah Purdy.
Description: First edition. | New York : Basic Books, 2022. | Includes
    bibliographical references and index.
Identifiers: LCCN 2021054813 | ISBN 9781541673021 (hardcover) |
    ISBN 9781541673007 (ebook)
Subjects: LCSH: Political culture—United States. | Democracy—United States. |
    United States—Politics and government—Public opinion. | United States—
    Politics and government—21st century.
Classification: LCC JK1726 .P87 2022 | DDC 320.973—dc23/eng/20220327

LC record available at https://lccn.loc.gov/2021054813

ISBNs: 9781541673021 (hardcover), 9781541673007 (ebook)

LSC-C

Printing 1, 2022

CONTENTS

INTRODUCTION

Imagine four history textbooks written in 2050, each one reflecting a different version of our future. They all explain that the 2020s began as a decade of crisis, plagued by a broken climate, deep inequality, and clashes over basic facts like whether vaccines work and how many votes were cast in recent elections. In these decades, the books recall, people around the world asked whether democracy had already failed. They blinked at the future and wondered who would save them.

The first textbook tells how strongmen saved us—some of us, anyway. Their enemies called them nationalists, populists, and bullies, and they gladly played the part. Some of their supporters didn't like the ways their countries were changing—in race, language, sex and gender roles—and wanted older codes back in place. Others felt that politics had become a joke, a charade whose only point was to keep well-connected insiders comfortable. They wanted leaders who talked straight even—especially—if they offended or alarmed the insiders.

In Poland, Hungary, Brazil, and the United States, these strongmen served their clans—partisan and ethnic. When politicians in the United States said "America first!" no one doubted which

Americans they meant. They treated the country as the property of the right kinds of people, and sometimes they looked after those people. Sometimes they left them to take their chances with pandemics, climate change, and a global capitalism that the strongmen occasionally decried but somehow never actually challenged. Popular loyalty survived these tests of faith. The strongmen—and women, soon enough—did what it took to make sure that only their favored candidates won elections.

In fact, this came to be what democracy meant. "Defend our democracy!" chanted supporters of Donald Trump Jr. in November 2032, as they mobbed the offices of election boards across the country. After that, the history books explain, it became clear that there was nothing sacred about getting more votes. The point was for the right people to win. After a struggle, they did. The years from roughly 1965 (when the Voting Rights Act became law and the Hart-Celler Act ended four decades in which immigration was tightly restricted and mostly confined to white Europeans) to 2024 are officially remembered as a failed experiment in political equality and cosmopolitanism. The year 2016 is remembered as the beginning of the end for the elite that orbited universities, the professions, nonprofits, political staffs, and legacy media.

The second history book tells the story of how experts saved us. Politicians couldn't solve the climate crisis. Their thinking was narrow and short term, and their constituents combined these limitations with flat-out ignorance and fantasy. Stepping into the breach, the central bankers of the rich countries joined technologists to create a sweeping innovation agenda that halfway saved the planet and was also very profitable. They even shaped their program to soften racial and regional inequality, likening it to a new New Deal, greener and more inclusive than the first. Some would-be strongman politicians railed against the bankers and techies, but the balance of public opinion was for solving problems, and the strongmen faded because they offered no solutions. Other politicians bowed to the experts, who barely bothered to return the courtesy.

The experts, the engineers, and the very rich had done what needed doing when governments could not. Their success put politics in its place—as a sideshow. In hindsight, the first decades of the twenty-first century were the time when a new global constitution grew in response to crises that traditional politics could not master. Historians explain that the emergency measures that central bankers took to avoid complete economic meltdown in 2008–2009 and to keep economies afloat during the pandemic that began in 2020 were premonitions of a new regime built on an old principle: the legitimate ruler is whoever can keep us safe. The COVID pandemic also showed, historians later relate, that it is madness to trust questions of life and death, *which have scientific answers*, to the whims of voters (especially the kind who, given the chance, might choose strongmen).

Elections continue in the experts' 2050, but the most important decisions are beyond the scope of politics: who can create money, whose debts or other assets get purchased by the Federal Reserve and its sister institutions, what limits on movement the current public health situation requires. The textbooks tell how, in the early decades of the twenty-first century, people of goodwill realized that democracy does not mean that majorities rule; it means a rational system of governance that shows concern and respect for every member of society. If some stakeholders (a term that has replaced the antique-sounding "citizens") see it differently, their governors will still take their interests—their real interests—seriously and hope their children will see things more rationally.

The third textbook is a mess of clashing stories and lessons. It is issued in almost unrecognizably different versions to satisfy the discordant expectations of schools and readers across a fractured country. In this future, no one saved us. There is endless quarrel over where to lay blame for the failure. Most countries have their own version of the Great Decline that began in 2016. Here, in capsule, is the American one. In some election years after 2020, waves of enthusiasm swept the cities, the countryside, or both. Partisans girded up to save the country from the other side. Sometimes they also had a program to restore it or to make it truly great for the first time. But the filibuster, the Supreme Court, the Electoral College, and social media all did their work. Every river of reform was lost in a great swampy delta of institutional vetoes and impassioned popular resistance.

Historians agree that the signal political facts of the early twenty-first century were the two presidential elections that Republican presidents won in 2000 and 2016 without popular majorities, the Supreme Court's 6–3 Republican majority after only one Republican president won the popular vote between 1992 and 2020, and the persistent belief among partisans that the 2020 election was stolen. As it slouched toward 2050, the country remained divided between what were, in effect, two minority parties— the right-wing one unable to win popular majorities, the center-left one unable to take control of a national government skewed to small states and rural voters—neither able to change much besides reversing each other's regulatory policies and marginally moving marginal tax rates. After a nationalist Republican won the Electoral College (losing the popular vote) and entered the White House in 2028, California's governor announced that their state would no longer recognize federal authority over certain matters, including immigration. Four years later, the woman whom many expected to be Texas's last Republican governor reciprocated amid claims that the Democratic president-elect had won by fraud. Talk of secession migrated, depending on which party dominated in Washington.

Meanwhile, the planet heated up, and more people died in every season of storms, heat waves, and crop failure. In 2050, those who are able stock up on what they hope will help them survive real breakdown: for some that means guns and solar arrays, for others second and even third passports. Those who don't have money hunker down and cultivate relationships with their neighbors, whose help they expect to need. Mutual aid studies becomes a major field in the remaining schools of public policy, and a book called *Dancing in the Ruins* is a best seller in what is called, for reasons no one recalls, Blue America. In Red America, which has its own best-seller list, *Joy in the End Times* is riding high. In international airports, Americans off to shop for real estate in New Zealand pass Chinese returning from doing the same in British Columbia. Depending on where you are, your history textbook will give you one story or another of how the Great Decline got started.

These three futures are already with us. The strongman scenario doesn't need much elaboration. It resembles what citizens of many countries saw, or feared, in the 2010s: in far-right electoral wins in Brazil, India, the United States, Hungary, Poland, and elsewhere and in nationalist irruptions from France to Burma. The experts-save-us future is a little less in the headlines, but two of the most important and creative political acts of the twenty-first century so far are the massive debt purchases that central banks launched during the economic near collapse of 2008–2009 and the beginning of the COVID-19 pandemic in 2020. This show of ingenuity and power, in a time of hobbled and inept government, has prompted a range of commentators to urge that the institutions that are able to govern should be encouraged to do so. In 2020, the historian and prominent interpreter of global economics Adam Tooze argued in *Foreign Policy* that "it is time to give our financial and monetary system a new constitutional purpose" to address environmental crises, inequality, and slow growth. In 2021, the *Financial Times* commissioned Kim Stanley Robinson, a beloved science-fiction author and self-described democratic socialist, to urge "carbon quantitative easing" in which central banks would effectively finance a Green New Deal. Both Tooze and Robinson took care to say that their proposals would need democratic authorization. But the logic of events may call for more. If voters and elected officials can't get their act together, will institutions that have the capacity to *do something* go ahead and take political silence, or cacophony, as a form of permission? Should they? After all, the next best alternative might be the no-one-saves-us scenario in which the political system spins the wheels of its own dysfunction in a world that can't afford inaction.

There is a fourth history book on the shelf. It tells how we saved ourselves, how, in the early twenty-first century, democratic citizens overcame their impasses and addressed their crises. This one is the hardest to forecast. The scenarios recounted in the other three textbooks all but write themselves as extensions of the events of the early twenty-first century. A democratic revival would be a change in direction powered by the creativity and action of citizens. It would be a reminder that history is not just something that happens to us or the cacophony of stories we tell about the mess we were born into: it is also something we make.

It is easy to disbelieve quietly in democracy, to treat it as a nice idea but one that, taken literally, would be impossible to achieve and dangerous to attempt. So we give it other meanings: endless conversation, broad consultation, the rule of law, the free market, or whatever set of policies we and our friends believe would be obviously good.

I argue that we should try taking democracy literally. In its Greek root it means rule by the *demos*, the ordinary free people of the polity, which today should mean everyone in our political order. Both roots of the word are essential: *demos*, people, and *kratia*, rule. At its core, democracy is a disposition of power. To be sure, it is not only that: it has ethical, cultural, and constitutional dimensions; there are rights that a democracy must respect and ways that the losers of elections must be protected. But the linchpin principle of democracy is that when there must be a decision binding on all, the people decide, and majorities are the best stand-in for the people. In a phrase, majorities rule.

Of course we don't need to make a collective decision—and shouldn't!—on the merits of James Joyce's *Ulysses*. But on policing and national health insurance, we do. On God's existence and Romare Bearden's paintings, people can live by their own judgments. But on the tax code and how to pay for education, there is no getting out of a shared decision. On those questions, which unavoidably set the terms of our common life, democracy means that the decision belongs to the majority of the people who will live with the result.

As I write in the years after Joe Biden's election to the presidency in 2020, the odds are often thought to be running against a democratic future. We are a country of people who have discovered that politics is wildly important, a matter of life and death, but who also feel abraded, assaulted, and exhausted by it and more than halfway wish it would just go away. Many of us both find ourselves more passionately attached to democracy than ever before and also suspect it is a childish dream, an ideal that humanity can't sustain. In 2020, the highest share of Americans voted since 1900, but what drove them to the polls was more grim worry than eager hope. As the election approached, 89 percent of Donald Trump's supporters said they believed that, if Biden won, he would bring lasting harm to the country. Ninety percent of Biden's supporters said the same about Trump. Fear of fellow citizens and the country they would create if they won was the fuel that fired the vote.[1]

Both before and after rioters in January 2021 stormed the United States Capitol to protest what they imagined was a conspiracy to deny Donald Trump the presidency, commentators warned that American democracy was undergoing a "near-death experience." In the Trump years, "Is Democracy Dying?" became a standard question, and a raft of books carried titles such as *How Democracies Die*, *How Democracy Ends*, and *The People vs. Democracy*. Biden's safe arrival at the White House on Inauguration Day didn't allay the anxiety. In February 2021, nearly a third of the country denied that he had won legitimately, including two-thirds of Republicans. They thought democracy *had* died. Not surprisingly, growing numbers of people said they expected political violence was likely to result from elections in the near future.[2]

In 2020, surveys showed the highest level of discontent with democracy ever recorded. In the United States, the share of people saying they are not satisfied with democracy as they know it climbed from under 25 percent in 1995 to over 50 percent in 2000. This sentiment began rising after the 2008 financial crisis and election and stairstepped up in the presidential election years of 2012 and 2016, suggesting that the more Americans' attention was drawn to politics, the more it alienated them.[3]

Dissatisfaction is not the same as despair. It can mean, rather, holding government to a high standard, asking more of it than it is doing. There is a strand of this constructive angst in attitudes toward democracy. Less than a quarter of Americans express confidence that the national government will do the right thing "most of the time," down from 77 percent in 1964. (This is not a steady decline. It was lower in 1994 and 2010–2011 than in 2021, but it has been below 25 percent since 2007—a long run of pessimism.) Nonetheless, people see the national government as having broad responsibilities, including ensuring clean air and water (87 percent), high-quality education through high school (79 percent), health insurance (64 percent), and adequate retirement (58 percent). It is quite a bind to believe that Washington needs to do these things but will probably do them badly or not at all. You might well conclude that a political system that didn't do its job was failing. If instead it produced a lot of political theater that seemed to make violence ever more likely, you might conclude that it was dying. You might wonder whether its dying could be for the best, or at least something to be accepted.[4]

Those who announce themselves the most passionately committed to the defense of democracy are often eager to confess (sometimes but not always quietly) that they do not, really, believe it can work. Sometimes they present these confessions as political wisdom. In February 2021, Democratic senator Chris Murphy explained his support for the second impeachment of Donald Trump, calling it necessary "in order for our democracy to survive." The previous summer, Murphy had told the *New York Times*: "I have a real belief that democracy is unnatural. We don't run anything important in our lives by democratic vote other than our government. Democracy is so unnatural that it's illogical to think it would be permanent. It will fall apart at some point, and maybe that isn't now, but maybe it is." Murphy's cultivated pessimism is emblematic. The casual declaration that "we don't run anything important in our lives by democratic vote," which is supposed to be worldly, suggests a failure to spare a thought to labor unions, quite a few religious communities, and many self-governing civic organizations that do decide important questions by majority vote.

In this light, the call to save democracy has the tone of proposing one last try for a relationship, emphasis on *last*.[5]

Yet we are asking more of politics than the country has in many decades. For the left, the calls include a Green New Deal, universal health care, free higher education, a jobs guarantee, deep reform of policing and public safety, and repair of the wrenching racial inequality whose roots run from slavery through Jim Crow and mass incarceration, and through decades of policy that have excluded working people of color from building wealth. On the right, they include various forms of taking back control, such as retrenching global capitalism in favor of candidly nationalist industrial and trade policy and cutting back dramatically on economic migration. These new demands on politics do not overlap in many particulars, but they start from a shared sense that in essential respects *things are not fine* and will not be unless we find a way to take them in hand.

The economy is not fine: globalization and automation have hollowed out industries and regions, inequality in wealth and income has spiraled upward for nearly fifty years, privileged groups find ways to hold on to everything from family wealth to seats in "meritocratic" colleges and professions, and many tens of millions of people go through life with low wages, little security, and fear that illness or injury, a lost job, or another piece of bad luck will sink everything. Those who have gathered some wealth know that their assets have been buoyed by more than a decade of bubbles engineered by monetary policy and expect another crisis, although no one can confidently say when or how it will come. Those who have little find themselves targeted by social-media misinformation and "innovations" in opioid marketing and compelled to take jobs driving for Uber or fulfilling Amazon orders. A global pandemic shook the lives of many workers but increased the concentrated wealth of billionaires and online merchants. The big get bigger. All of this is the result, more or less, of the "natural" play of capitalism. It will go on this way unless we find a politics that can get control of it and give it a different shape. Politics—whether left or

right, aimed at taxing "the billionaire class" or high-salaried professionals, for or against affirmative action—has become fiercely
distributional because the economy is fiercely distributional, and
we are past the time when majorities could be persuaded to pretend otherwise.[6]

The planet is not fine. In 2021, record-breaking and deadly heat
waves, forest fires, and floods seemed to come weekly. These are
only a glimpse of what climate change promises in the next century. Yet despite weak-tea promises to cut greenhouse gas emissions,
those emissions increased by 50 percent in the first two decades of
the twenty-first century. For many adults reading this book, global
carbon levels have risen more in their lifetimes than in all previous
human history. Other pressures on the planet's health are rising
at similar rates: demand for fresh water, exploitation of farmland
and fisheries, manufacture of plastics and concrete, use of toxins.
If we somehow managed, almost miraculously, to stabilize global
climate trends, we would need to turn to a host of looming and ne-
glected crises. It is painfully clear that the environmental politics
of the coming decades will center on doing less than we need to
do and struggling over who bears the consequences and over how
best to mitigate what we fail to prevent.[7]

Society is not fine. Fifty-eight percent of Americans say they
believe that others would take advantage of them if they got the
chance. Social trust is declining with each new generation. Almost half of people younger than thirty express low trust in others
across the board, compared to less than a fifth of people over sixty.
Rising rates of suicide and drug overdose deaths have driven life
expectancy down overall in recent years, a reversal of many decades of steady gains. The pandemic that began in 2020 was a stress
test on social trust: almost overnight, it was impossible to know
who might be dangerous—including oneself—and new practices,
from masking to distancing to vaccination, were the only remedy. Yet suspicion and conspiracy theories slowed and sometimes
thwarted the effort to be, as the hopeful signs had it, "in this together." Cultivating mistrust was a political strategy in itself. There
is a larger lesson here. Part of the reason politics is frightening is

that through it we change ourselves, and the change can be for the worse as easily as for the better. Democracy can work only if people are willing to hang together, at least enough to master the crises they can't avoid. It requires a certain kind of civic feeling, including a willingness to abide by the majority's decisions. But democratic politics can perversely reward electoral strategies that destroy this willingness and make democracy itself impossible. We seem to be experimenting now with this self-canceling version of democracy.[8]

The stakes of politics are high, yet there is reason to believe politics is failing and will fail to rise to the occasion. So an age of political passion is also haunted by varieties of political nihilism. The most visible and corrosive version is the politics-as-entertainment trolling of the Trumpist right, which is two parts menace, one part sick joke, and often content to settle for the joke—if all of this comes to nothing, at least we sold some merch and owned the libs. Seen as an episode in the careers of grifters, the Trump presidency began when an entertainer's branding campaign accidentally won the Electoral College and met its poetic denouement when Trump's early strategist, Steve Bannon, was arrested for embezzling funds from a supposed nonprofit that promised to finish Trump's ballyhooed wall on the Mexican border.

But this way of putting it understates the seriousness of the new right-wing politics. Seen in terms of the base that rallied to him, Trump's presidency began when a novelty campaign became a social movement, more charismatic to those who felt it than any since Obama's 2008 run, and ended only when the hard core of that movement stormed the Capitol trying to overturn by force an election loss they found so intolerable as to be obviously illegitimate. One of these time lines describes a bad joke that gets worse, the other an upheaval that almost breaks democracy. But there is a unity to the seeming opposites. The Trump administration was in many respects an assault on liberal and democratic government, but it was also so lazy, slipshod, and shambolic that hardly anyone involved developed a program for using the power of the state, other than for self-enrichment. It was, to the relief of many, a singular political victory that ushered in four years of willful incompetence and neglect. The arc of the Trump years fed on and reinforced the feeling, already widespread, that politics is cathartic theater, occasionally jolted by episodes of public violence. We all now live with this species of nihilism, which denies itself nothing and offers the same. Talk of a coming civil war, sometimes a touch ironic and sometimes not ironic at all, can be a way of giving up on politics, whose basic fact is coexistence. Taking your gun, or your laptop, and going home is a personal secession.

Among those who fiercely opposed the Trump administration, there is also nihilism, although it is compatible with high-mindedness. It takes the form of living as if the American experiment had already failed, perhaps even while talking about the need to keep it alive. It means piling up what resources you can for your family and friends while quietly cutting ties of common fate with people, regions, histories that you have decided are irredeemable. It may mean taking a certain satisfaction in "knowing" that the country has never been good and is living on borrowed time—an emotional alchemy that splits outrage into cynicism and self-righteousness.

The phrase "burn it all down," which gets voiced mostly on the left and mostly online, is the objective end of all shades of political nihilism. If politics fails, everything burns in time. A failed politics will even start the fire. Yet the nihilistic temptation offers the relief of giving up on something that has felt both obligatory and impossible. It cuts the knot of believing that we cannot escape politics yet cannot make it work, offering the briefly sweet release of "Fuck it. Fuck those people."

Here I am going to ask a favor of you, the reader. I would like you to consider your own feelings and those of the people around you—family, friends, coworkers, whoever. Do you sometimes feel anxious, worried, repelled by other citizens who seem, in your estimation, to be doing their best to wreck the country? Do you wonder whether our politics is going to destroy itself and take some of us with it? Do you turn back to daily life—parents, children, sports, entertainment, quiet—with a sense of relief, hoping public life stays boring for a few days, even a few months, but seeing no way to avoid the fires flaring up again? Do you fear, when you think about it, that we are living on borrowed time? If so, please hold those feelings open and keep them in mind. In this book, I am writing about politics, history, economics, philosophy, and the law, but I am also trying to address those feelings, to understand where they come from, what truth is in them, and whether, in fact, we have a way to get beyond them. I have those feelings, too.

This book is a response to political nihilism and, I hope, a partial remedy—not because it shows that everything is actually good or is going to be OK but because it shows something about how we got here, the ways we have misunderstood democracy and allowed it to be weakened and distorted. This is not a book about the Trump years but about a longer and slower-burning set of crises, which prepared the way for the Trump presidency but did not begin in 2016.

Our political crises did not just befall us like fate. They were conjured up by politics. Sometimes—not always, contrary to certain hopeful formulas—what we have made we can remake once we understand it. The point of politics is precisely that: to turn collective life from fate to shared choice. This is what we have to do now if we are to turn our politics back from a miserable fate to a way of choosing a future.

Politics is not optional, even though we may wish it were. Political life has been the petri dish of many pernicious and vile fantasies, but the most dangerous political fantasy is the antipolitical conceit that we can do without politics. This conceit fosters the neglect of politics, and the cynical practice of it, which worsens its deformations just when we need to ask the most of it. So we tighten the knot of our dilemma, in which politics is both necessary and impossible. We must decide in favor of its necessity if we are going to weaken the grip of its impossibility. Otherwise, we really shall have to give up on it. That loss would be very great— greater even than we tend to realize.

What is often called the crisis of American democracy is not the result of too much democracy but of too little. Too few Americans are able to vote, and those who do vote are prevented from ruling. The national majority that voted for Hillary Clinton in 2016 was thwarted by the antiquated Electoral College, which is prescribed by the Constitution. The national majority that elected a Congress that expanded Medicaid to the working poor in 2010 was thwarted by a Supreme Court that ruled in 2012 that the means of funding the expansion was unconstitutional. As I write in 2021, national majorities that support paid parental leave and public support for childcare are being thwarted in the Senate, where identical representation for each state gives extra power to older, more rural, and whiter voters and therefore, in a polarized country, to Republicans. These are partisan examples, partly because the Republican Party is presently a minoritarian party adapted to an antimajoritarian political system; but tens of millions of Donald Trump's supporters voted to express their own version of the perception that, as a pair of political scientists put it in 2014, "under most circumstances, the preferences of the vast majority of Americans appear to have essentially no impact on which policies the government does or doesn't adopt."[9] The pathologies of contemporary politics—angry partisan clannishness, overheated elections combined with weary doubt that government can do anything—are not evidence that democracy is failing but symptoms of our failure to be democratic.

Our crises are rooted in a decades-long depoliticization, a collapse of political vision, energy, and faith, whose hinge was, most ironically, the democratic victories of 1988–1991, when the Soviet Union disowned one-party rule and dissolved its empire, and "velvet revolutions" swept away autocracies, tore down the Berlin Wall, and dissolved the Iron Curtain between West and East that the wall symbolized. A world that had seemed permanently divided now rushed together, as people were churned by the freedom to move around, to buy and sell, to have a voice and a life on their own terms. In the two decades that followed, many people found it easy, even natural, to imagine that politics had done its historical work, carrying nations to the threshold of what some dissidents from the former Soviet bloc poignantly called "a normal society": a liberal, capitalist order where voters would tack between the reasonable right (a little more market competition, a little more military spending) and the reasonable left (a little more social spending, a little more attention to the environment). The point of elections was mainly to rotate politicians before they got too comfortable and, besides that, to affirm that things were on the right track.

Our understanding of democratic politics is still shaped by those decades, in which it was easy not to think closely about what so many people took for granted. Some Americans came to imagine politics, if they thought about it at all, as a free-form activity that blurred effortlessly into entertainment, dialogue, or entrepreneurship. For others, politics seemed a basically moral enterprise whose goal was to make sure that the right set of human rights was respected, whether through elections or courts or treaties. The apex of democracy—a word that often meant nothing more specific than "good politics"—was not a collective decision among equals about how to live together but a constitution that enshrined the right answers from the start. Images of democracy as basically identical with capitalist markets, the rule of law, or endless conversation threaded through all these ideas. What united these otherwise varying attitudes was a consistent evasion: a turning away from the ideas that politics is centrally about deciding how we will live together and that democracy is the politics in which the power to make those decisions belongs to majorities.

During the same years that liberals and centrists drifted toward these conflict-free visions of politics, in which history seemed to promise consensus among people of goodwill, right-wing politics was coming to be all about conflict, decision, and power. Beginning with Republican scorched-earth campaigns against moderate Democrat Bill Clinton in the 1990s, and culminating (for now) in Donald Trump's refusal to acknowledge defeat in the 2020 presidential election, its creed has been: whatever power our side does not control is not legitimate. Its democracy is an identity politics of "real" Americans and a claim that the country belongs to them.

Drained of conflict or drunk on it, each of these political trends distorted democracy. Democracy is not another name for markets and civil rights, for managing society toward a proper outcome that is already set, let alone a synonym for eternal conversation. And it is, most certainly, not an ethnic "real people's" control of a country.

Democracy is rule by equals. This phrase captures two commitments, which are also two sides of the same coin: to be ruled by majorities of our fellow citizens and to regard all those citizens as our political equals. Democracy is the only form of politics that makes real what we modern people, Americans and others, often say that we believe: that people are equal and free and can shape our shared lives accordingly. This shared power is what makes us citizens. For that power to fall instead to judges or economists or others who are thought to know what the future expects of us, or what the past requires, is a usurpation. So is hoarding that power for a favored group. The soft consensus of experts and jurists can undercut democracy and so can the hard populism of nationalists, who do not see their fellow citizens as genuine equals.

Rule by equals is the keystone of democracy. The core question of politics is who has the power to make a shared world. The democratic answer is that the people who live with those choices should control them and that majorities are the best stand-in for the whole people. The two strongest reasons for this are *plurality* and *equality*. We live in a deeply plural world, made up of many desires, plans, points of view, and histories (personal and collective) of feeling and experience. This plurality is a good thing: it arises because we ourselves are not all the same and we care about our lives. Unlike ants, we must decide how to live together: our common life is not just a fact but a perennial question. And the people who must live together are one another's equals. Equality is not just a fact about IQ scores or physical strength or gender but a moral commitment, indeed the fundamental moral commitment of democracy: that I have no greater or lesser right to decide how we will live together than you have. Anchoring legitimate power to the vote of the majority is not enough to make this equality real, but a democrat believes it is the only and indispensable way to begin.

Unless I say otherwise, I use the word *citizen* to refer to anyone who lives in a political order that, like ours, calls itself democratic. I do not restrict it to those who have the legal status of citizenship. This usage fits democratic principles. The power of citizenship, joint authorship over the conditions of common life, is too essential to be limited to a politically privileged caste.

If democracy is the rule of majorities, what about individual rights? May majorities do whatever they want and still call their governments democracies? No: there are limits. They are the limits necessary to protect democracy itself. Democracy is a form of political freedom partly because a genuine democracy produces no permanent majorities. It is always open for the lines of social conflict and solidarity to shift, through deliberate argument and organizing, so that anyone who has been out of power may find themselves in power instead. To make this principle real, a democracy may not deny full rights to vote and to participate politically to any of its members for any reason. American disenfranchisement of prisoners and people convicted of felonies is a serious mark against the country's standing as a democracy. So is the denial of voting rights to noncitizen residents.

For the same reasons, a democracy must not sustain a caste system in which members of some electoral minority are pressed into dishonored positions, denied the resources and support for full social participation, and generally treated as people who could not plausibly rule their "betters." The possibility of composing a new majority must be socially real, not just theoretically conceivable, and caste systems make it unreal. A democracy must prepare us to live under one another's sovereignty. A democracy also must not permit those in power to suppress criticism, undermine opposition groups, or prohibit the discussion of ideas they regard as dangerous. Democratic principle demands respect for the peaceful transition of power. In these ways, democracy is linked to the rule of law and the protection of individual rights, values central to modern liberalism, including the liberal traditions of social democracy and democratic socialism.[10]

What do these qualifications leave majorities? A great deal—indeed, everything that is legitimately up for decision. Because the cornerstones of democracy are the recognition that there are shared questions we must answer, and the commitment to answering them as equals, majority rule is not a license for any majority to do whatever it wants with everyone else. There must be, for every democratic citizen, a genuine and perennial chance to be a part of ruling, to give answers to unavoidable questions. A majority that denies *that* denies political equality and kicks the strut out from under its own claim to democracy.

All of this may seem unduly abstract. We live in a time that likes to think of itself as practical and unapologetically technical. *Nerd* and *geek* are terms of pride for people who understand how complex systems work. From politics to sports, we listen to statisticians and technicians. There is no better way to catch the attention of self-consciously smart people than to announce that you are about to talk about something boring—which is to say, technical and specific. After all, our everyday reality is that small technologies solve problems while big ideas drive people mad or make them, well, actually boring. In politics, the preference for the technical can foster a sense that we don't need to talk abstractly about democracy, let alone blockier ideas like sovereignty; we need to get into the weeds of voting systems and legislation, where the gearheads go. I share in all of this. I study and teach law, particularly constitutional and environmental law, because I believe we don't understand anything until we see how it works—and, ideally, how to take it apart and put it together a little differently. But decades of work on these questions persuades me that we also need to think clearly about some big questions, such as what we mean when we talk about defending, or achieving, democracy and why it matters so much.

Some of our shying away from thinking too hard about democracy expresses an understandable impulse to shy away from political life altogether. The chief human experience of politics has been to hope to avoid being harmed by it. To be ruled less, and less actively, is a normal and widespread desire, rooted in both the value of everyday life and the rational fear of things getting worse. Everyone has something to lose from politics: work, a home, loved ones, life itself. Much of modern political life is the story of people's efforts to shrink, confine, or get out from under the state and the mass of their fellow citizens who might use it to get power over them. "You must first enable the government to control the governed; and in the next place oblige it to control itself," James Madison wrote, and he reckoned his constitution had achieved this by "THE TOTAL EXCLUSION OF THE PEOPLE IN THEIR COLLECTIVE CAPACITY" from American government. (Yes, he capitalized it this way, as if the Constitution's antidemocratic machinery had prompted a very excited text message.) What saved the American idea of popular sovereignty from tyranny and disaster, Alexis de Tocqueville argued nearly fifty years later, was that Americans did not really mean what they said about the supremacy of the people and lived actually in a rather stable political culture of property rights, limited government, and racial solidarity. Only the horizons of their culture kept democrats within safe bounds.[11]

This skepticism toward politics, and democracy in particular, continued in the twentieth century. The "dogma of democracy," Walter Lippmann wrote in 1930, promised to make people their own enlightened masters, but in reality the effort to build majorities from disparate and distracted citizens only created "an intensification of feeling and a degradation of significance." That was not a misfire but the nature of the thing: "We must assume that a public is inexpert in its curiosity, intermittent, that it discerns only gross distinctions, is slow to be aroused and quickly diverted; that . . . it personalizes whatever it considers, and is interested only when events have been melodramatized in a conflict." A democratic public, Lippmann concluded, was the worst thing in the world to confront the problems of modern economics, technology, or international affairs—or, really, any matter requiring competent knowledge and sustained attention. The only sane thing to do was to confect a system of governing that would direct people mostly to their private affairs, where they were more likely to be prudent and take the trouble to get informed.[12]

Madison, Tocqueville, and Lippmann: the first the preeminent constitutional framer and an early president; the second a literary genius and arguably the most influential interpreter of Americans to themselves; the third perhaps the most important American intellectual of the first half of the twentieth century, when the country took its place astride the world and launched the short American Century. Their three formulas epitomize the touchstone strategies for putting democracy in its place. Madison, the classical liberal republican, proposes a constitutional design to keep the people out and recruit responsible elites who, in turn, will check and balance one another's accumulation of power. Tocqueville, the liberal conservative (not a paradox, except in our parochial lexicon), looks to *mores*, the deep culture of a people, to baffle radicalism and constrain democratic power. Lippmann, who in 1938 helped coin the term *neoliberalism* for a social philosophy that aimed to tamp down democracy's alleged excesses, looks to shift attention to personal affairs, especially economic ones, keeping competing visions of society out of politics except as decoration and enabling competent administrators to oversee stable market competition.[13]

Each begins by saying that the people cannot rule. The very idea is dangerous nonsense. Each then shifts the work of social order someplace else: constitutional design, culture and norms, the economy and private life (properly administered from above). These formulas ebb, flow, and shift, but they have been the perennial antipolitical counterparts of the age of democracy. And, to a great degree, they converge: all hope for the stabilizing effects of responsible elites, all celebrate the narrowing and attenuation of political decisions about the shape of social order, all seek buttresses that will preserve private life and settled custom from the purview of the state. Still today, the familiar guardrails of politics are the putative wisdom of the Constitution and its interpreters at the Supreme Court, the norms that bind responsible politicians and voters, and the more or less autonomous rationality of the economy, which makes its own demands and which no politician can afford to ignore or abuse too far.

These ideas are not just the ideological excuses of people who would like to avoid change. They might well appeal to anyone who is not sure they trust any given majority in their country or any given congress or president. (At the time of writing, in the United States these categories include, not to put too fine a point on it, everyone.) An antidemocratic insult of the Lippmann variety is sure to strike many partisans as a sharp description of the other side. This is why we who live in the age of politics also live in the age of antipolitics. Our institutional and intellectual life, our culture and common sense, are made up substantially of warnings against politics and appeals to alternative sources of order: enduring constitutions, sober norms, the wisdom of markets. These are *antipolitics*, not just nonpolitics, because they are formulated in reaction to modern politics, with its dangerous promise of world making and because—as the examples I have given suggest—they are actually a form of politics themselves, a series of agendas for using and understanding the state.

In the abstract, the back-and-forth between politics and antipolitics could populate an unending seminar on modern life. In practice, antipolitics is killing us. Antipolitics can have value, even a kind of wisdom, when it points to ways of peacefully, safely, and decently ordering our lives without going through politics and the state. But today, it is the global capitalist economy that makes humanity the enemy of the only planet we have. The economic order now remakes the planet itself, at every scale, from the chemistry of the global atmosphere to the risk of fires or storms in every region, on every mountainside or plain. These changes sort people into wildly varying ecological fates: as hedge funders who can buy refuge in favored climates, as farmers' children who can no longer farm, and as refugees from land inundated by rising seas or from places inhabited for tens of thousands of years that are becoming too hot for human life.

Rather than cooling democratic passions, as it was once imagined to do, constitutional antipolitics is heating up the worst political energies. It is the constitutional order that, along with an infusion of oligarchic energies, has given Americans spurious right-wing majorities and rewarded minority-rule strategies that feed on fear. Our common culture, such as it is, has not buffered us from these troubles but increasingly taken their shape, as commodified partisan clannishness. In these conditions, the assurances of antipolitics are unavailing. There is no reason to trust that we can secure the order we need outside the hazards of political change.

Politics is not optional. It is not optional because certain questions arise inevitably from our living together, and the shape of our lives depends on the answers we give them. How is the world's wealth shared—this landscape, that city, these rivers, that power to create money at a keystroke? Who may show up at a hospital and get care? Who may cross a border for work? What kind of power can owners have over workers, what kinds of agreements may those workers enter, who can fire whom and when? Is education a public good or an expensive commodity? May internet platforms choose preferred vendors or speakers and shut down the rest? Is vaccination mandatory? For what might you go to jail? For what might you be ordered to risk dying, and what happens if you refuse? What distinguishes these questions is that they are so involved in our interdependent lives that we cannot each have our own answer. We must live with shared answers, to the disappointment, or worse, of many who would have liked to see things go differently. Politics is how we provide that shared answer. Even if you would like to see some of these questions dissolved out of existence, that project would be a political one.

Democracy is scary. It means that the people we live with rule us and vice versa. And every effort to make it real must grapple with deep problems: the people can't literally decide anything. The *demos* is always artificial, a name we give certain institutions and practices, such as elections and constitutional conventions. It isn't surprising that Richard Posner, one of the most influential legal scholars of the late Cold War and its aftermath, called the idea that the people can achieve a common will "a pipe dream hardly worthy of the attention of a serious person." Many serious people have thought this, more openly or more privately.[14]

Democracy also sets a high standard. Because we are all potentially one another's rulers, a democracy must ensure genuinely equal political rights for all, reject social caste and exclusionary definitions of the national community, and treat no group as unworthy of ruling as well as being ruled. Another way to put this is that genuine democracy must produce no permanent electoral losers, no population whose fate is to be ruled. At the same time, there must be enough mutual loyalty, enough embrace of a shared and chosen fate, that each citizen can find a way to perceive an election outcome as speaking for them, even if the result, in any given cycle, also feels like an affront. None of this is easy. None of it is impossible. To the extent that we achieve this sort of democracy, we can say that we have chosen our common world. A community of equals who choose how to live together: this is the possibility that goes out of the world if we drift, tumble, or are dragged away from democracy.

Democracy provides a way of answering inescapable questions on the basis of human equality and social solidarity. Its ambition is to overcome the half-random hierarchies and divisions we are born into and move toward a world that we can see ourselves as *building* together. Democracy aims at creating a life in which we are less fundamentally strangers, less one another's problems and threats, and more nearly collaborators—even when we disagree, even if we detest one another. This may seem abstract, even romantic. But we live in a world shaped by the largely peaceful political revolutions that democracy allows. American civil rights laws repudiated Jim Crow and set in motion the uprooting of legalized white supremacy. Labor law turned workers' unions from often illegal "conspiracies," dangerous for those who tried to organize them, into pillars of the twentieth-century economy. The New Deal lifted fear of abject poverty from tens of millions, especially the elderly and disabled, who had often lived and died poor.

These watershed events, in which political majorities changed their world, are examples of what I mean by choosing how we shall live together. The fact that all three are, in various ways, battered and even crumbling is only a reminder that democracy needs constant renewal.

There is another reason to embrace democracy, one that its first theorists saw clearly in classical Athens but which has become more obscure recently: democracy is a politics of class. It is the only system in which those who make up the people are also the ones who do most of the work and suffer most of the injuries of common life. Because we live in complex and stratified societies, a political order always has a class composition. Sovereignty tends to belong to some set—the experts, the scholars, the generals, the captains of industry, the financiers, or some blend of these. Only democracy offers what its earliest students sometimes candidly called "the rule of the poor"—the free, male poor, anyway, in ancient Greece. We can update that formula, in our rather different world, to something like the rule of the great middle, of people who work and worry, who wish they had more control over their lives and could promise more to their families, who feel sometimes that the world must have been made for other people. The quietest, most ordinary form of tyranny is government in which these lives are invisible, these voices silenced. Democracy is the only political order in which they cannot be ignored for all that long, and the power to make the world is really theirs if they can take it.

To make these ideals even partway real, we have to do what no polity, including the United States, has ever done: we have to put democracy first. Holding a few cycles of successful elections does not, it turns out, mean we can expect stable elections into the future. History does not move in only one direction and certainly not only toward what we regard as progress. A resilient democracy is not a side effect of economic growth or posttraditional or postmaterial values. Democracy does not take care of itself, any more than the economy, society, or the environment does. If we need democracy to address crises in all of those areas, we also need to tend democracy's own crises.

What does it mean to put democracy first? It means asking whether our culture, our economy, and our politics help us to see one another as equals who can rule together. It means recognizing how culture, economy, and politics can undercut both democratic equality and the civic solidarity and trust that people need if they are to rule together. It means unlearning the habit of imagining that things will take care of themselves and crises will ease spontaneously, that political responses are unnecessary and dangerous, and that in any case we really cannot rule ourselves and should not try. These ideas have worked themselves deep into our thinking. We cannot afford to assume they are true.

1

A POLITICAL HISTORY
OF THE PRESENT

W hen the Berlin Wall fell in November 1989, the people who
would define the first two decades of twenty-first-century
politics were already adults, products of a polarized world who
suddenly found themselves in one that seemed destined for Amer-
ican-led unity. As the Soviet Union collapsed, Donald Trump pro-
moted a ghost-authored advertisement for himself called *The Art
of the Deal* and recast his inherited real estate enterprise into a
business model based on pure self-promotion. He first appeared
on the cover of *Time* magazine—a hard-to-imagine big deal in
that pre-internet world—in 1989, some months before the wall
fell. Bernie Sanders had recently served two terms as the mayor
of Burlington and was preparing his first run to represent Vermont in Congress, which he won in 1990. Hillary Clinton lived in
the Arkansas governor's mansion, where her husband was serving
his fifth term, and sat on the boards of the Children's Defense
Fund and Walmart. In Cambridge, twenty-eight-year-old Barack
Obama was considering a bid for the presidency of the *Harvard
Law Review*. He became the first Black president to preside in

Harvard's Gannett House nineteen years before he entered the White House.

The wall's demolition began the short epoch in which these political rivals all made the careers they will be remembered by, a time that half ironically called itself the end of history. The phrase was elevated by a young political scientist and State Department official, Francis Fukuyama, who published an attention-getting article titled "The End of History?" in summer 1989, when the wall still stood but Soviet-led communism already looked to be in terminal crisis, and a follow-up book in 1992, whose title dropped the question mark. Because the claim of that title was so grand, it was de rigueur when discussing it (as many prominent people did) to insist that, of course, no one could really believe such a thing. The phrase kept coming up, however, because so many people did believe something like what Fukuyama actually spelled out: that the basic questions about how to organize political and social life had been resolved. The liberal, capitalist order, whose regular elections were essentially housekeeping, came to seem natural and inevitable to the gatekeepers of respectable opinion.

It also seemed inevitable to some who might have been a tougher audience, visionaries who had seen beyond the Cold War world. When Soviet-backed regimes fell through mostly bloodless transformations, which were dubbed velvet revolutions, the people who stepped into the political vacuum were often reflective, idiosyncratic, and very brave misfits who had spent their best years resisting an empire that most observers expected to outlive them many times over. Their revolutions, unlike most that came before them, were bids for an ordinary life, aimed not at remaking the world order but at joining it. Czech president Václav Havel, a long-imprisoned dissident playwright, wrote: "Though my heart may be left of center, I have always known that the only economic system that works is a market economy." To many who saw dissidents like Havel step into power as an empire fell apart in the background, it seemed that the countries once dominated by Soviet power had simply unfolded into the modern form of human coexistence, like flowers blooming. A few so-called strategists, and many more ideologists, contended that something similar would ensue from Afghanistan to Iraq, once American power stripped away anachronistic tyranny. The thought that both markets and elections could conspire in new (and old) forms of tyranny was hard to conjure.

The task of government seemed to be supervising, expanding, and maintaining markets. The work of cultural life, meantime, seemed to be to adapt to the perennial disruption that markets brought—disruption that was often named with the more euphonious "openness." If politics had been about deciding what sort of world to make together, a world in which that question was settled seemed to need a politics at once more modest in its ambitions and more definite in its program. Words like *governance* and *administration* seemed the better fit—not choosing among open futures but keeping the present on track for a future whose only viable shape we already knew. Elites and would-be elites prided themselves on being postideological, which is to say, not pretending more was at stake in politics than marginal disagreements over the shape of good governance. Accordingly, they tacked toward becoming postpolitical altogether. "Running government like a business" was taken to be an obviously good thing, even through the economic crises of 2008–2009 and very nearly until 2017, when the country began to learn more about what that might imply to someone actually interested in profit.

The seemingly solid post-1989 world was shakier and less preordained than it seemed, and the vision of the future that came with it was accordingly incomplete. It mattered immensely which version of the West was poised to collect history's laurels at the end of the Cold War. Ronald Reagan in the United States and Margaret Thatcher in the United Kingdom represented very particular versions of their own nations. If the oligarchic Soviet autocracy had collapsed in the mid-1960s or the mid-2010s, communism's failure would not have seemed to imply that capitalism posed no existential threats of its own. Rather, those who survived World War II or learned from its survivors often concluded that capitalism's recurring crises, grinding inequality, and disorienting cultural churn had produced a global depression and European fascism. The British Labour Party, which had helped win the war in coalition with Winston Churchill's Conservatives, threw out Churchill and built a modern welfare state, including the National Health Service and millions of units of public housing. Germany's Christian Democrats built a social market that buffered capitalism with public spending and strong unions that helped govern their companies. In the United States, Dwight D. Eisenhower, Republican president and former Allied supreme commander in Europe, spoke in the 1950s about the dangers of corporate power and the importance of a strong state in ways that earlier—or later—Republicans would have dismissed as socialism.[1]

That generation was on its way out by the 1980s, and in the meantime, a sea change had occurred. A strand of American politics that had always resisted the New Deal, lionized the market, and seen government mainly as a problem had a renaissance in the 1970s when it made the Republican Party its own. A similar change, led by future prime minister Margaret Thatcher, shifted Britain's conservatives from oligarchic caretakers of the welfare state to its dismantlers. Both Thatcher and Reagan were ideological cold warriors, and at the end of the 1980s the countries they had spent a decade reshaping were tribunes of the West that had "won." With an assist from post–Cold War euphoria, they scored their biggest ideological victories by stamping their embrace of the market on the opposition parties that succeeded them. Asked to name her most important legacy, Thatcher once snappily replied, "Tony Blair"—the Labour Party leader who had defeated her Conservative Party but adopted much of her promarket perspective. Reagan might have said something similar when Bill Clinton announced, in 1997, "the era of big government is over." The Democrats and New Labour might have found their hearts beating slightly to the left of center, as Havel had put it, but their minds and, increasingly, their funders were solidly on the side of market-making governance. A smarter and more tolerant path to the same future was what they promised. What came after ideology was competence, and they were the parties of the meritocrats.

By the time the centrist Democrat Bill Clinton was rounding out his second presidential term in 2000, it was all too easy to imagine that American politics had arrived at a great convergence. The "compassionate conservatism" that Texas governor and Republican presidential nominee George W. Bush advertised suggested a leftward tilt of the heart, and there were hardly any ideological fireworks in his race against Clinton's vice president, Al Gore. Both seemed to be candidates of continuity, and it was considered astute political analysis to ask whether Gore's stiffness and propensity to be a bore about such personal hobbyhorses as catastrophic global climate change, combined with the teetotaling Bush's imagined congeniality to a beer-drinking voter, might upend the usual course of democracy: Could this be the presidential year in which the shorter candidate won? In the event, the officially six-foot Bush defeated the officially six-foot-one Gore, suggesting posthistory might still offer a few interesting plot twists.

Behind the appearance of more or less consensus, trouble was brewing in several forms. One was a politics of force, a bareknuckled political nihilism that turned every issue of principle or pragmatism into a tactic and managed at the same time to yoke every tactic to a demagogic crusade with apocalyptic overtones. This politics as force, the tell-any-lie, break-any-rule approach, describes the Trump administration, of course, but it was already well adumbrated in the mid-1990s when Republican Newt Gingrich, Speaker of the House of Representatives after the 1994 midterm elections, launched an impeachment campaign against President Bill Clinton, a cynical set piece of partisan polarization and the capstone to a long anti-Clinton war. Gingrich had engineered a 1994 midterm sweep for his party by devising the "Contract with America," a short campaign platform that promised to combat "illegitimacy" (in which readers would have recognized a racist image of young, Black mothers), achieve an "effective death penalty" (the race of the condemned was also clearly implied), and stave off such feverish nightmares as "U.S. troops under U.N. command."[2]

What really defined Gingrich's innovation, beyond these particulars, was that governing, as well as campaigning, became a zero-sum battle for partisan power at every point. Gingrich was a kind of grotesque version of Clinton himself, whose White House was also on a "permanent campaign"—a phrase from the Clinton adviser Sidney Blumenthal. Clinton didn't hesitate to pander to race baiters, dumping Justice Department nominee and legal scholar Lani Guinier after the *Wall Street Journal* called her a "quota queen," staging a scolding of rapper Sister Souljah, and flying home to Arkansas in the middle of the 1992 presidential campaign to oversee the execution of Ricky Ray Rector, a Black man who had murdered a police officer. But Clinton struck a certain balance between principle and opportunism, maintaining his own version of the mixed moral ledger that most politicians keep. The cynicism with which Gingrich came for him was less qualified. It only presaged that of later Republican Senate leader Mitch McConnell, whose fixation on partisan power has an Iago-like purity.

When Donald Trump was in power between 2017 and 2021, it became standard to say that the country was suffering a crisis of political "norms." The word, which went from social-science esoterica to the standard jargon of the NPR class, referred to often unspoken restraint among elites that kept politics from breaking into open conflict and made government possible even amid intense disagreement and dislike. The reminder that any political system needs these kinds of self-control was correct and important, but it did not quite capture the depth of the crisis. The political norms at issue here, such as not lying about election results or seeking to make criminals of your opponents, are not just customs or habits, like saying good morning to strangers or walking the same path to work every day. They are fragments of a moral worldview, based on the understanding that it is less important for you to win today than for the politics of the country to go on. The political nihilism that runs from Gingrich to Trump and McConnell gives up on any idea that politicians have a responsibility to keep the system itself viable. It has the Miltonian quality of someone who would rather be majority leader in hell than minority leader in heaven.

That nihilism was easier to cultivate in the shadow of the end of politics than it might have been during the Cold War or another active crisis. If the world has become postpolitical, if market society is a machine that runs pretty much of itself, then what is politics besides a protection racket that skims the surplus? This had long been the vulgar version of some economists' take on politics: that it was a relatively decorous form of looting, conducted under cover of legislation. In that atmosphere of thought, with no crisis to avert, who but a sucker would not seek their share of the goods? Or for those who cared less about wealth and fame than power itself, what would hold them back from taking it by any means available? Politics had long existed in the tension between selfish and public-oriented action and between pandering and principle. Now, for a certain political strand that was especially pronounced on the right, the tension began to seem gratuitous. Selfishness increasingly became the principle, manipulation the essence of the practice. They were, at least, not suckers.

A second political style to emerge in the 1990s was the opposite of this politics of force: it reduced the struggle to get and use power to words, words, words. One version of this politics, the more radical in style, can be distilled in the phrase "Speak truth to power." The formula supposes that "truth" and "power" are separate and opposed, that truth is pure and power oppressive, and that speaking truth nonetheless can shake power's ramparts. Such testimonial speech seemed to take on a new force in the velvet revolutions, when literal walls fell, Jericho-like, and authoritarian governments yielded to dissidents whose lifelong campaigns had seemed hopeless. Václav Havel had written of "living in truth" and "the power of the powerless" in spelling out a politics that was mainly about existential commitment and personal integrity. Testimony, it seemed to some, could bring down empires.[3]

Another version of politics as speech was conversational rather than testimonial. Politics, according to a mainly liberal disposition that grew in the 1990s, was a very long dialogue, which ultimately tended toward consensus. What would it mean to reckon with Americans' legacy of racial injustice? A "national conversation about race" was the Clinton administration's response. What was the worst thing you could say about an argument in those years? That it was "a conversation-stopper," as the influential American philosopher and public intellectual Richard Rorty complained of those who wanted to bring religion into public life. Generally unspoken in encomiums to conversation was the premise that, when people took on public questions in a spirit of good faith, listening to others' perspectives and holding their own views open to challenge, they would converge on broadly liberal principles.

Politics as conversation willfully overlooked two central aspects of political life. One is that politics is largely about difficult contests over material distribution. The farce of a conversation about race was that race in the United States is a deeply material reality, entangled with inequality in family wealth, health, neighborhood safety, and vulnerability to police violence and incarceration. A politics of conversation is a dematerialized politics, which for many of the most important purposes is no politics at all. Second, because politics aims at decisions about questions that a polity can't avoid, it succeeds only if it is "a conversation-stopper." For these reasons, politics as conversation appealed mostly to relatively comfortable people whose interest in politics was more abstract than material. It had particular plausibility for those whose institutional worlds were talking shops such as universities, consultative oligarchies like the European Union, or interpretive hierarchies such as constitutional courts. It also appealed to those who, while they regarded themselves as eminently reasonable and open-minded, seldom encountered anyone who actually disagreed with them over important political questions. The trick to believing in politics as conversation is keeping up confidence that reasonable people do not disagree when the chips are down. This is far easier to believe if you keep company with the like-minded.

History happens twice, Karl Marx famously wrote, first as tragedy and later as farce. Testimonial politics has its farcical version in abundance. In 2020, when Avril Haines, Joe Biden's pick as director of intelligence, announced, "I have never shied away from speaking truth to power," the slogan of dissidents was repackaged as a promise of accuracy in spying. Truth was not the antithesis of power but what power needed. (Imagine if Havel had meant by "living in truth" that he always gave the KGB verifiable facts.) More than a decade earlier, however, testimonial politics met real politics not as farce but as tragedy. Barack Obama's splendid 2008 campaign showed the emotional vitality and human energy of testimonial politics. The limitations of what he subsequently achieved showed the failings of all versions of politics as talk.[4]

Was there anything to compare with Obama 2008, at least for those of us who believed? "We are the ones we have been waiting for," he promised, and his first presidential campaign brought to life something that had been dormant in American politics: the conviction and feeling—beyond abstract belief—that mobilized people could remake the rules of common life and could become different and better people through politics. The campaign became the platform for a movement. Solidarity felt, for the first time in my life, like something young, vital, and American. Treading the back roads of South Carolina in the days before Obama dominated its 2008 primary and through the long months that followed until November, I felt I was living in a political time as never before, maybe as it had felt in Eastern Europe twenty years earlier. I cannot, obviously, speak for everyone who worked for the campaign or watched it with enthusiasm, but I know I was not alone.

It may be difficult to believe in the hindsight of the 2020s, but the first Obama campaign went beyond the familiar rhetoric of unity to touch a more personal chord. Although he was significantly older than those of us who poured out to support him (many of us falling somewhere on the boundary of Gen X and Old Millennial), the campaign and Obama's biography seemed to embody a new experience of the social world, which was ours. We children of the 1990s, unlike our Boomer parents, had grown up amid the diversity of every continent. We had first encountered borders—we Americans, anyway, in marked contrast to people from poorer countries—as flexible, almost nominal marks on the land across which curiosity and desire poured. It is shocking to recall how easily the assumption came, then, that American life was simply the future of the world. Obama was just a little too old to have grown up in this world—he went to college in the Reagan years, when the Cold War was ending but no one knew it yet—but he managed to embody it, child of Kenya, Kansas, Indonesia, Hawai'i, and Chicago.

There is a lot of hindsight scorn for the short-lived conceit that Obama's presidency ushered in a "postracial" America. The impatience is right if postracial means the same thing as color-blind, a way of denying the burden of inequity today. But what the campaign itself suggested, and what the candidate contended, was that race did not need to be fate. Racism had injured every-one who lived with it, he argued. Black people suffered most by far and in qualitatively different ways from others, but Obama followed James Baldwin in appreciating that all Americans, when divided from one another by fear and dislike, could not help also being divided from themselves and ill at ease in their coun-try. Obama's own blackness, as he described it in *Dreams from My Father*, was partly a matter of deciding to identify with one strand of American history, one part of the country's life, while refus-ing to adopt the fear and bitterness that the older men in his life had proffered as a legacy, from his white grandfather's re-sentment to the hardness his Indonesian stepfather had learned in the Suharto genocide of the mid-1960s. Identity, he insisted, was a problem, a question, a task. If that were true for a person, could it also be true for a country? *Why not?* a political generation seemed to ask.

I am documenting a political fantasy that Obama invited the country to participate in and without which his insurgent 2008 victory would probably have failed. Calling it fantasy is not to de-ride it. All politics has a lot to do with how participants imagine their world, and the kind of imagination that Obama offered was much better than the "organization of hatreds" that Henry Adams had defined as the essence of politics and which would return to the center of national life before Obama left office in 2017. The point of limning the fantasy is to diagnose where the country's understanding of politics was so that a testimonial, conversational, existential politics—a politics whose central act was to ask *Who am I? Who, then, are we?*—could have such force.[5]

It was a formula for people with more of an idea of how politics ought to feel than of what it ought to do. Its premises were emblems of their time. Political division seemed perhaps illusory, rooted in misunderstanding. Meritocracy seemed almost natural: *of course* the new emblematic American had double Ivy League degrees. Obama's 2008 campaign was a distinctly meritocratic version of a peace movement, powered by disgust and exhaustion that grew as the American involvement in Iraq deepened without succeeding and crystallized in the candidate's proclamation that he was "not against all wars," just against "dumb wars." A campaign rooted in the feeling of democratic transformation, but without a program to make such transformation real, drew once in power toward what was, at least, certifiably smart: the technocratic authority of generals, bankers, and economists, along with hardball political fixers of the Rahm Emanuel variety. So the politics of talk, which was at once revolutionary and reassuring in its promise, ended up as a conventional form of governance by the credentialed.[6]

The result was a marriage of two political modes, one rhetorical, the other administrative. The rhetorical side was redemptive constitutionalism, the creed of Abraham Lincoln's Gettysburg Address and Second Inaugural, Martin Luther King Jr.'s "I Have a Dream" speech, and Lyndon Baines Johnson's nationally televised speech on the Voting Rights Acts of 1965, in which he promised, "we shall overcome." It holds that the nation really was founded on democracy and equal freedom, that slavery and Jim Crow were terrible deviations from these principles, and that, if we manage to live by our principles, Americans will finally be free together. In one sense, Obama's victory and inauguration unavoidably embodied a version of this idea: a Black man speaking the constitutionally prescribed oath, as Lincoln had done, and invoking the Declaration of Independence, not to promise equality but, at long last, to pronounce it. The short-lived fantasies of a postracial America were one symptom of this moment. A Tom Toles cartoon quoted the iconic "all men are created equal" and added, as in a note of legislative history, "Ratified November 4, 2008."[7]

The administrative side of the Obama presidency was technocracy, the treatment of government as a problem of expertise. Deference to the professional culture of economists led, in particular, to trade policies that pressed aggressively toward liberalization and harmonization, until a political rebellion against the Trans-Pacific Partnership drove even Hillary Clinton to repudiate it while campaigning. Obama's policymakers had accepted that there is a right way to manage major policy questions and that much of the point of electoral politics is to keep the way clear for expert administration.

Obama's persistent refrain—from his speech at the 2004 Democratic National Convention, which first brought him to national attention, to his elegiac address after five police officers were murdered in Dallas in 2016—was that unity is deeper than division. Both redemptive constitutionalism and technocracy promised reconciliation among different groups of Americans. If citizens can just live by the right principles, hope and history will finally rhyme. If smart policy can just plug the holes in the economy, the rising tide will lift all boats. But these promises glossed over too much. There was a sharp coming apart between the America that Obama untiringly evoked and the country that people experienced. New forms of radicalism grew up in that gap.[8]

Bernie Sanders's 2016 presidential campaign reminded observers of the insurgent Obama 2008 campaign but not always in a good way. Paul Krugman, the resident economist on the *New York Times* opinion pages, had warned in 2008 that the Obama campaign "seems dangerously close to becoming a cult of personality" whose supporters were spewing "venom." Returning to the same well to denounce the insurgent Sanders campaign in 2016, Krugman warned that governing is simply too hard for an idealistic democratic socialist: Sanders didn't seem built for compromise, and his proposals lacked detail. *Grow up!* was the bottom line here: as the economist told his readers, invoking the most basic methodological wisdom of his field, "politics, like life, involves trade-offs."

Meanwhile, the *New Yorker* featured a cultural take on Sanders's appeal to young voters: it must be his air of "purity" and "nostalgia for an imaginary time of simpler, more straightforward politics," curiously like the Wordsworthian "very heaven" back in 2008 of imagining young Barack Obama "entirely pure." Whether it came dressed as neoclassical political economy or as style criticism, the point was the same: adults learn not to take campaigns, promises, or political hopes too seriously. They learn that the real work is tedious, often invisible to the public, and highly constrained. This is the alternative to fantasizing about unblemished leaders or utopias of free stuff.[9]

There was a thread connecting the first Obama campaign with the first Sanders campaign, but it was not woven from a naïve cult of personality. Sanders's anticharisma did have a certain gruff appeal, but his campaigns were not powered by style. Obama's political magic had essentially to do with the ways the candidate embodied his own picture of the country. In Sanders's campaigns, his supporters—who by the end amounted to something like a political generation among Democrats—took the candidate as their vehicle to claim ideals and make demands that had long been boxed out of serious politics: for truly universal health care, truly open higher education, relief from the debt and anxiety that had become the engines of economic life. This kind of ideas-based campaign hadn't been seen on the left for many decades. Its nearest historical parallel had been on the right, and even that was vanishingly remote to most Sanders supporters: in 1964, Republican nominee and Arizona senator Barry Goldwater ran a hard-right, libertarian campaign against Lyndon Johnson, the sitting Democratic president. Goldwater was routed, but sixteen years later his ideas rode into Washington with Ronald Reagan's victorious presidential campaign.

The first Sanders campaign followed on Obama's in a more complicated way. It represented a different view of how political transformation begins: not with rhetoric, atmospherics, or feeling alone but with a program. Skeptics had decided that the gap between the charisma of the first Obama campaign and the limits the victorious candidate met in real-world governance meant that the ideal of political transformation was childish. The Sanders campaign took Obama's goal, democratic self-transformation, but rejected his means, choosing instead a clear agenda that proposed a sharp break with how the country had been governed since the Reagan years. The Sanders campaign also reversed Obama's style by setting out lines of conflict and naming enemies, as Obama had strenuously declined to do. Many politicians and voters had come to hate Obama, some for—might as well say it—deplorable reasons, but in speeches and interviews, he always aspired to embody a decent and reasonable American consensus, whose critics were an unspecified "those who disagree" or "those who see it differently." Sanders, by contrast, denounced "the billionaire class" and Democrats as well as Republicans who catered to it, as well as "the racist criminal justice system." He sought a new and different majority but not a consensus. The politics of conversation was over.

Devotees of comity, like the *New York Times*'s mild-mannered centrist David Brooks, compared Sanders to Donald Trump and called him a voice of his followers' id, a "tool for supporters' self-expression," a walking, talking angry meme. But an essential part of democratic politics is the struggle to interpret social conflict in relation to a picture of the common good. Obama had sought to do that in a maximally conciliatory way, which gave a moving but underspecified image of the common good he sought, and nonetheless failed to stave off enemies. Sanders was more specific about what he sought and about who stood in the way. Such line drawing, the constructive interpretation of social conflict, is at the heart of democratic politics.[10]

Despite everything they got wrong, there was a way that commentators were right to see something in common between the Sanders and Obama campaigns and between Sanders and Trump. And the transitive property holds: there was also something in common between Obama and Trump. All three campaigns offered ways for supporters to build up and act out new political identities, convictions, vocabularies, even ways of feeling. In each campaign, with very different results, each candidate spoke in ways that broke with standard political language and tone: generationally hopeful and emotionally incisive for Obama (others tried to hit his notes but couldn't); polemical and unapologetically radical for Sanders; and logorrheic, boastful, and sadistic for Trump. In each case, some core of listeners felt, "Yes! This is real. This is what it's actually about!" The campaigns grew through the discovery that the listener was not alone: this political epiphany was shared. People felt freer to say things they had kept to themselves or not quite known they believed and to take stances they had shied away from, assuming no one would join them. Now, for better or worse, it turned out that others had the same hopes, the same grudges, the same relief and delight at seeing them turned from half-secret things to points of solidarity. Each campaign became a movement, partly because it became a way for people to be unapologetically together what they had suspected they could only be alone.

It is a very different epiphany to find that you can be part of a cross-racial movement of constitutional patriots or a rebirth of social democracy than to discover that your inner misogynist does not need to stay private, or that you can chant demands for violence against your political opponents. David Brooks was right to recognize that both the Sanders and Trump campaigns represented the return to politics of something that had been suppressed. Obama's worldly-wise critics in 2008 were right, too, to see that he was conjuring a desire for change that politics as they understood it could not deliver. All three campaigns were revivals of political energies that had receded far from the center of public life. Some of those energies may yet help to reclaim democracy. Others may destroy it.

The twenty-first century began with the idea that democracy was more or less inevitable but also more or less superfluous: inevitable because capitalist democracies with liberal constitutions and regular elections had turned out to be the natural shape of common life in the modern world, superfluous because this system presented no great questions about how to live or epochal crises to confront: it required expert maintenance and public quiescence, not acts of collective will. Two decades into the new millennium, democracy seems, all at once, dangerous, fragile, and indispensable. It seems dangerous because its ferment can produce exclusionary, violent, and nihilistic movements, which may simultaneously threaten to restore "America for real Americans" and insist that talk of violence is a self-affirming game, a meme for making bad friends, not serious because nothing in politics is serious.

Nihilism's irony does not mitigate its antidemocratic gestures. Rather, each amplifies the other. Refusing responsibility does not mean avoiding consequences. Politics really is dangerous, even when the dangerous ones pretend otherwise. And it can be a crucible of clannish irrationality. In 2021, tens of millions of Americans put themselves, their children, and their elders in danger from a deadly pandemic because they found it congenial to believe that effective vaccines did not work or were more dangerous than the pandemic they aimed to stop.

Democracy seems fragile because the same antirational and nihilistic energies can erode even the most basic shared facts, such as the results of elections. Wild scenarios loom: competing presidencies, like medieval contests among claimants to the papacy, and fights in Congress over which candidates to seat. People whom politics has taught to mistrust and even hate one another will, it turns out, find reasons to deny that their opponents can ever rule them. If that denial succeeds, democratic politics is over.

There are collective choices to make: how to roll back an unfolding climate catastrophe and other ecological crises, how to reckon with our massive and multifarious inequality, how to restore democracy itself so that these problems can become projects, rather than succumbing to fate. Our lives depend on the choices we make and those we are unable to make.

2

MAKING DEMOCRACY UP,
MAKING DEMOCRACY REAL

Thomas Hobbes's schoolmates called him "Crowe," for his dark hair, his sharp eye, and a certain aloofness in his manner. A tutor and tennis player, a daily walker who favored boots of Spanish leather laced with black silk, and a theorist of optics, he led a life that was refined, sociable, anxious, and long—long enough to see from one world into another.[1]

Hobbes was born in 1588, in the age of William Shakespeare, into an England that had been Catholic within living memory and whose first North American colony would not be founded until Hobbes was a young man. Shakespeare was only a quarter century older than Hobbes. A quarter century after Hobbes's death in 1679, Benjamin Franklin would be born in Boston, a merchant, publicist, and revolutionary, whose blend of entrepreneurship, self-promotion, and statecraft still feels contemporary today.

Hobbes watched the shattering of an old world and the first pained movements toward something new from the uncomfortable vantage of a political refugee. He was a tutor in mathematics to Charles, Prince of Wales, when his pupil's father was imprisoned, then executed, in a revolution that seemed all but unthinkable until it happened. Hobbes was in Parisian exile with the remnant of the royal court when the executioner's axe fell in London. He was soon a double refugee: his philosophical radicalism alarmed the pious royalists around him. He fled back to England in 1651 and swore an oath of loyalty to the revolutionary commonwealth. When that government fell in 1660, and his former pupil returned to London as King Charles II, Hobbes feared he was a marked man. His friend and first biographer, John Aubrey, reported that "in Parliament, not long after the king was setled [restored to the throne], some of the bishops made a motion to have the good old gentleman burn't for a heretique."[2]

Little wonder, then, that Hobbes's political thought, the main reason he is remembered today, dwells on the menace of politics. Hobbes liked to joke that he had been born a twin with fear. He had been delivered when the country was in a panic at the expectation of a Spanish invasion—soon reversed by fortunate weather and a dramatic English victory at sea—but the quip also contained a key to his philosophy. Hobbes was all his life a theorist of fear, a student of the reasons people have to be afraid of one another and of the ways our fear makes us even more dangerous. He was also an educator of fear, who worked to bend it to good use, ultimately turning it against itself. He hoped to show how the world could be made less fearsome, and people grow less fearful, by concentrating anxiety on the real source of danger, which was political disorder and confusion.[3]

Reasons for pessimism arise in the course of any life. Hobbes's reasons were unusually vivid and momentous, but the real interest of his thought is in its acute delineation of the balance of menace and promise in political life. He described, with a lucidity that no one since has exceeded, why human beings need politics and also why it is so dangerous in our hands. His thought remains invaluable in understanding the power and limits of a quintessentially modern idea: that politics is the way to make collective choices, the Archimedean lever that can move the world.

This idea has been neither perennial nor universal. Much less has the idea that democracy is the uniquely legitimate mode of politics. Both ideas emerged in early modern Europe and its colonies, notably Haiti and the United States, between the early 1600s and the late 1800s. They grew up alongside and in response to such distinctively modern phenomena as capitalism, racial slavery, and the Industrial Revolution. But there is one institution from which these ideas of politics and democracy are all but inseparable: a certain kind of state, one in which it is possible to form and carry out an agenda for a territory and the people there, to set the terms on which they shall live their lives. Such a state has *jurisdiction*: through it, rulers can speak the law. As they grew, these states—national, imperial, and colonial—produced what historian Sven Beckert calls "war capitalism," the forced movement of peoples and large-scale expropriation of land in service of a world system of production and exchange. They made the system of race that powerfully persists, drawing lines among different "kinds" of people through the laws of slavery, crime, migration, and marriage, producing the world in which children learn to see race as a fact.[4]

But not all was menace and exploitation. The modern idea of politics was also intertwined with doctrines of universal equality and personal freedom. Radical thinkers saw that the state could provide a new form of community, in which people could meet as equals to decide how they would live together. In this way, it might become a uniquely effective way of overcoming inherited and arbitrary domination.

Such a state was Janus-faced. It was the most effective vehicle of domination and exploitation ever devised. It also offered the chance to begin the world again on new terms. By implementing law over a territory, the state could quiet the predation and fear that marred human life. The question was whether the chaos would give way to a more systematic predation or to a different order of things. Hobbes remains invaluable in grappling with this problem.

To understand politics, Hobbes contended we must see what it adds to the world, which requires imagining life without it. This is the point of his famous "state of nature," which, without government, becomes a "state of war." In such a state, according to one of the most famous (if misunderstood) lines in political thought, life is "solitary, poor, nasty, brutish, and short." It is often thought that this phrase bespeaks a pessimistic view of human nature. In fact, Hobbes believed that human nature, in the sense of people having good or bad motives, was less important than many supposed, and political order was more important. Without an authority to organize their actions, even decently motivated people would fall into suspicion and conflict. The reasons were simple. We all have the same needs, desires, and goals: to stay alive, to have enough resources for security and comfort, to enjoy the respect of others. Because we need and want the same things, we come into conflict: What is mine? What is yours? Who decides? Without an answer, these ordinary questions flare up into bloody disputes—or, at best, keep people huddled in reciprocal mistrust.[5]

The prospect of these disputes haunted everyone, all the time. The hell of it was that people were, as Hobbes ironically put it, equal: any of us could be dangerous to anyone else, whether through sheer force or by trickery and betrayal. As long as we are one another's problems, no one is ever really safe. Hence Hobbes defined life as a search for power that ends only in death—because no one can ever be sure they have enough power to stay alive. Hence, too, Hobbes's unsettling conclusion that, outside government, everyone has a natural right to everything—including the bodies of others. If we have a right to anything, Hobbes reasoned, it must be to keep ourselves alive, life being the precondition of anything else mattering to us. As long as anyone else might pose a mortal threat, the right to self-preservation means the right to strike first. Because everyone has that right, no one is safe, and because no one is safe, everyone has that right. The very reason that we need security keeps us from achieving it.

On one level, what solves these problems for us is law. The law of property distinguishes mine from yours, drawing and enforcing boundaries that enable us to coordinate around our appetites and needs. "Keep off." "Come in." "Tomatoes, $1.79/lb." These are signposts to getting around peacefully in a world full of other people. They tell us where we can be, what we can use, where to get permission to take what is not already ours. Rules against murder, battery, and harassment provide security that annuls the right to strike first. When rules do their work, they establish and police the line between my body and yours.

But where does law come from? Hobbes argued that laws arise from political choices. They are made by people. Law is not written on the world, waiting for us to learn to read it. And, unlike language, it does not arise organically from social life. Rubbing up against other people for years, or even generations, will not securely sort out mine from yours or put a brake on violence. Even if a small community does build up stable customs for a while, it is always just waiting for trouble: an upstart who wants to claim more than custom allows him, intrusions from a neighboring community, an enmity or passion that sets people at odds.[6]

Nor are general principles of morality enough to keep order. We may agree in principle that some religious text or tradition tells us how to live, but disagreement over what, exactly, a community's religion requires is one of the richest sources of conflict and violence. Anyone living in the seventeenth century understood this. Religious warfare had convulsed Europe in the century before Hobbes lived. The English Civil War, the defining crisis of his lifetime, was motivated as much by clashes among Catholics, Anglicans, Presbyterians, and Puritan independent Christians as it was by the struggle between royal and parliamentary rule.

So we cannot *find* law because it is not there, or at least we are not equipped to see it. If a body of law is going to be clear enough to turn us from ubiquitous threats to possible collaborators, we have to make it. But how? The answer has to be one that avoids just re-creating the same old disagreement in new language: my law versus yours, like my catechism versus yours, or my judgment that you are dangerous to me and I need to take you out. Hobbes proposed that, to avoid recurring cycles of disagreement and conflict, *someone* must have the power to say what the law is. The rest of us, that is, must agree to treat their word as law and accept that it may be enforced against us; we must comply even if the law goes against our interests and keenest hopes, even if we believe it is wrong. Otherwise, we can never have resolution, only conflict. Hobbes called this power to pronounce the law sovereignty and the one who holds the power the sovereign.

Although Hobbes himself preferred royal government, it was essential to his thought that a sovereign need not be a person. Sovereignty is, like the law it pronounces, an artificial thing. A sovereign might be an individual, but it might equally well be a representative body like a parliament or a democratic assembly in which every member of the community participates. The point for Hobbes was not to have a king but to have a procedure to say what the law is when conflict threatens.

And how should sovereignty come to be? What could transform incorrigible conflict into what Hobbes called a commonwealth, a people under a sovereign and so a people with law? Hobbes proposed that sovereignty must be justified to each person who will live under it and justified in terms of their most fundamental interest—avoiding violent death. He sketched a story in two stages. First, there must be unanimous agreement among a set of people that they will be subject to a shared law. No one can be bound to such an agreement who has not freely entered into it. Second, the group must then decide how it is going to make decisions; that is, it must choose a form of sovereignty and so decide whose word will count as its law. This is the first act of politics.[7]

Hobbes presented democracy as the primordial form of politics: "Each member of a crowd must agree with the others that on any issue anyone brings forward in the group, the wish of the majority shall be taken as the will of all." Elaborating the idea, he continued: "When men have met to erect a commonwealth, they are, almost by the very fact that they have met, a *Democracy*. From the fact that they have gathered voluntarily, they are understood to be bound by the decisions made by an agreement of the majority" (italic in the original). By majority vote, then, the gathered people would decide how they would be ruled: by monarchy, by legislature (what Hobbes would have called an elected aristocracy), or by themselves, in continuing majorities, as a democracy. At this point, Hobbes believed democracy lost its primacy. As a form of government, it had problems of unwieldiness, ignorance, and corruption, to name a few, that might well give a majority good reason to hand over sovereign power to a monarch or assembly. But democracy lay at the root.[8]

In *Leviathan*, Hobbes analogized the founding of a commonwealth to the divine act of creation. In *On the Citizen*, he gave a subtler and less grand description of the power that sovereignty conjures: in a commonwealth, "a crowd of citizens both exercises power and is subject to power, but in different senses." Sovereignty, in other words, put people into two roles. As subjects of sovereignty, they lived within the order that their country's laws produced; they followed commands. As members of the sovereign that exercised power, they shaped their country's order; they gave commands. The same person might occupy both roles by turn or at the same moment. Although Hobbes was no democrat in our modern sense, he described a way in which people could imagine themselves as the authors of the laws that gave order to their common lives—in which, that is, they could imagine themselves democratically.[9]

Hobbes did not intend his new form of democratic imagination to rally people to what we would consider democratic action—particularly not dissent or resistance. He aimed his political polemics at anyone who thought their own intellect or conscience could pick out legitimate power from the illegitimate kind. Indeed, all established governments legitimately commanded their subjects, Hobbes argued, because any political order was better than the lawless state of nature, and there was no solid middle ground between the two. (The limit of this defense of established order lay where the government tried to kill you. At that point, you could assert your inalienable right to save your own life. Of course, by the time the government is unmistakably trying to kill you, your odds are likely poor.) Addressed to someone living under the monarchy of Charles I before he lost his head, perhaps someone inclined to reject that dynasty's doctrine that kings ruled by divine right, Hobbes's arguments would recommend submission. From the point of view of someone living under the revolutionary republic that followed Charles's execution, the argument for obedience was the same. When Hobbes returned to England and swore loyalty to the new government, he was making a philosophically consistent decision that would haunt him politically, as he had shown himself committed to no particular government, only to the principle that any sovereign is better than lawlessness.

For all the bleakness of his thought, which laid to waste the attractive conceit that you are entitled to a government that meets the requirements of your conscience, Hobbes was radical in portraying politics as arising from an originally democratic act of self-rule. That idea laid a dynamite charge of popular sovereignty at the cornerstone of political order. A century later, the Genevan polymath Jean-Jacques Rousseau set off Hobbes's dynamite. Agreeing with Hobbes that government must be justified to each person who is subjected to it, Rousseau posed the problem this way: "find a form of association that defends and protects with all common forces the persons and goods of each associate, and by means of which, each one, *while uniting with all, nevertheless obeys only himself and remains as free as before*" (italics mine). For Hobbes, political power found its justification in the tragedy of the state of nature: subjection was better than insecurity. Rousseau proposed something more positive: the political state as a condition of freedom.[10]

How could this work? Others had proposed ways of limiting state power to make it less menacing to personal freedom, but their solutions depended on denying just how much politics added to common life. They sought to escape politics, while Hobbes saw no way but through it. John Locke, the influential seventeenth-century English philosopher who is often counterposed to Hobbes, had portrayed prepolitical life as being already full of law. Rights of personal security and even private property existed before politics, with fairly certain metes and bounds, and were apparent to anyone who cared to look for them. Life outside politics was not life without law. It merely presented certain "inconveniences," as Locke put it, disputes over boundaries and trouble arising from lack of enforcement to punish violations of natural rights. Locke's state was akin to a commercial arbitrator or a hired security agency, enlisted to enforce a set of already existing rights, subject to firing and replacement if it stepped beyond its role. His theory was a favorite of English Whigs, who used it to rationalize the so-called Glorious Revolution of 1688–1689, in which the Stuart King James II was forcibly replaced by the more reliably Protestant William of Orange. In Lockean terms, this revolution was a basically orderly act of constitutional housekeeping rather than a hazardous dissolution and reconstitution of political order. It appealed for similar reasons to American revolutionaries, who liked to portray their "unalienable" rights as stable and permanent, their government as optional. They abhorred the Hobbesian idea that rights could have no reliable meaning without sovereign endorsement. Locke's social contract is the formula for revolutionaries who aim at changing governments without calling into question the rest of the legal and social order—the rights, for instance, of landlords and patriarchs.[11]

Rousseau agreed with Hobbes that the world was not already lawful before politics. If it seemed otherwise, this was, ironically, because you had the good fortune to live in a stable political order—and, probably, to be one of the fortunate few whose interests that order served well. Outside political order, human life was marked by pervasive insecurity. *Homo homini lupus*, Hobbes had written: man is a wolf to man. Slaving, looting, rape, massacre: these were the everyday shadows that the stronger cast over the weaker. To this, Rousseau added what Hobbes had tended to downplay: life under the state was often not much better. "Man is born free, and everywhere he is in chains." A ruler, after all, could be a very large wolf, as insurrectionaries, egalitarians, outlaws, or simple political opponents of Europe's monarchies had long recognized. During his late and anxious years back in England, Hobbes could have seen the decaying head of Oliver Cromwell, lord protector of the republic to which the refugee philosopher had once sworn loyalty, blind and mute on a spike above Westminster Hall. Cromwell's body had been disinterred, and his head removed from his body and mounted on a pike by Hobbes's former pupil, the restored Charles II, as a symbol of sovereignty that Hobbes could hardly have gainsaid.[12]

Rousseau believed he knew how to turn the chains of political life into gentler bonds, which—to recall his phrase—would leave everyone free and secure. He adopted Hobbes's formula for the origin of political life: a unanimous agreement to make a "total alienation of each associate together with his rights to the entire community." This agreement, identical with Hobbes's contract, created a sovereign and split each person into subject and sovereign: "each individual . . . finds himself under a twofold commitment, namely, as a member of the sovereign toward private individuals, and as a member of the state toward the sovereign." But there was a key difference: Rousseau held that sovereignty, once created, must remain with the entire community. Hobbes's image of a majority decision to hand over sovereignty to a king or council portrayed a transfer that, Rousseau insisted, would be quite illegitimate or, put differently, would destroy sovereignty. This is so, Rousseau believed, because what gives sovereignty its power over each individual is the fact that everyone stands in the same relation to it: as both lawmaker and subject of law. If that bond is broken,

> if the populace promises simply to obey, it dissolves itself by this act. It loses its standing as a people. The very moment there is a master, there no longer is a sovereign, and thenceforward the body politic is destroyed.

For Rousseau, political life was not just originally democratic. It was also, and for the same reason, perennially democratic.[13]

Hobbes had argued that once an individual agrees to abide by the judgment of the sovereign, their individual will is absorbed into the collective will. People will have their own views, of course, but only the sovereign can make authoritative judgments, and those judgments have binding power over each person. "You agreed,"

Hobbes says in effect throughout his work, "or rationally should have agreed, to substitute the sovereign's will for your own. This means that, as far as your legal rights go, *it is* your own." Rousseau reformulated this to say, in effect, "you stand in a relation of political equality to all your fellow citizens, and in this relationship, you agree to let the judgment of the whole stand in for yours." For Hobbes, a unanimous initial decision makes everyone the author of political society, part of the choice to bring it into being. Here Rousseau agrees. Next, for Hobbes, a democratic decision assigns sovereign power to some body or, in the rare case of a democracy, preserves it for future majorities. Rousseau takes the argument in a very different direction: democracy remains the key to legitimacy at every stage of politics. Only decisions that arise from sovereignty of this kind deserve to be called laws. "On close examination, very few nations would be found to have laws," Rousseau reckoned, taking aim at the European heartland of "civilization."[14]

What was so special about the political relationship of sovereignty? Rousseau described it in a variety of ways. Sovereignty established equality: it "substitutes a moral and legitimate equality to whatever physical inequality nature may have been able to impose . . . however unequal in force or intelligence they may be, men all become equal by agreement and by right." It also established freedom: "Obedience to the law one has prescribed for oneself is liberty." Because the will of a sovereign was, as a political matter, one's own will, Rousseau asserted that he had satisfied his own standard: to describe a form of political subjection that is not subjection at all but liberation because in it the citizen-subject "obeys only himself." In this combination, political society "substitutes justice for instinct" and gives lawful actions "a moral quality they previously lacked." To be free does not mean simply avoiding obstacles, dodging commands, and getting what you want. In a world in which boundaries and obligations are the alternatives to chaos and danger, freedom means drawing the boundaries yourself and choosing the obligations.[15]

Rousseau lent a sharp blade to his critics by concluding his discussion of sovereignty with this formula: "Whoever refuses to obey the general will, will be forced to do so by the entire body. *This means merely that he will be forced to be free.*"[16] Bertrand Russell gave one of the twentieth century's more temperate judgments on this sentence when he remarked, "Rousseau forgets his romanticism and speaks like a sophistical policeman." In this light, Rousseau seems to have dressed up Hobbes's absolutism with democratic moralizing, making it all the more dangerous because it is less stark and more seductive. But absolutism remains absolutism.[17]

It's worth pausing over the easy condemnation, though. Maybe it is the *rejection* of coercion that is seductive and deceptive moralizing? Consider: Does it make sense in some cases to say that "forced to be free" is exactly how we see the situation of people who want to opt out of the political order but may not? Take the Trump supporters who stormed the US Capitol on January 6, 2021, some of them seemingly bent on stopping the certification of Joe Biden's victory in the Electoral College. The political community has a perfect right, and certain officials have an obligation, to reprotect elections and the peaceful transfer of power that they should make possible. Without them, the United States would have no claim to be a constitutional polity. By obliging dissenters to abide by the community's decision, don't we force them to be free, that is, keep them inside a constitutional order rather than follow them into the chaos of competing claims to rule? Or consider the segregationist opponents of *Brown v. Board of Education* and the Supreme Court's other civil rights decisions of the 1950s and 1960s. Don't we think that by enforcing these, and laws such as the 1964 Civil Rights Act and the 1965 Voting Rights Act, we are obliging people to treat one another as equal citizens? Isn't being an equal citizen among equal citizens at the heart of political freedom? Don't we take the same attitude when the First Amendment requires a town government to permit a demonstration by people most locals would prefer to keep out, whether it is the Republican Party in Portland or climate activists in the Texas oil fields?

I worry only that these scenarios may seem too easy and readers may suspect I am playing some sort of trick on them. But I am not playing tricks, just taking clear, core examples. It would be easy to multiply these examples—and as they increased, more of them would seem controversial, or different ones would seem controversial to different readers. But they highlight that these questions—Who rules? What does equality mean? Who may speak?—require answers, and we believe that the answers we enforce should—and, for now, around here, do—have a core of political legitimacy. To say that you want to opt out of these principles is to say that you want to opt out of the polity altogether and deny the rest of us the power to live by a shared law that has some claim to ensuring freedom and equality. We will, however, keep you within the law. We will force you to be free. This may involve policemen, but it is not sophistical. The sophistry, as Hobbes in particular would have insisted, is in pretending political order can persist without force.[18]

Hobbes and Rousseau have often been regarded with diffidence, or worse, by the founders and theorists of American political order. They have the reputation of being dangerous thinkers, reckless inspirations to dogmatism. Rousseau takes some blame for inspiring the Terror of the French Revolution ("forced to be free") and Hobbes for defending the kind of royal absolutism that the American revolutionaries rejected. The American habit has often been to describe this country's federalism, which purports to locate concurrent sovereignty in the state and national governments, as a homespun Copernican innovation, a bit of Yankee ingenuity that leaves Hobbes and Rousseau's political metaphysics in the dust. "Federalism was our Nation's own discovery," Justice Anthony Kennedy wrote. "The Framers split the atom of sovereignty." Similarly, the US Constitution's separation of powers is often described as the key principle of the system, one that James Madison and his fellow drafters adapted from the Baron de Montesquieu, a far less worrisome Francophone source than Rousseau.[19]

But if the answers Hobbes and Rousseau gave are sometimes unsettling, that may be because they stated the questions so clearly. Hobbes gives us a way of understanding the need for politics. There are inescapable questions in human life: What is mine (or, if you prefer, what may I use, what may I have)? What may I do? Whom can I trust? The questions are inescapable because we are similar to and interdependent with one another. Everyone has the same questions, and my answer relies on your answer, and vice versa. The problems arise spontaneously, but they do not get solved spontaneously. There is no agreeing on a natural or divine answer: if we appeal to those, we only recreate the conflict in different terms. Politics is the way we make a solution. Its essential, necessary task is to set the terms for our cooperation.

The political solution is built out of the same materials that produce the problem. Hobbes opened his *Leviathan* with a discussion of language, noting especially the ways that it tricks us. Because we can express an idea in words, we are easily confused into imagining that those words name something real. But often these are only verbal will-o'-the-wisps, gleaming nothings to which we lend confused meaning. Or they are centaurs: concepts sutured together, like the upper body of a man and the lower body of a horse, that we can join in our minds but that do not actually exist. Religious wars were powered by wisps: a principle hallucinated like a desert mirage that was then taken as a reason to defy a king or murder a neighbor. Political theories were built on centaurs. It is easy to make a sentence defining a "natural right" to property and security, the kind of inherently legal and orderly right that John Locke and the American founders would later describe as existing outside and before politics, but that does not mean that the concept has the shape and strength to save a political order from confusion. Only sovereignty can do that, by using the powers of speech and imagination to erect a set of rights and rules that people can live by.[20]

Hobbes, an educator of fear who sought to turn it from the engine of disorder to the linchpin of order, was also an alchemist of political imagination. He laid into the fanciful ideologies of legitimacy and rebellion that had driven England into civil war and sent him scurrying between countries and camps. He despised the grip that priests and rhetoricians could get on the minds of the unwary. (He would have been unsurprised by the lurid conspiracy theories that have entered US politics in the twenty-first century.) But for all his warnings about the dangers of rhetoric and imagination, his political theory is a rhetorical and imaginative triumph. It proposes a new way of understanding oneself and others: as the ultimate authors of political order, subject to it, but only because we have created it. The law, clearly understood, is our law. Hobbes's image of the social contract that establishes sovereignty, and then takes a majority vote to assign sovereign power to a monarch or institution (to choose a constitution, we might say without distorting the idea), is meant to be entirely rational. But it is also as speculative, almost as metaphysical, as the theories that Hobbes rejected for their superstitious irrationality. At no point in English history, or anywhere else we know of, did the entire populace swear a solemn oath to live under joint sovereignty. Hobbes's was a just-so story that invited readers to treat the decisions of rulers as if they were their own.[21]

In Hobbes's mind, the meaning of this imaginative exercise was a conservative one: whatever state you lived under was legitimate, unless it failed to keep order. But we do not control the meaning of what we make. Hobbes's origin story for sovereignty generated new stories, whose tellers built on his cornerstones. His ambition was to end political cacophony. Instead, he launched a new dispute over just what it meant for a people to make their own laws and set the terms of their own interdependence. His idea of sovereignty, basically authoritarian in intent, contained the seeds of democracy.

Not all seeds grow. Democratic sovereignty had to be made up but also made real. Without a way for millions of people to act as one, it could be only a just-so story. The innovation that made this idea real was mass election as the institutional vehicle of majority rule. Mass election gave institutional reality to the notion that the people could act as one, even while dispersed across a large country and mainly engaged in their private pursuits. In some cases, election by the masses emerged by fits and starts, becoming something like a sovereign voice nearly in hindsight. This was the case, for instance, in British parliamentary elections. Originally not much more than a form of class representation for the gentry, these elections finally became a site of universal suffrage in 1918, after a series of watershed expansions of the franchise in the nineteenth century. In other cases, the mass election was an innovation aimed from the outset at giving life to the idea of a sovereign people. This was so in the early United States.

It has been conventional for a long time to talk about nations as "imagined communities" and to trace the ways that traditions, languages, national dress, and patriotic stories get invented and enable people to believe that they are somehow essentially linked with others hundreds or thousands of miles away, leading different lives—but on the same side of the border. Political sovereignty is also a form of imagined community, made up through a certain vision of political power, which is made real through institutions that translate that picture into action. Imagined sovereigns, as we might call them, have some moral advantages over imagined nations. They are not obsessed with linguistic, racial, or cultural commonality. Instead, they begin from individuals, here and now, who decide how they will live together. Imagined sovereigns base their appeal not on who their citizens are but on what those citizens do.[22]

We have already seen that democratic sovereignty inspires doubts and fears. Those fears are many and strong. They loom as large in modern politics as democratic sovereignty itself. Democratic sovereignty can be hard to take seriously, let alone literally, and to take it seriously can be frightening. Yet it persists at the center of modern politics.

Part of the reason may be its stark contrast with the alternatives. If we do not believe we can be the authors of our own common world, then what do we believe about politics? We would then be back to accepting what has seemed, to most thoughtful people in most of history, the only realistic view: that one hopes to live in a time with good rulers or, in the rarest circumstances, to be born in a country with decent institutions that have not yet fallen into their inevitable corruption. These are questions of fortune. In the great drawing of straws, more are short than long. When it comes to politics, most of us will keep our heads down and hope that it does not come to politics too often.

How, in this attitude, would we understand the economic, social, and ecological crises that are wearing away our lives? Those, too, are a kind of fate—created by human effort and activity but, ironically, quite beyond our control. We would suffer them as we would suffer our rulers, only a little more impersonally. Maybe we hope a new technology or a new religion will sweep onto the scene and change the course of things. That, too, would be fate.

In light of the alternatives, the moral and emotional appeal of democracy becomes vivid. It seeks an escape from fate and fatalism, from a passive stance toward the history of one's time. It proposes to make that escape at the price of a new fate, an artificial common fate. Is the price worth the dangers? And, apart from its appeal, does democratic sovereignty make sense? Is it merely the most recent political myth, replacing the divine rights of kings and organic wholeness of peoples with something equally implausible and not much less dangerous? Or is it the way, uniquely, that we common people can shape our shared lives? Arguments over that question have made our world. They are still our arguments today.

3

THE CONSTITUTION
VERSUS DEMOCRACY

When Joseph R. Biden was sworn in as the forty-sixth American president on January 20, 2021, in a Washington thinned out by pandemic restrictions and monitored by twenty-five thousand National Guard troops, he was quick to praise "the resilience of our Constitution." Biden's encomium to the Constitution was standard talk for the day. Eight years earlier, Barack Obama had launched his second inaugural address under the same slogan: "the enduring strength of our Constitution." Eight years before that, George W. Bush had begun with "the durable wisdom of our Constitution." Biden also called his inauguration "democracy's day," saying that "the cause of democracy" had proven fragile but had prevailed. George H. W. Bush had called his own inauguration "democracy's big day," and Obama in 2013 equated the Constitution with "the promise of our democracy."[1]

In the common tongue of the American political mainstream, as these examples highlight, the Constitution and democracy mean pretty much the same thing. Under the palpable strain of multiple crises, Biden spoke the same civic language as his predecessors. In one respect, his heavily guarded inauguration, haunted by fear of some new eruption of violence, showed the truth of the formula that democracy equals the Constitution. What political scientists call the minimalist definition of democracy focuses on the peaceful transfer of power following an election: if voters can send the party in power packing and choose its replacement, they live in a democracy, and if they can't, they don't. January 2021 was haunted by fear that, even by this modest definition, democracy would fail. During the campaign, Donald Trump persistently re-fused to say that he would leave office if he lost the election. After he lost, he denied that the result was legitimate, hurling claims of fraud and hinting that he would find some way to stay in office. The pro-Trump rioters who briefly took control of the Capitol building two weeks before the inauguration had the same idea, to the extent a mob has an idea: to keep the president in power by jamming the constitutional machinery of transition. They had no chance of achieving their goal, but the goal itself, and the fact that the president in office had cultivated it in them (while also patronizing any lawyer who claimed to have a trick for reversing the election), amounted to a sledgehammer aimed at the gears of minimalist democracy. It isn't hard to see why Biden was moved to say that the Constitution and democracy had fought through a dangerous season together.

But democracy's relationship to the Constitution looks more vexed if we take just one step back. Suppose when we said *democracy*, we meant something just slightly less minimal than "a peace-ful transfer of power to the winner of the electoral college vote," which is the rule the Constitution sets. Imagine if by democracy we meant, instead, "a peaceful transfer of power to the candidate that the most voters chose." Through most of the twentieth cen-tury, these two formulas reliably came to the same thing. They came apart in 2000, when George W. Bush won the presidency (with help from the Supreme Court's 5–4 ruling in *Bush v. Gore*) but lost the popular vote to Al Gore by about half a million votes, and in 2016, when Trump won 304 electoral votes to Hillary Clinton's 227, but nearly three million more voters supported Clinton than Trump. The popular vote and the Electoral College tally nearly came apart again in 2020: Biden won seven million more votes than Trump, a lead of almost five percentage points in the popular vote but would have lost the Electoral College if about seventy-seven thousand voters had switched to Trump in Nevada, Wisconsin, Georgia, and Arizona.

The Constitution prescribes the Electoral College as the means of selecting the president—just one aspect of James Madison's "total exclusion of the people in their collective capacity" from their own government. Madison meant that under the Constitution the national majority does nothing directly, including picking the executive. So in 2000 and, more dramatically, in 2016, there was a genuine sense in which the Constitution and democracy were not on the same side. If Trump had pulled out those seventy-seven thousand extra votes in four states, the election would have put the Constitution and democracy into an extremely tense relationship: Trump would have been the plain winner by constitutional rules, after a clear majority repudiated him in the highest turnout election in a century. (Even narrower and more arcane: with a difference of forty-three thousand votes, Trump could have tied Biden with 269 electoral votes apiece and thrown the race into the House of Representatives, which would likely have chosen Trump.)[2]

The problem isn't just that the Constitution's rules for peaceful succession are not, in the usual sense, democratic, although that is serious in a country that has the habit of regarding democracy and the Constitution as two cornerstones of the same political structure. The Electoral College also creates the artificially narrow margins that feed conspiracy theories. Even a world-class huckster would have trouble keeping up a story about seven million stolen votes, but a difference of ten thousand votes (Arizona in 2020) is a difference on a scale that conspiracy mongers can handle. By fragmenting the national polity and making the most important national political decision turn on state-by-state majorities, Madison's constitution contributed a great deal to the near crisis in 2020 whose passing (for the time being) Biden at his inauguration chalked up to the same Constitution's resilience. The signal quality of the Constitution in this case is not resilience but rigidity.

A mechanism for selecting a chief executive among propertied elites in the late eighteenth century persists into the twenty-first, now as a key choke point in a mass democracy.

In the course of thwarting actual majorities, the Constitution also produces spurious ones. These, in turn, feed back into the conditions that produced the Trumpist riot of January 6, 2021, and the politics of alienation and mistrust behind it. The modern Republican Party depends existentially on the Constitution. It is a minority party, not just in its share of the national presidential vote but also because only antimajoritarian constitutional structures keep it viable. The year 2004 was the only time since 1988 that a Republican candidate has led in the national vote, yet Republican appointees dominate the Supreme Court by 6–3 because the justices are appointed by the president and confirmed by the Senate, which, by representing each state equally, gives extra influence to conservative, rural, and white voters in less populated states. As noted earlier, the Republican Senate majority that confirmed Trump's two nominees to the court represented just about 45 percent of the country.[3]

The Constitution is also designed to inhibit lawmaking, slowing down politics and making meaningful initiatives hard to undertake. Passing a law requires majorities in both houses of Congress and the support of the president, plus surviving the gauntlet of creative legal argument that controversial laws must run at the Supreme Court. Few elections result in the sweeping legislation that builds new constituencies and lasting majorities, as the social protections of the New Deal did. So campaigns have shifted into a symbolic and defensive mode. The way to mobilize voters is not to promise a better world (they know it isn't coming) but to impress on them the urgency of keeping the other candidate and party out of power. This was the bipartisan strategy in 2016 and in 2020, when large majorities of voters from both parties told pollsters they doubted the country could survive if the opposing candidate won. They did not come to that worry accidentally: it was each party's central message. If enough people believe it is their responsibility to resist and disable any government they did not help to elect, self-rule can become impossible. The Constitution's inhibition of lawmaking fosters this situation.

Donald Trump's presidency arose from all of these dysfunctions. He cultivated the sense among his supporters that they were at once an endangered minority and the natural, proper majority, and promised to protect them from the other side. As we have seen, only the antidemocratic anachronisms of the US Constitution gave Trump the presidency and his party control over most of national government, despite his losing the popular vote and consistently attracting more disapproval than approval in polls.

—— ——

So American democracy, still habitually identified with its Constitution, is also vexed by it. How did we come to this, and why has it been so hard to see? The answers are in the origins of the US Constitution and its place in the larger history of constitutions. The concept of a constitution goes back to Aristotle's use of *politeia* to describe the institutions of political rule in the Greek city-states. He and his students are credited with assembling accounts of the constitutions of as many as 170 of these *poleis*. The only surviving example is the Constitution of the Athenians, thought to have been written about 350 BCE and recovered in an Egyptian papyrus codex in 1879. It is one part political history of Athens and one part an account of the sequence of institutions that arose after successive waves of conflict. Each constitution was a recasting of collective power, a new way for the *polis* to take action.

Aristotle's treatment of constitutions established several themes that have persisted ever since. Constitutions both define a polity's forms of political action and themselves arise from political action. In Aristotle's meaning, a constitution is a polity's set of authoritative institutions, the ways it answers its political questions. Confronted with a political dispute, do citizens look to an assembly, a citizen jury, or a leading magistrate (archon) for an answer? A constitution answers these questions, which have no answer outside a constitutional order.

But creating a constitution, which is the quintessential political act, must often happen outside constitutional order—sometimes quite dramatically, such as after a civil war. Constitutions thus tend to involve a paradox of authorship: they authorize the decisions that count on behalf of the polity but must often find their own authorization somewhere else. The Athenians squared this circle, with some damage to its shape, by assigning individuals to author new constitutions at the end of conflicts that had broken the previous regimes. This solution depended on a good deal of preexisting political unity among the Athenians, whether because of their relatively small and homogeneous polity or because of the solidarity that can bind the winning side at the end of conflict.

Aristotle's treatment also highlights that constitutions have what we can call, at the cost of a little anachronism, a deep class element. Aristotle identified the prohibition of debt slavery as the most democratic feature of the constitution that the statesman Solon is credited with writing for Athens in the early sixth century BCE. A "democratic" constitution for Aristotle meant a regime of popular control and also meant protecting poor and middling citizens against economic domination. (In the same spirit, it would seem natural today to say that one of the most democratic features of the US Constitution is the Thirteenth Amendment's prohibition of slavery and other forms of forced labor.) The *demos* of classical democracy was not the abstract body of citizens but the free poor and small landholders in contrast to the rich. Oligarchy was, and is, plainly a form of class rule, but democracy was, for the ancients, just as plainly a different form of class rule. Because classical Greece was a slave society, the class character of a democratic constitution involved a downward contrast as well as an upward one. Classical democracy was political rule by the free over those who were not treated as members of the polity at all (the enslaved) and also over the wealthy. The wealthy found ways to resist, not always directly. The aristocrat Plato attacked democracy as feckless, piggish, and the enemy of both justice and excellence, and his *Politeia* (translated *The Republic*, but the word is the same as Aristotle's "constitution") is world history's most lasting indictment of a political system.

The more recent history of constitutions began in the monarchies of early modern Europe, which were larger, more commercial, and in many cases more religiously and linguistically divided than the classical city-states. One paradigm of the modern constitution is a document issued from within the government of such a society—usually in the name of the monarch—to define, reassign, or limit political power in a concession to other social forces. These are not, mostly, the kinds of refoundings of political society that Aristotle described the Athenians as launching but reiterated reforms within a continuous order. Much of English political history from the medieval Norman period into the seventeenth century is a string of such constitutional shifts, often royal concessions to the landholders who wanted control (chiefly) over how they were taxed and took advantage of fiscal crises (often rooted in war) to press their case. Parliament, now the site of British sovereignty, grew up as a vehicle for the landed class to weigh in on government and for centuries was called chiefly to authorize extraordinary taxation. It was a vestigial parliament of that kind, the Estates-General, called by Louis XVI in 1789 to try to remedy a debt crisis rooted in the War of American Independence, that turned itself into the crucible of the French Revolution. The *Nakaz* that Catherine the Great composed for Russia in the 1760s and had approved by representatives from across the empire, was a constitutional document of this familiar species. It combined modest reform with a reaffirmation of the monarch's central place in the political order, anchoring absolute rule in the conceit that the peoples of Russia had all assented. (It did not outlive Catherine's reign.)

That appeal to the people was in line with the general understanding of constitutionalism in monarchical early modern Europe. It was widely argued that legitimate government must be traced back to some kind of agreement by the people governed, but this idea was almost never taken to imply democracy. The idea of popular consent worked more as a political myth than as a way for living people to criticize or change their government. There was no way for a people to revisit the agreement that had, ostensibly, placed it under its government. A people was not, in practice, an entity that could act. It was closer to a group defined by subjection to a given government—a conveniently packaged object for rulers, who swapped territory and often regarded it and the people living on it as a sort of plantation. Constitutionalism, that is, was not at odds with the rule of kings.

In the late eighteenth century, constitutions took on a new significance: They became vehicles of a special kind of democratic action: the whole people of a political community making fundamental law for itself—not mythically, in the irretrievable past, but now. The results were, in principle and to a varying extent in reality, acts of popular sovereignty. They made real a version of the sovereignty that Rousseau, drawing on Hobbes's thought, had helped to make up. But, of course, it took much more than ideas to make this new form of action real.

What happened? For one, revolutions. England's two seventeenth-century revolutions, particularly the violent and ultimately defeated one of 1647–1662 that is more often called the English Civil War, presented a novel problem: how people who have dissolved their government can create a new one, typically under pressure from social unrest and actual or incipient war. The constitutional theorizing that flew around these revolutions—in particular the first, which was longer and bloodier, the one that sent Hobbes into exile and ended with Oliver Cromwell's exhumed head on a pike outside Westminster—was a fantastical miscellany, including a wild array of sectarian and speculative religious appeals, myths of pre-Norman Anglo-Saxon liberty, and demands that, by natural right, "every man that is to live under a government, ought first by his own consent to put himself under that government." The last claim comes from Colonel Thomas Rainsborough, an officer in Oliver Cromwell's army and a member of the Leveller movement (so called by its enemies for its alleged plans to redistribute property). In practice, the Levellers, who had their base among the artisans of London, saw this principle as requiring universal male suffrage. It also resonated (perhaps ironically) with the royalist Hobbes's image of political order beginning in primordial democracy and anticipated Rousseau's search for political bonds that would leave the governed free.[4]

More temperate and more influential was philosopher John Locke's rationalization of the Glorious Revolution of 1688, which justified Parliament's power to exclude the Stuart succession by appeal to a hypothetical contract between the people and their rulers. Locke was not a democrat, but he did argue for a right of revolution, which came into force when the government violated certain fundamental interests, such as life, liberty, and property, or broke constitutional constraints on power. Locke traced all these limitations on legitimate authority to an idea of what the people would originally have signed up to obey. Imagined foundings, which theorists had pushed safely back into the mists of time, were now in the foreground of events, unsettling regimes they had more usually bolstered.

Even this paled beside the constitutional supernova of the French Revolution. Declaring themselves the rulers of France on behalf of the ultimately sovereign French people, the Estates-General and subsequent revolutionary legislatures issued a series of constitutions that aimed to make popular sovereignty an institutional reality. In France and wherever radicals took inspiration from its revolution, including France's own colony, Haiti, the principle that the people should make their own law was no longer a philosopher's conceit but a design principle for inventing a constitution.

Meanwhile, in the British colonies of America, a successful colonial revolt created a new political situation that resembled the theorists' image of the social contract more, perhaps, than anything before in world history. John Locke's position on the Glorious Revolution provided the argument, and a good deal of the rhetoric, of the American Declaration of Independence of 1776: "That to secure [natural] rights, Governments are instituted among Men, deriving their just powers from the consent of the governed,—That whenever any Form of Government becomes destructive of these ends, it is the Right of the People to alter or to abolish it, and to institute new Government, laying its foundation on such principles and organizing its powers in such form, as to them shall seem most likely to effect their Safety and Happiness." With their rulers expelled, the colonists confronted in practice a question that centuries of reflection had merely hypothesized: How, *actually*, should they establish a political society? In such circumstances, there was no getting around the thought that political power came ultimately from the people. Where else would it come from? The question was not whether they should decide but how. Events thus presented real-life versions of a theoretical problem: how people might decide on the terms of their collective lives when those had become an open question. How could the people become their own sovereign?

Another development was essential to giving popular sovereignty a life outside the philosopher's chamber. This, as noted earlier, was the mass election, in particular the large-scale up-or-down judgment on a proposed constitution. It had long been standard to say that democracy, whatever its other strengths and weaknesses, was only possible where citizens could gather in person, as the ancient Greeks had done, and so was out of the question for the large countries that dominated the European scene. By voting without coming together in person, the people really could act collectively to authorize a new government, as surely as Athenian assemblies and juries had decided political disputes. This new way of authorizing a constitution made it not just a different kind of legal document from royal pronouncements and negotiations between crown and parliament but also a different kind of political act, coming not from the present rulers, but from the people who—in theory but never before in practice—authorized government and were ultimately their own rulers.

The idea of a constitution created by the people who would live under it expressed a specific, limited, but powerful idea of popular sovereignty. Dispersed and engaged in their personal affairs, modern citizens could not rule en masse on every public question, as Athenians were often imagined to have done. They could, however, stand as the authors of their fundamental law, embodied in a constitution. This idea was in full swing in the insurrectionary colonies of North America. So, more than a decade before the Philadelphia constitution was drafted, the North Carolina constitution of 1776 opened with "all political power is vested in and derived from the people only [and] the people of this State ought to have the sole and exclusive right of regulating the internal government and police thereof." The Vermont constitution of 1777 begins with a statement of social contract theory reminiscent of the Declaration of Independence: "Government ought to be instituted and supported, for the security and protection of the community only . . . and whenever those great ends of government are not obtained, the people have a right, by common consent, to change it." The Pennsylvania constitution of 1776 contains substantially the same language as both the Vermont and North Carolina documents. Revolutionary theory was as constructive as it was destructive, a formula for establishing as well as dismantling governments by appeal to the people.

In the same spirit, the short-lived French Constitution of 1791 declared that "sovereignty is one, indivisible, inalienable, and imprescriptible. It appertains to the nation; no section of the people nor any individual may assume the exercise thereof. The nation, from which alone all powers emanate, may exercise such powers only by delegation." In the Jacobin (or Montagnard) Constitution of 1793, which lasted an even shorter period, the left wing of the National Assembly declared: "Popular sovereignty includes all French citizens. It directly appoints its deputies . . . deliberates upon the law."

Suspended at the start of the Terror, the period of dictatorship that saw some seventeen thousand people executed as enemies of the state, the Constitution of 1793 was, by its language, the most democratic of French revolutionary constitutions. It was also a mess from the point of view of constitutional authorship. It was adopted by the Jacobin faction of the national legislature after the expulsion and, often enough, execution of their more moderate revolutionary allies, the Girondins, in an insurrection powered by the street-fighting radical artisan *sans-culottes*. It combined the ideology of popular sovereignty with the reality of one-party rule. The actual origin of the 1793 constitution was not, then, all that different from those of earlier monarchical or parliamentary attempts to create a new fundamental law: an elite-driven adjustment of institutions offered up as being, in some hard-to-specify way, an expression of the will of the people. It simply happened that this elite was a revolutionary one, a small band of lawyers, journalists, and other radicals, many still in their twenties, often working at night in wine-soaked gatherings, in an episode of political mania in which the will of the nation seemed (to them) to run through them.

Kings and emperors had made the same claim for centuries, with no more basis in reality. But the revolutionaries had taken on the goal of linking the fundamental political law of the country— the constitution—to popular sovereignty, the self-rule of the people. When they failed to make that link real, leaving it a heady rhetorical costume for their new constitution, they failed at their own purpose. They also performed a sleight of hand that would recur in the politics of "popular sovereignty": without any clear way for the people to act, and in a country divided to the point of civil war, they effectively treated a mobilized demographic splinter, the *sans-culottes*, as a stand-in for the public.

The idea of popular sovereignty, without an institutional expression, practically requires something like this. Either one can identify the people with (some of) their present rulers, or one can identify the people with some dissenters, with one's favored activists. In a social world that is always cacophonous and divided, these are the alternatives to babble, unless there is some cogent and authoritative way to say that the people have spoken.

This was the problem that the modern form of the constitution solved, imperfectly and contentiously but still with revolutionary results. It offered the direct insertion of popular sovereignty into politics, not as a diffuse legitimating rhetoric but as fundamental law, the source and limit of all political power. That is the meaning of the phrases about the people and popular sovereignty in the revolutionary constitutions we have been surveying.

How credible was the conceit that the people authored their fundamental law through constitution making? Most of the American revolutionary constitutions, like their French successors, were simply written and adopted by revolutionary state legislatures—a form of political action indistinguishable from ordinary lawmaking except for the *ipse dixit* assertion that it made fundamental law. The stronger link between constitutions and popular sovereignty relied on two institutional innovations, the constitutional plebiscite and the constitutional convention. In voting, majorities could issue an up-or-down vote on a proposed constitution and so actually do what Hobbes had imagined them doing in the original act of popular sovereignty and Rousseau in the ongoing ideal of lawmaking: directly authorizing certain laws of general and fundamental importance. In this form, constitution making could be seen as an act of sovereignty distinct from ordinary lawmaking and government, a higher order of political action for a more fundamental decision. Massachusetts held a referendum on a proposed state constitution in 1778, the first plebiscite in the modern world. New Hampshire soon followed suit. (Voters rejected both proposals, approving a different fundamental law for Massachusetts the second time and on the third try for New Hampshire.) More than a decade later, some Girondins proposed that a French constitution should similarly be approved by plebiscite, although their call went unanswered. A few decades into the nineteenth century, it had become standard in American state constitutions that amendments or new constitutions should be approved by referendum. The people could finally speak in their own voice. Popular sovereignty became a lever, not a ghost, in the political machine.[5]

The second innovation was the constitutional convention, a representative body created especially to propose the fundamental law that voters would then adopt or reject. A few states called conventions for their early constitutions, and the parliamentary assembly that immediately followed England's 1688 revolution was styled a convention, but these were not clearly distinguished from

73

ordinary legislatures, and they ratified their own proposals rather than submitting them to popular vote. New Hampshire once again marked out the new path, establishing an amendment process by which special conventions proposed new constitutional language and a popular vote approved or rejected it as fundamental law. This is not direct democratic action, but it creates a distinct institutional pathway for constitutional change. Where a convention is staffed by delegates who are popularly elected for that purpose, there is an institutionally real sense in which popular majorities both compose their own forums for constitutional reflection and proposal and then ultimately decide whether the proposals that the conventions issue will be fundamental law.

The US Constitution has a momentous and peculiar place in this development. It was written in the summer of 1787 by delegates sent from the thirteen state governments to consider changes to the Articles of Confederation. Adopted by the thirteen states upon independence in 1781, the Articles had done a notably poor job of holding the states together. They created a sort of congress, staffed by representatives of the state governments, in which each state had one vote, and which could raise funds only by going begging to the state legislatures. The inability to raise money by taxing created a debt crisis, as the colonies had borrowed a great deal of money at home and abroad to finance their war of independence. Besides this signal deficiency, the Articles created only weak coordination in the essential matters of defense, trade, and foreign affairs, in which political elites felt the urgent practical need to present a common front to European partners and rivals. The barrier to overcoming these inconveniences was high: the Articles stated that they could be amended only by unanimous agreement of the states.

As is well known, the delegates in Philadelphia went far beyond their assignment to propose amendments within the terms of the Articles of Confederation. A bit like the Jacobins a few years later, they staged what legal historian Michael Klarman calls a "framers' coup," putting themselves in the place of the people without quite being asked and setting out fundamental law well beyond what they had been authorized to write. James Madison made no apologies about this, arguing that "the transcendent and precious right of the people" to peaceful revolution required that fundamental "changes be instituted by some INFORMAL AND UNAUTHORIZED PROPOSITIONS, made by some patriotic and respectable citizens" (capitalized in the original). After all, "it is impossible for the people spontaneously and universally to move in concert towards their object." In other words, since the people must rule, but they cannot rule, let us, here and now, rule on their behalf and count our decisions as theirs. Madison's appeal showed the power of the idea of popular sovereignty and its wide acceptance but also highlighted how dangerously open it was to factional abuse. The Jacobins at least looked to their favorite rioters as stand-ins for the people, rather than simply offering themselves for the job.[6]

The way the Philadelphia convention sought authorization for its proposals also showed the power and influence of the theory of popular sovereignty that some states had already put into practice in their constitution making. Besides the Articles' deficient design, Alexander Hamilton wrote, they had a debilitating democratic deficit:

It has not a little contributed to the infirmities of the existing federal system, that it never had a ratification by the PEOPLE. Resting on no better foundation than the consent of the several legislatures, it has been exposed to frequent and intricate questions concerning the validity of its powers. . . . The possibility of a question of this nature proves the necessity of laying the foundations of our national government deeper than the mere sanction of delegated authority. The fabric of American empire ought to rest on the solid basis of THE CONSENT OF THE PEOPLE. The streams of national power ought to flow immediately from that pure, original fountain of all legitimate authority.[7]

75

The words, of course, do not make the reality. Hamilton and Madison were perfectly capable of attacking the Articles of Confederation for problems that their Constitution also failed to solve. They denounced the Articles' congress for its one-state, one-vote principle, which Hamilton said "contradicts the fundamental maxim of republican government, which requires that the sense of the majority should prevail," while advancing a one-state-two-vote principle in the US Senate. They dismissed the Articles' combination of state and federal authority, writing "a sovereignty over sovereigns, a government over governments, a legislation for communities . . . as it is a solecism in theory, so in practice it is subversive of the order and ends of civil polity." It is a powerful point, rooted in a Hobbesian insight that order requires knowing where the last word resides, a point that resonates today in the recurrent crises of the European Union's government of governments. The Constitution's compromise of federalism did not, however, really solve the problem by adding national power alongside that of the states. The Civil War was only the most dramatic of the many crises of authority that have grown up in the uncertain space between federal writ and state autonomy, from the fight over Congress's power to pass New Deal legislation in the 1930s to the states' rights revolt against civil rights reforms in the 1960s to the multilevel failure to manage the COVID pandemic.[8]

But the Philadelphia delegates did more than just assert popular authorization: they sought it in the ratification campaign that brought the Constitution into force in 1789. Ratification by specially elected conventions (selected in some states with broader suffrage than ordinary elections) put the Constitution on a special lawmaking track. While it was not as direct a popular act as the referendums of Massachusetts and New Hampshire, ratification in conventions did give institutional life to the principle of popular sovereignty, adoption of fundamental law by the people, that Madison and Hamilton accepted rhetorically as the standard their proposal must meet. "We the People," as the Constitution's text begins, is not just a flourish or conceit. It identifies the author of the document, the sovereign people, which, when they act through the proper channels, can make law as surely as Congress can. Just as Congress is the author of a statute even though an anonymous staffer has drafted the language, the popular sovereign of the United States can be the author of the Constitution and the source of its authority, even though the drafters were the delegates sweating out the Philadelphia summer in their closed meeting rooms.

Advocates for the new Constitution advanced many arguments for it, from natural rights (often those of creditors: some state legislatures were seeking ways to lift the burden on debtors, particularly by issuing paper money, which was unconventional and suspected of being a kind of fiscal swindle) to the benefits of commerce in a single national market to the threat that European powers would invade a divided United States. There were, too, many reasons that the Constitution took root once adopted. Written charters were a familiar legal form across the history of English and colonial government, so what was new in some ways was very familiar in others. Many of the political elites in the new republic were already linked by extensive networks of trade along the Atlantic coast (a fact to which the authors of the *Federalist Papers*—Hamilton, Madison, and John Jay—drew attention in their early installments), so national unity was hardly strange to them. So there were many reasons the Constitution was approved, and many reasons that it succeeded as well as it did. These, however, were all distinct from what gave it authority as fundamental law. Here the answer was clear in what the Constitution's supporters did (and believed they must do) as much as in what they said: the Constitution became fundamental law when it was adopted by the people in an act of popular sovereignty. Appeal to the people was not just rhetorical: it had institutional life in the elected conventions, where the proposed Constitution would succeed or fail.[9]

That is what popular sovereignty meant to its drafters and ratifiers. What did their new Constitution mean for popular sovereignty? The answer is complicated and, on the whole, not positive. The ratification of the Constitution called into being a new popular sovereign, the people of the United States, and also laid down rules of constitutional change that made it exceedingly difficult for that sovereign to act again. These constitutional barriers to constitutional lawmaking have several dimensions. First, according to Article V of the Constitution, an amendment requires much more than majority or even supermajority support. It must be proposed by a two-thirds vote of both houses of Congress or by a convention requested by two-thirds of state legislatures, then ratified by majority votes of the legislatures of three-quarters of the states—once again passing both state houses, as nearly all states have both a senate and a more numerous house. Thirteen states can block a proposed amendment. In theory, states representing less than 10 percent of the national population would be enough, and the sharp political divide between rural and urban regions means the reality could somewhat resemble the theoretical extreme. Second, the fact that proposed amendments begin in supermajority votes of Congress means they cannot express popular sovereignty, as something distinct from the ordinary processes of government, without first achieving something approaching a consensus within the ordinary processes of government. This is a paradoxical requirement. Under these rules, a country that needs sovereign action because its government has drifted away from democratic accountability will be precisely the one least able to take such action.[10]

In both cases, supermajority requirements (two-thirds, three-quarters) interact with the most basic incoherence in the Constitution's design: the dispersal of authority between the states and the national government, both styled "sovereigns." Having denounced the Articles of Confederation for trying to create the "solecism" of a sovereign over sovereigns, the authors of the *Federalist Papers* described the authority behind their proposed Constitution as "neither wholly NATIONAL nor wholly FEDERAL." Tellingly, Madison thought it obvious that "were it wholly national, the supreme and final authority would reside in the MAJORITY of the people of the Union; and this authority would be competent at all times, like that of a majority of every national society, to alter or abolish its established government." That is, if "We the People" really were the national people, then the same principle of popular sovereignty that gave the Constitution its authority would also entail a much more flexible form of constitutional amendment and, behind it, a much stronger authority to revisit the Constitution. Instead, the Constitution fractured that sovereignty into states that must be cobbled together to change fundamental law. The Constitution called on popular sovereignty for its authority but baffled, inhibited, even imprisoned its sovereign. The result was to found a polity on an act of fundamental lawmaking, anchored in popular sovereignty, while setting that fundamental law apart from the ongoing life of the country's majority, making it, in reality, an ever more remote, alien, even mystical authority. This initial combination of reliance on and denial of popular sovereignty produced a constitutional paradox from which centuries of confusion have flowed.[11]

Certain principles seemed all but self-evident in the theory of popular sovereignty that powered the adoption of the Constitution—the same principles that its text undercut. The first was popular authorship: a constitution is fundamental law if the people can be said in a nonobscurantist, institutionally concrete way to have adopted it. The second principle was present consent: what gives fundamental law its continuing authority is the agreement of the people now living under it who constitute the present sovereign, not the fact that it was originally adopted through an earlier sovereign act. Constitutions are for the living. Taking these principles together, popular sovereignty must be ongoing and self-renewing or else fail as a practice of self-rule.

Constitutional lawmaking was not imagined to be a one-time affair. A sovereign majority had no legitimate power over later generations. What gave inherited constitutional law its authority in the present could only be the present consent of those now living under it.

St. George Tucker, the prominent founding-era jurist, expressed this idea in his edition of *Blackstone's Commentaries*:

> That mankind have a right to bind themselves by their own voluntary acts, can scarcely be questioned: but how far have they a

right to enter into engagements to bind their posterity likewise? Are the acts of the dead binding upon their living posterity, to all generations; or has posterity the same natural rights which their ancestors have enjoyed before them? And if they have, what right have any generation of men to establish any particular form of government for succeeding generations?

The answer is not difficult: "Government," said the congress of the American States, in behalf of their constituents, "derives its just authority from the consent of the governed." This fundamental principle then may serve as a guide to direct our judgment with respect to the question. To which we may add, in the words of the author of Common Sense, a law is not binding upon posterity, merely, because it was made by their ancestors; but, because posterity have not repealed it. It is the acquiescence of posterity under the law, which continues its obligation upon them, and not any right which their ancestors had to bind them.[12]

Tucker quoted Thomas Paine's *Common Sense*, which was enormously influential during the American Revolution, though Paine was clearest on this point in his later *Rights of Man*, in which he defended the French revolutionary experiment against Edmund Burke's attack:

It requires but a very small glance of thought to perceive, that altho' laws made in one generation often continue in force through succeeding generations, yet that they continue to derive their force from the consent of the living. A law not repealed continues in force, not because it cannot be repealed, but because it is not repealed; and the non-repealing passes for consent.

Founder and jurist James Wilson observed a corollary of this point when he insisted around the time of the Constitution's adoption that "the people may change the constitution . . . whenever and however they please. This is a right of which no positive institution can ever deprive them."[13]

The principle of popular authorship and the principle of present consent fit together in a vision of popular sovereignty. Popular authorship means that people should make the fundamental laws that they live under. Present consent means that the people who must authorize or reject fundamental law are those who live under it today. Self-rule is a present and continuing project, or it is the rule of the dead over the living.

There is no natural way that the many individuals, families, and groups that share a polity can unite to act as the people. In this sense, politics is always made up. But that does not mean that it is false. Some things that are made up are also made real. When constitutional amendments, even conventions, are possible, popular sovereignty is as real as an ordinary electoral victory. (There is no natural way that voting—marking a piece of paper and putting it in a scanner—makes you part of a majority that replaces a senator, say, but the act is real.) It is as real as judicial review. (Getting five other people to cosign your opinion that a law violates the Constitution has no natural effect on anything, but the effects of Supreme Court rulings are certainly real.) It is as real as the World Series. (There is no natural way that running around a field with sticks and balls produces winners and losers, but baseball is real.) On the other hand, some things that are made up, widely believed, and strongly felt do not become real. You can get a million people to march on the National Mall and anoint you archbishop of Montana or mark ballots declaring war on Mars. The world will be the same tomorrow. Without a way of making popular sovereignty institutionally real, such acts would belong to the category of things made up but not made real. We would be back to the world that medieval theorists envisaged, in which the people could not directly act but could only be represented by rulers and interpreters. The idea of the people would be more a legitimating myth for competing agendas of rule than a version of popular collective action.

In light of the antidemocratic structure of American constitutionalism, we should ask whether we are there already. As we have seen, the Constitution's claim to legitimacy as fundamental law is a democratic one. This was clear to its architects and promoters, even as many feared democratic power in practice and sought to countermand state majorities and baffle national ones. They used the Constitution to shut down popular sovereignty with one hand while relying on it with the other. The concrete effect is in the Senate and the Electoral College, where what Americans have long called "democracy" produces rule by an institutional web of spurious majorities. The minority-rule strategies that have defined US politics in recent decades, particularly on the right, depend on this constitutional design. A more diffuse, ideological symptom is a political culture defined by constitutionalism, powerfully attached to the idea that popular sovereignty and fundamental law are the roots of the polity, but ironically imagining that the power to make constitutional law is always elsewhere: far back in the eighteenth or nineteenth century or in the esoteric recesses of the Supreme Court's chambers.[14]

Depending on our political outlook, we may talk about the Constitution as something handed down from ancestors as inheritance, woven into our political culture as tradition and identity, contested in the rhetoric of movements and the grammar of protest, or discerned in the scholarly statecraft of nine justices in the secular temple at 1 First Street, NE, in Washington, DC. No matter which way we tell the story of constitutional meaning making, the key chapters will always return to the courts, where the made-up claims of constitutional imagination (Rights for future generations! The right to carry a handgun!) are made real in institutional action or are not: "We are under a Constitution, but the Constitution is what the judges say it is," averred Charles Evans Hughes, himself a chief justice of the Supreme Court. None of these stories ends with the people, made real by the institutional form of a majority or supermajority, reauthorizing or revising their own fundamental law. *That* idea—the one at the root of it all, which made it legitimate in the first place—now strikes many as a dangerous fantasy. With the Constitution's text effectively frozen, the first principle of constitution making—popular authorship— is no longer an aspect of democratic power over fundamental law but is instead caught in an ever-receding past. An authoritative text whose authors cannot change it will inevitably be renewed and revised by its interpreters: hence Chief Justice Hughes's bland statement of sovereign transubstantiation.

For a very long time, the Supreme Court's justices have accepted the mantle of constitutional oracles, drawing controversial judgments from competing versions of the document's design and spirit. In 1842, Justice Joseph Story declared that, because the Constitution was a compromise that could be achieved only by protecting "the safety and security of the southern states," it must create "a positive, unqualified right" in a slaveholder to "immediate possession" and control of an enslaved person who had escaped into a free state. Pennsylvania laws preventing particularly cruel acts of kidnapping and family separation by slave catchers were therefore unconstitutional interference with the enslaver's rights. Four decades later, Justice Joseph Bradley rejected the 1875 Civil Rights Act, which forbade racial discrimination in public accommodations, holding that it would betray constitutional design by "mak[ing] Congress take the place of the State legislatures." In 1918, Justice William Day turned away a child labor law, holding that if Congress could forbid children from working in North Carolina's fabric mills, "all freedom of commerce must be at an end, and the power of the States over local matters may be eliminated and thus our system of government be practically destroyed." Nearly a century later, Chief Justice John Roberts cut the legs from under Congress's expansion of public health insurance for low-income people, holding that federal fiscal pressure on states to offer more generous health coverage would "undermine the structure of government established by the Constitution" and put "a gun to the head" of state legislatures deciding whether to go along with the expansion. Returning to the theme in the next Supreme Court term, Roberts struck down a key enforcement provision of the Voting Rights

Act, explaining that it undercut the states' "sovereignty under the Constitution" and, in particular, the "fundamental principle of *equal* sovereignty among the States."[15]

I have picked examples that show the Supreme Court using the boundary between state and national power to protect enslavers, racial discrimination, the prerogatives of factory owners, and limits on voting. It would be easy to give a litany of cases defining national power in ways that have more progressive effects such as authorizing antidiscrimination laws, voting rights, and economic regulation and redistribution. Either way, the Supreme Court sits as ultimate arbiter of constitutional design, drawing and redrawing the implications of that old solecism, a sovereignty over sovereigns. I have also picked examples that have to do with the Constitution's assignment of specific powers to certain institutions, rather than the interpretation of the individual rights set out in the Bill of Rights and the Reconstruction Amendments. There is a fierce and long-running argument over how to understand rights: how strict or flexible their protections should be, what happens when they clash, whether there is any "correct" way to give specific meaning to broad terms like *liberty*, which appears in the Fourteenth Amendment and which the justices have taken as the basis of the rights to choose abortion and same-sex marriage, among others. Those attention-getting controversies are instances of a deeper problem: a fundamental law, supposedly democratic in origin and authority, whose authors are remote and whose interpretation is now in the hands of a tiny institution.[16]

Most citizens, even most practicing politicians, can go years without thinking very hard about whether the Constitution, democracy, political legitimacy, and Supreme Court jurisprudence are more or less synonymous. When circumstances force them to pay attention to the problem, they may find their thoughts unsettled, as when Al Gore reflected on the Supreme Court ruling handing the 2000 presidential election to his opponent: "In the U.S. system, there is no intermediate step between a final Supreme Court decision and violent revolution." Intended as a wry piece of tragic wisdom, Gore's musing would have struck the thinkers, revolutionaries, and institutional architects of popular sovereignty as a concession of defeat for their project.[17]

But the problem of constitutional legitimacy is especially vivid from within judicial chambers. So Justice Antonin Scalia, dissenting from his colleagues' embrace of a right to same-sex marriage in 2015, declared that the content of the case did not matter very much to him, but "it is of overwhelming importance . . . who it is that rules me. Today's decree says that my Ruler, and the Ruler of 320 million Americans coast-to-coast, is a majority of the nine lawyers on the Supreme Court." Scalia was overstating it with "Ruler"—the Supreme Court won't be passing legislation anytime soon—but he was right that the sovereign authority to define fundamental law has migrated, via the Constitution, from the people to the court.[18]

Scalia's plaint captures the impetus of one major strand of US constitutional politics: originalism, the school holding that the Constitution should mean today what it meant to those who ratified it. From the originalist perspective, any other approach empowers today's judges to rewrite fundamental law, usurping popular sovereignty in the process. Originalism embraces and defends the principle that legitimacy arises from popular authorship. Its core problem is that defense of popular authorship is not the same as defense of popular sovereignty: it is one half of a broken whole. The other half, were it not absent, would be present consent. Originalism has nothing to say to this *originally* coequal principle except that whoever would dissent from the old Constitution should try to amend it—and good luck to them. This blasé attitude toward present consent means that originalism makes constitutionalism into a dogmatic defense of the past. In a country where ideas of freedom, equality, and the role of the state have changed profoundly, this defense of the past is also defense of a constitutional vision that is distinctly conservative. In its modern form, originalist jurisprudence arose only in the 1970s, in response to liberal rulings on individual rights and racial and gender equality, and its basic stances have been against constitutional equality for women, against LGBTQ rights and especially same-sex marriage, against abortion rights, and for gun rights. In purist formulations such as Justice Clarence Thomas's, original-ism would mean striking down a great deal of the modern law that governs labor and employment, environmental protection, and social spending.

So it is hardly surprising that present consent, too, has its champions in constitutional politics. Before there was original-ism, there were varieties of living constitutionalism, the approach of judges and scholars who assumed that the Constitution's prin-ciples must change along with values and needs. "In approaching this problem" of school segregation, Chief Justice Earl Warren wrote in 1954, "we cannot turn the clock back to 1868," when the Fourteenth Amendment was adopted with its guarantee of "equal protection of the laws." "We must consider public educa-tion in the light of its full development and its present place in American life." The question here is still Scalia's: the importance of determining "who it is that rules me." But for a living consti-tutionalist, "my Ruler" cannot legitimately be those who ratified constitutional text long ago, when the people were restricted to white men (and often to property holders) and official racial and sex discrimination was widespread. Whatever "equal protection" or a "right of the people" might have meant to the people who ratified those phrases, legitimacy requires that *our* fundamental law be acceptable to *this* twenty-first-century polity. Let the dead obey their dead.[19]

Varieties of living constitutionalism have been the theory of abortion rights, LGBTQ equality, and constitutional equality for women. Constitutional law "respects our history and learns from it without allowing the past alone to rule the present," wrote Justice Anthony Kennedy in the 2015 decision that established the right to same-sex marriage. "The nature of injustice is that we may not always see it in our times," and when "new insight reveals discord between the Constitution's central protections and a received le-gal stricture," the justices may conclude that this insight gives the Constitution a meaning never before envisaged. Justice Kennedy went on to link the "new insight" (roughly "Love = Love," in the phrase of a popular yard-sign catechism) to "pleas and protests," arguments among citizens and experts, and LGBTQ-friendly rulings in other countries' courts, lower federal courts, and those of some states—in short, the argument among the living about what it means to treat the intimate lives of everyone with equal respect.[20]

It is a stirring opinion, and I was one of millions of readers who celebrated on the day it was announced. But although its political morality is charismatic, its theory of constitutional authority is vexed by the equal and opposite problem to that of originalism. Living constitutionalism does snatch constitutional authority from the past, but it is not a victory for the democratic principle that the living control their fundamental law. It can seem to be such a victory because its jurists draw on contemporary diversity and moral creativity, invite social movements to lend new meanings to liberty and equality, and encourage courts to take guidance from cultural ferment. In these ways living constitutionalism is an antithesis to originalism's stark insistence that constitutional meaning does not change unless the constitutional text changes. But all of this makes living constitutionalism the second horn of the American constitutional dilemma. Judges may seek to channel the terms of the political community's present consent, but they cannot *give* that consent, cannot authorize changes in fundamental law. In substituting their own best moral and political judgment for the democratic act of the people, which the constitutional system relies on but also suppresses, judges claim the sanction of the people, who, regrettably, could not act politically and so had to be represented by their faithful betters.

More charitably, everyone here is caught in a dilemma. Fundamental law based in democratic popular sovereignty makes sense only if the twin principles of popular authorship and present consent coexist. A constitution like the American one deserves democratic authority only if it is realistically open to amendment. Then we can know that what has not changed in the old text still commands consent. Silence can have meaning, but only when it is the silence of those free to speak. When the popular sovereign cannot speak, silence is ambiguous. It definitely does not mean that old constitutional provisions still have the consent of the people whose political lives they govern. But neither does it authorize any particular new principle of fundamental law. In facing this dilemma, there are creditable reasons to be either a living constitutionalist or an originalist. But neither approach can keep up the connection between the people and their fundamental law. Both are symptoms of a constitutional order that shuts down the source of authority that powered it in the first place, training citizens to believe both that their constitution is the highest law and that making such law is something done by giants long ago, scholarly statesmen at the Supreme Court, or social movements whose claims a majority of the justices find persuasive.

Partly because neither originalism nor living constitutionalism can give legitimacy to American constitutional practice, constitutional judging recurrently takes a different and more candidly elitist direction. If judges cannot trace their decisions to popular lawmaking, this approach suggests that constitutional law can have a different basis: the special insight of the legal profession, the wisdom of the judge. First developed in ancient Rome by the priests who adjudicated disputes and the imperial aristocrats who succeeded them and created what has come down to us as Roman law, this approach holds that the finest lawyers can discern distinctly legal truths through a process of judgment that is qualitatively different from the will or mere decision of political choices. The principles that judgment develops over generations, with perennial refinement and application, can frame and restrain politics, like reason governing the passions. Ever since its priestly origins in early Roman law, this idea of fundamental law has had a savor of aristocratic domination: it is always a specific elite, whether of birth or of training, that claims special access to the content of reasoned judgment, in contrast to the untutored political impulses of plebians and their tribunes. Tocqueville understood this when he described lawyers as the "aristocracy" of American democracy, a tradition-minded caste with the function of checking the impulses of the moment.[21]

Viewed skeptically, substituting judgment for will looks like a set of rhetorical tricks for dressing little revolutions and restorations in the clothing of principled continuity. Tact covers up rupture and makes politics look like professionalism. For instance, when Chief Justice Roberts ruled that Congress's constitutional power to regulate "commerce" did not authorize the portion of the Affordable Care Act that requires individuals to purchase health insurance, he drew a new line through old precedents, limning distinctions that hardly anyone would have discerned before 2010. Yes, the court had ruled in 1942 that the "commerce power" authorized Congress to bar a farmer from consuming wheat grown on his own land because the prohibition served to support the price of wheat by driving growers onto the market as buyers. Surely the same principle authorized Congress to require buying coverage to keep healthy people in the insurance pool, which health care, economists argued would make premiums affordable? *No*, Roberts quietly replied, the situations are different. The farmer, you see, when he started farming, crossed an invisible threshold that made him susceptible to regulation. But the person who is required to purchase insurance has not freely entered the field of health care, and requiring her to buy insurance would drag her into that field. The farmer's situation falls within the power conferred on Congress to "regulate commerce among the several states" in Article I, section 8 of the 1789 Constitution. That of the uninsured person does not.[22]

These distinctions were pretty much cut from whole cloth, but they *felt* like judgment rather than will, like the use of expert technique to spy a line that was already there and just had to be drawn out. To quarrel with it, you would have to follow Roberts through the old cases and give the dusty facts and language a different meaning. Even the terms of the potential challenge are basically those of elite professional training: the challenger must out-craft the master craftsman. And—here is the real bite—the craft's standards are largely circular, defined by what the dominant justices of the time do and what their professional and political allies honor. Good luck unseating them with semantics. The mystifications of originalism and the moralizing of living constitutionalism look candid by contrast. They at least return, however unconvincingly, to the ground of democratic sovereignty to renew their authority. The rhetoric of judgment hovers indifferently over that ground.

So in 2013 Roberts coined the principle of the "equal dignity" of the states as "sovereigns." In his hands, this meant that the Voting Rights Act could not place Justice Department supervision over the election laws of states and counties with histories of suppressing the non-white vote. It was a fiercely partisan question that touched on the character of American democracy and the legacy of the civil rights movement. To read the opinion, however, is to float in soothing currents of reasonableness, constitutional balance, the preservation of tradition. The result is to give the appearance of deciding a political question without politics—by judgment, not will.[23]

American constitutionalism has become, then, a form of antipolitics: a politics defined by the way its practitioners conceal the political character of their decisions, putting its topics outside democratic contest. What sustains this use of a constitution whose authority, by its own declaration, comes from the people? Part of the answer is that partisan advocates devote energy, intelligence, and money to developing legal arguments like the one Roberts embraced in limiting the Affordable Care Act and whole ecologies of interpretation in which these thrive. All interpretive practices depend on communities of interpreters. In a country where judges often have the last word on important disputes, economic and ideological fortunes depend on what those communities find obvious, plausible, laughable, or shocking. Those who have both resources and reason to care what judges do invest accordingly, from law schools to law firms to the "public interest" litigation groups and institutes that represent every possible etiolation of the concepts of the public and its interests.

Another part of the answer is civic fear. The foremost constituencies of constitutional review are those who fear being victimized by their fellow citizens. Fair enough: in danger, you need security, as Hobbes insisted. For perfectly understandable reasons, since

World War II the courts have become the patrons of religious objectors to secular regulation and secular objectors to religious practice, of unpopular speakers and gun owners, of the right to choose abortion (hanging by a thread at the time of writing) and the right to spend big money in political campaigns, of LGBTQ people and opponents of affirmative action, of the ACLU (some of the time) and the Chamber of Commerce and the National Federation of Independent Businesses. All that these constituencies have in common is cause to see the federal courts as standing between them and hostile political action.

Threaded together with the self-interest of mere politics and the self-protection of civic fear is a subtler ideological bind. The Constitution and democracy are the twin symbols of American political legitimacy. Since World War II, several generations have learned to treat them as synonymous. Our mainstream political language still lacks ways of saying, with unapologetic conviction and even patriotically, that the Constitution may be the enemy of the democracy it supposedly sustains. Our civic talk runs into the confusions of Joe Biden's 2021 inaugural address. We can hardly imagine having the power to refound a genuinely democratic constitutionalism. Reclaiming that power would take a confrontation with the Constitution, not to reject constitutional order but to renew it.

4

CULTURE AND CONSENSUS

Since its imperfect beginnings, modern democracy has been shadowed by suspicion that it cannot be what it seems. In the clear light of reason, the idea that large groups of ordinary people can rule themselves is implausible, the argument goes, and so some other principle must be lurking beneath the semblance of democracy. In the American setting, this idea goes back to the early revolutionary stirrings of 1775, when Edmund Burke, viewing the restive colonies from London, denied that the language of social contracts and popular sovereignty that poured from the Atlantic seaboard could provide the basis of a political order. For people to live together, they needed stronger cornerstones and buttresses than these airy phrases could provide.

If the Massachusetts colonists had managed to keep their society together after British troops withdrew and the colonial government lost its power—as they seemed to have done—they must be relying on some sturdy but unacknowledged supports. Burke speculated, like an astronomer inferring a distant planet's existence from the wobble of something nearer and visible, that these supports must lie in the invisible bonds of custom and imagination. If "anarchy is found tolerable," as Burke conceded it seemed to be, this must be because it was no anarchy at all. Gently, quietly, custom was holding together a restive people, flowing steadily like deep water beneath a squall. Burke pointed to several strands of British colonial culture and emphasized especially that English common law, with its strong regard for rights of property and contract, provided Americans with a grammar for order. The colonists were, he thought, a people shaped by a particular legal culture, one in which the state could recede for long periods because law was present in the habits of the people.[1]

Decades later, another European interpreter of American politics made a similar argument, with more lasting influence. Popular sovereignty was terrifying, Alexis de Tocqueville wrote, in part because it could not be what its enthusiasts claimed. In reality, it could only amount to one segment of the country doing something to another segment, perhaps quite abruptly and roughly. There was no cogent sense in which this could be justified as a matter of consent or the joint action of the whole people. "I regard it an impious and detestable maxim that in matters of government the majority of a people has the right to do everything," he wrote. "What is a majority, in its collective capacity, if not an individual with opinions, and usually with interests, contrary to those of another individual, called the minority?"[2]

Fortunately, Tocqueville continued (sounding like Burke), the Americans did not really mean it when they talked about popular sovereignty. Probably no people could stand to mean it: they would then have too much to fear from one another. (Here the Hobbesian threat, where we become one another's dangers, is not in prepolitical social life but in political life itself.) Like Burke's colonists, Tocqueville's Americans were held together by *moeurs*, or mores: shared moral intuition, political imagination, habits of judgment and feeling absorbed so deeply they felt natural. For the Americans, these included (Tocqueville thought) an inheritance of Christianity and a legal culture that gave them a common sense of right and wrong, of who owed what to whom. This common sense included a faith in rights—of private property, religious conscience, and free speech—and a willingness to let certain hard questions find their answers in courts, which, we might say, "speak law," the language of judgment rather than the harsher terms of political will. Americans, in Tocqueville's understanding, generally wouldn't think of using the terrible tool of popular sovereignty for the kinds of disruptive ends to which it might otherwise be put. Mores were the ballast that kept their craft stable on democracy's tumultuous seas.[3]

Tocqueville's work seemed from the beginning a warning about the tyrannical potential of democracy. Henry Reeve, the English journalist who produced a standard translation of *Democracy in America* in the 1830s, warned his readers that "the book of 'The Prince' is closed for ever as a State manual; and the book of 'The People'—a book of perhaps darker sophistries and more pressing tyranny—is as yet unwritten." The English should read Tocqueville, he urged, because of "the necessity of study of that element which threatens us"—the democratic element: "the democratic element must be met, and to be met it must be known, before the unhallowed rites of destruction have begun . . . before the vertigo of conquest has seized the lower orders, or the palsy of dejection fallen upon the aristocracy."[4]

When Reeve's translation appeared in the United States, the publishers replaced his Cassandran introduction with a more sanguine one by John Canfield Spencer, a New York lawyer who had met Tocqueville during his American travels. Spencer took care to present Tocqueville as a friend and educator of democracy, not a guide to those threatened by it. The book "explained, with a pencil of light, the mystery that has baffled Europeans and perplexed Americans"—how democratic self-rule had proven compatible with order. Tocqueville had found the answer "in the manners, habits, and opinions of a people who had been gradually prepared, by a long course of peculiar circumstances, and by their local position, for self-government." By understanding these sources, Americans would find "the means of preventing their decay or destruction." The key was to replace "general and indefinite notions of our own liberty, greatness, happiness, &c." with "precise and accurate knowledge of the true merits of our institutions, the peculiar objects they are calculated to attain or promote, and the means provided for that purpose" so that "every citizen" could "discharge his great political duty of guarding those means against the approach of corruption, and of sustaining them against the violence of party commotions." In other words, the duty of citizenship was essentially conservative: to preserve the inherited "manners, habits, and opinions" that had made Americans suitable for self-government. This would become the model for receiving Tocqueville—as an aristocratic sage who could teach American democrats lessons about their own institutions that they could not see themselves. It was also a template for a larger genre of argument: the lesson for democrats from a skeptic of democracy, intended as a diagnostic "pencil of light" to save us from excesses of confidence or enthusiasm for our own principles. Tocqueville is a beginning point of the American tradition in which democrats have tended to take lessons on democracy from its enemies, or at least its skeptics.[5]

Tocqueville's admirers took him to mean that the promise of democratic self-rule—that people can use the technology of law and the state to transform their shared life—is an illusion, and a dangerous one. Peaceful cooperation has other bases, which are more organic, more diffuse, less open to intentional transformation. Tocqueville's arguments became a way of baffling reform, especially radical reform, by warning that it would run against the unspoken mores of the people.

Take the politics of racism and slavery. It was apparent to many from the beginning that there was a cruel contradiction between the announced political premises of the United States—equality and self-rule—and the slavery system. Tocqueville took this as a given and tended to note that his descriptions of American egalitarianism applied only to whites, while an entirely different logic governed relations among "the three races" of North America (the third "race" being Indigenous peoples). John Spencer, in his preface to the first American edition, turned Tocqueville's sagacity against abolition: "his remarks on slavery," Spencer assured readers, "will be found to present a masterly view of a most perplexing and interesting subject, which seems to cover the whole ground, and to lead to the melancholy conclusion of the utter impotency of human effort to eradicate this acknowledged evil." It was a convenient view for anyone who wished to disown the moral defense of slavery but also to resist any call to eliminate it, let alone to overcome white supremacy wholesale. In Spencer's hands, Tocqueville taught the tragic lesson that principles of equality and self-rule could not be extended across the color line because they were the organic cultural norms of a dominant white population. Custom and culture were a hard brake on principle. Democracy was a culture of, by, and for white Americans. It did not promise to make the world afresh for everyone, as Thomas Paine had once insisted, but instead preserved a very specific inheritance, a skein of norms and practices without which it would become just another form of boundless power. Better, apparently, to accept racial tyranny than to cut American democracy out of its cultural soil.[6]

This theme was still vital in 1899, when the Colonial Press of New York City issued a lavishly colored and illustrated edition of *Democracy in America* in a series called the World's Great Classics. The editors solicited "special introductions" to the volume from two US senators, John Morgan of Alabama and John Ingalls of Kansas. Ingalls had fought with Union forces in the Civil War. Morgan had been a Confederate general. The structure of the volume was to model the reconciliation of the white South and the white North around a common set of American mores.

Morgan took up Toqueville's famous definition of democracy as the "equality of conditions"—roughly the absence of caste: What could this mean after the Thirteenth, Fourteenth, and Fifteenth Amendments to the Constitution had abolished slavery and extended citizenship, voting rights, and "equal protection of the laws" to all Americans alike? This was a radical change to a body politic that Tocqueville had seen as defined by equality "among the people of the white race, who are described as 'We, the people,' in the opening sentence of the Constitution," Morgan observed. In this phrasing, the Alabama senator accurately recounted Tocqueville's sociological portrait of American white supremacy, but by linking it to constitutional language, he did more than that. The point of the Reconstruction amendments had been, in good part, to repudiate the ruling and reasoning of *Dred Scott v. Sandford*, the 1857 opinion that had found—or embedded—white supremacy in the Constitution itself. Morgan used Tocqueville to make *Dred Scott* true again—not in the letter of the law but in the mores that were democracy's real nerves and muscles—and to make this culturally authoritative white supremacy the basis of white reconciliation. The Reconstruction amendments, he wrote, were "intended to be radical and revolutionary," and for that reason their egalitarian principle would ultimately fail "because it has not the sanction of public opinion." There was no longer a written fundamental law of white supremacy, Morgan acknowledged, but wise Tocqueville would have known to "find it in the unwritten law of the natural aversion of the races . . . in public opinion, which is the vital force in every law in a free government." Public opinion, especially in the local governments where Tocqueville had seen the taproot of democratic life, would absorb and "negative"—veto—the principle of equality.[7]

Morgan offered this proof that mores mattered more than law: "At the end of the most destructive civil war that ever occurred, when animosities of the bitterest sort had banished all good feeling from the hearts of our people, the States of the American Union, still in complete organization . . . took up the duties of local government in perfect order and without embarrassment."[8] In other words, the heart of American democracy was the local governments, where mores endured through mere changes in constitutional text or national party politics. Morgan's view was particularly ironic because, in denying that politics could change culture, he was appealing to a culture that politics had done much to create, not all that long before he wrote. The first effort at multiracial democracy in the South was defeated under the flag of "folkways," but those were always mythic and obscurantist. The southern whites who took control of state governments across the former Confederacy after Reconstruction—with bipartisan collaboration from northern politicians and capitalists—were not organic avatars of regional civilization. They were a new economic class invested in railroads, utilities, and banks and pressing for state subsidies, freedom from regulation, and low taxes, especially on the rich. They revised their state constitutions to give central government—the legislature or the governor—control over the counties, bringing to heel both Black-majority counties (where the right to vote was at least nominally intact until late in the nineteenth century) and the Republican and later (sometimes) populist counties of mostly white upland farmers. So much for the localism of norms.

That political history was still being made at the time that the Colonial Press released its version of *Democracy in America*. Two years after Morgan's introduction appeared, his state, Alabama, adopted the "redemption" amendments to its state constitution that, in line with other southern states, buried the legal legacy of Reconstruction and erected the Jim Crow system. Three years after that, in 1904, the state Democratic Party adopted the motto "white supremacy," which helpfully appeared on the party's line on state ballots in case voters were unsure about Democratic principles. The "redeemed" southern governments were working busily to create extensive segregation, legal architecture that lent seeming obviousness to what Morgan called "natural aversion." Although white supremacy was an old American ideology, Jim Crow was the newest, not the oldest of American systems, grim testament to Edmund Burke's dictum that revolutionaries must conceal their work.

The Supreme Court had done its part to lay the groundwork for Morgan's embrace of localism as the bulwark against egalitarian democracy. In 1883, as described briefly in the previous chapter, the court invalidated the 1875 Civil Rights Act, a federal statute that desegregated trains, hotels, and "places of public amusement," creating a principle of equal treatment in the public sphere of commerce and transportation. It was the most ambitious antisegregation legislation until the 1964 Civil Rights Act, eighty-nine years later, and the Congress that passed it was the last before racial reaction broke Reconstruction in the election of 1876. The justices ruled that the law intruded too deeply on the sphere of state sovereignty and local control. They also denied that the merely "private" segregation of a business owner could offend the Constitution. This defense of local control and culture was turned up to eleven in 1896 when—amid the disenfranchisement wave of the "Redeemers" and the restoration of elite white rule in the South—the Supreme Court upheld official segregation, observing that "in the nature of things" legal equality could never mean racial equality or integration, which "racial instinct" forbade. Two decades earlier, segregation had been a closely fought political and legal question. Now what lawmakers had made, the country's highest court declared a fact of culture and human nature, a norm too deep for mere law to reach.[9]

These developments resonated with a broader shift in the way self-government was understood in American law. In his influential *On Civil Liberty and Self-Government,* published in multiple editions before and after the Civil War, the jurist Francis Lieber proposed a comprehensive recasting of the idea of self-government along lines closer to Tocqueville's than to the original conception of constitutionalism as democratic sovereignty. Lieber, a liberal who had done his early study in Germany and ended his career at Columbia University after teaching in Boston and South Carolina, denied emphatically that self-government could mean the people legislating for themselves. This, he insisted, could only be "the people-despot . . . a dictatorial multitude." Throughout his work, he warned against "the idol of . . . popular despotism." Instead, he agreed with Tocqueville that "without local self-government there is no real self-government." Self-government could only be "organic," for "it consists in organs of combined self-action, in institutions, and in a systematic connection of these institutions . . . the opposite at once of a disintegration of society of into individual, dismembered, and disjunctive independencies, and of despotism." In other words, self-government was more a sociological than a legal or political phenomenon, a web of more or less local forms of self-organization in which individuals interacted and which they should never take it on themselves to unmake or recast in radical ways.[10]

Lieber's position was culturalist and nationalist. Under the lifelong influence of the *volkish* theories of law and society that circulated in the Germany of his youth and early education, he invoked an Anglo-American "we," insisting that "we belong to that race whose obvious task it is, among other sacred and proud tasks, to rear and spread civil liberty over vast regions in every part of the earth. . . . We belong to that tribe which alone has the word Self-Government." Americans, he thought, were susceptible to the dangerous confusion of forgetting that talk of the rights of the citizen "means our own white race," with its stabilizing customs and web of institutions, and instead taking seriously the more abstract version of popular sovereignty. To resist that idea, Lieber advocated a different standard of legitimacy, not collective self-rule but the supremacy of the law even over democratic decisions. And where did the law, in turn, come from? It had no precise earthly source; instead, it was the implicit moral grammar of the many institutions in which individuals were able to arrange their own affairs. It was the logic of neighborhoods and commercial relationships, churches and clubs, in which the state had no need or authority to intervene often or deeply. If self-government was organic, so was the law. It did not require—indeed was in danger from—the Archimedean fulcrum of sovereignty. What Tocqueville had proposed of politics, Lieber contended for law.[11]

This idea was in no way new, but Lieber helped to transmit it to the United States from the civil law systems of Europe. In waves of reform after the French Revolution, an increasingly commercial, liberal, and middle-class European legal profession revived a "Roman" conception of law. European reformers found it in the *Corpus Juris Civilis*, or "Body of Civil Law," a compilation of Roman jurisprudence completed by scholars in Byzantium around the years 529–534, under the direction of the emperor Justinian, and often called, after its patron and one of its sections, the Code of Justinian. The code interpreted and consolidated nearly a millennium of Roman jurisprudence, which began in the ritual and magical origins of social regulation but developed into the classical world's most elaborate and professionalized legal system.

Recovered in Bologna in the eleventh century, the code figured thereafter in the gradual development of a medieval and early modern European jurisprudence, which came into its own when nineteenth-century reformers put it at the center of national legal systems. In this conception of law, legality was the uniquely effective and legitimate form of social ordering, the way that people's lives and work could be stitched together in a peaceful and productive fashion. The rules of law combined public power with private cooperation, turning the imperial hand, and later the administration of the modern state, to the definition and enforcement of personal rights of property and contract, which, properly designed and overseen, could extend across vast territories, even attain global reach. The arrangements that Romans made in this legal grammar were paradigmatically ones of ownership, exchange, and labor contracts—the ligaments of a commercial economy. Ancient Rome fostered considerable long-distance trade and commodity production, and the law of ownership and contract was at their heart. When Adam Smith and his fellow early modern theorists of "commercial society" developed a concept of social ordering around market-style reciprocity (such as the agreement of buyer and seller), they looked to the terms of Roman law, which they naturalized into a social theory. Just as important as these uses in philosophy and early economics, however, was the revival of Roman law as an account of law itself.

This account managed to evade what might seem to be central questions about the origin and legitimacy of the law. Law as figured here—as Lieber's example highlights—is based in the custom and "common sense" of the people but is not reducible to these. Instead, it is also a specialized, technical field, subject to professional rationality, providing jurists with the concepts and patterns of reasoning that enable them to resolve disputes of property and contract in a spirit of objective justice, not arbitrary decision. Yet the character of its rationality cannot be traced to any precise axioms of deductive reason, nor can its concepts be rooted in the rigorously specified facts of empiricism. Instead, it floats between the two, its reasoning essentially conventional, its principles—who may own what, what kinds of contracts are valid, how a contract gets binding meaning in a case of ambiguity—rooted in historical facts and widespread practice. It both stands above social life and inheres in it, having no other basis of its own but claiming a special authority over the whole.

What enabled the law to play this role—rationalizing mores but also obscuring the political character of its own rationalization—was in good part the simple fact that it was a vehicle of social power. Legal pronouncements are performative: a judge speaks a phrase, a contract recites a formula, and someone loses their wealth or freedom, someone else gains power over them, the world shifts a bit on its pillars. It is only natural to suppose that there is some power in the words themselves and the professional codes they invoke. How else could they rule us?

As classicist Aldo Schiavone explains in a study of Roman legality, this sense of law worked in contrast to another: the Greek democratic conception of law as the codification of the decisions of popular majorities. As we have seen, a revival and adaptation of this Greek idea was at the heart of the early American experience of constitutionalism, which contained the first popular referendums on basic law (or any law) in the modern world and designated this procedure as the institutional vehicle of popular sovereignty. It was telling, then, that jurists such as Lieber, along with popularizers of Tocqueville, shifted the American practices of law and self-government generally toward a diffuse communitarianism, an impressionistic idea of the people that served mainly to authorize the specialized work of professional jurists. In the nineteenth century, those jurists were increasingly involved, too, with the work of political economists who presented the market as the natural form of social life, giving the commercial categories of Roman law a putative natural foundation. Political intrusion on these organic legal orders could be easily presented as folly and tyranny.[12]

During the Cold War, "democratic theory" emerged as an American scholarly pursuit, and the Tocquevillean tradition helped some of its most influential practitioners to explain how the eighteenth-century Constitution, marked by Madison's "total exclusion of the people in their collective capacity," could offer a paradigm of self-rule for the twentieth century. The answer was an institution-minded version of what Tocqueville had written about popular sovereignty and Lieber about law: the genius of the Constitution lay in its simultaneous appeal to the people and blockage of popular action, which shunted the work of social ordering from political *decision* to a kind of perennial political *negotiation*, facilitated by a common culture that was doing much of the real work of holding everything together. Take the argument of Robert Dahl, probably the most influential American democratic theorist of the twentieth century, in his 1967 work, *Pluralist Democracy in the United States: Conflict and Consent.* Dahl argued that American politics was founded on a deep consensus about the goodness of the country's political and economic institutions. At most times in the country's experience, Dahl asserted, political conflict was "moderate" and changes in policy "marginal," not just because the US Constitution set up a variety of checkpoints to stop reform but just as basically because "in the United States there is a massive convergence of attitudes on a number of key issues that divide citizens in other countries." Americans, he went on, tended to believe that their own lives and prospects were good, that the country's constitutional arrangements and economic system could be counted on to deliver fair results, and that any reforms should be incremental and in keeping with the spirit of the inherited system. They personally identified themselves as middle class and believed that the American economy tended to reward talent and effort.[13]

Dahl argued that this tacit American consensus propped up political cooperation. The country's political institutions thwarted the decisive formation of a "popular will," sending the quest for the people's judgment ricocheting from place to place. If you lost in the House, you could appeal to the Senate. If you lost in both places, you could appeal to the president. If you lost all down the electoral line, you could go to the Supreme Court. American politics drove its participants toward a search for consensus, which its institutions could not generate. Fortunately, that elusive consensus emerged instead from cultural reserves of overlapping agreement: "If Americans converged on a single principle it would be this: unanimity, though unattainable, is best." So long as Americans had this disposition, political institutions could "foster incremental adjustments . . . generate politicians who learn how to deal gently with opponents, who struggle endlessly in building and holding coalitions together, who doubt the possibilities of great change, who seek compromises." The artificial unity of clear majoritarian democracy was unattainable but, fortunately, was also unnecessary in a polity with a more organic unity of outlook and accompanying norms.[14]

In this way Tocqueville's cultural theory of democracy was translated into the self-understanding of Cold War liberalism. Democracy was not real if by democracy one meant the actual and ongoing rule of majorities, but the American constitutional order enabled a mix of competing and overlapping interest groups and other constituencies to bump along in good-enough agreement. Any effort to empower majorities to a greater degree would, Dahl asserted, put unmanageable strain on the country. It was a good thing that the constitutional framers, who had spoken wantonly of the sovereignty of the people, had not tried to give it institutional life. No one, after all, liked being subject to the will of others. The solutions that Rousseau and other democratic constitutionalists had given were, Dahl implied, self-evidently myths. No sophisticated modern citizen could take them seriously.

Yet for all this, Dahl argued, it was important that Americans not become too worldly wise about the limits of their political powers. A certain wild faith in democratic capacity was still somehow the animating spirit of the whole enterprise, the source of the energy that the antimajoritarian institutions baffled and redirected. It was true that "the citizen interested in political action may feel himself to be a helpless victim of forces over which he can exert no control" or even "believe that there are no alternatives to naked opportunism or alienation and despair." But this was "too one-sidedly pessimistic a view of man's fate." Dahl invoked Clarence Earl Gideon, the drifter, accused burglar, and named plaintiff in *Gideon v. Wainwright*, the 1963 Supreme Court case that established a criminal defendant's right to legal representation: "The dawn of victory may be long in coming; for some ideas that day may never dawn. But unless individuals were to act, like Gideon, in the confident expectation that their actions had significance, if not now at least some day, then the changes we all witness in our own times may never come." It was stirring prose, but the promise it offered was oddly flat, its exhortation curiously abstract. Against all the evidence of sophisticated political realism, you must believe that your actions matter. After all, you might be the occasion for reformist judges to expand the rights of people like you![15]

It was a fragile democratic equilibrium that Dahl described, one in which people had to have faith in the system (but not too much faith, lest they make impossible demands) and share enough unspoken premises that they could work out their remaining disagreements and clashing interests through institutions that had made clear decisions hard to reach. Dahl's moderate Tocquevillean optimism all but invited a bleaker riposte. One came a few years later in a 1975 report by the prominent political scientist Samuel Huntington and two collaborators, titled *The Crisis of Democracy: On the Governability of Democracies*. Huntington wrote in light of political conflicts that must have been salient in 1967, when Dahl published his book, but seemed not to have pressed themselves on Dahl's attention: the fierce fight over racial hierarchy, the increasingly desperate contest over the Vietnam War, and widespread challenges to patriarchy, priesthoods, and other forms of everyday authority. A shadow of conflict on Dahl's landscape of consensus was itself the landscape by the time Huntington turned to the condition of American democracy. He contended that the fragility of Tocquevillean order was being revealed, and the system must be reconsolidated or risk collapsing.[16]

Huntington returned to one of Tocqueville's central themes, the tendency (as Tocqueville thought) of equality-loving citizens to make demands on government that end up undercutting democracy itself. Tocqueville had warned against not just the tyranny of the majority but also "democratic despotism," a government that achieved equality at the cost of personal liberty by micromanaging everyday life in a soft administrative authoritarianism. This was the prophecy that made Tocqueville an icon for small-government conservatives in the twentieth century. He seemed to anticipate the administrative state (France, after all, had one when he wrote—not terribly effective but entrenched and fiscally burdensome) and to predict what its critics claimed, that it would leave its citizens isolated and passive—the opposite of the can-do self-organizers that Tocqueville famously saw in American civil society.

What did this picture of democratic malaise look like in the 1970s? The authors identified three trends in American culture (and those of Europe and Japan as well). One was the rise of an "oppositional culture" among the highly educated, "value-oriented intellectuals who often devote themselves to the derogation of leadership, the challenging of authority, and the unmasking and delegitimation of established institutions." This development was "potentially at least as serious as those posed in the past by the aristocratic cliques, fascist movements, and communist parties." Norms are, after all, inarticulate moral premises, unspoken theories of authority and right conduct. A pervasive skepticism about inherited and familiar roles and about the disposition of power in society could weaken these social ligaments like acid. Dissolve too many of them, and you might find that abstract ideas, about democracy or rights or anything else, were too weak to hold a social order together.[17]

Second was the rise of "post-materialist" culture, with its emphasis on "belonging and intellectual and esthetic self-fulfillment," which tended to be "privatistic in . . . impact and import," turning people inward to their own lives and concerns and posing a challenge to government's "ability to mobilize its citizens for the achievement of social and political goals and to impose discipline and sacrifice." Huntington, for his part, must have had in mind the contrast between the mobilization of World War II and the resistance to the Vietnam draft that shook universities and eventually put the military on a volunteer (hiring) basis. Teaching at Harvard during the most radical period of student activism, when self-expression and militancy went hand in hand— "Strike because your classes are a bore, strike to smash the corporation," urged the iconic poster of the 1969 student strike—he seems to have seen the withdrawal of institutional loyalty as a kind of individualism gone mad. Mores mattered more than law. As a new generation's habits of the heart changed, the real reach of political authority would also have to recede.[18]

In key ways, it was the entrance into political life of populations that had been excluded from real power that sparked Huntington's alarm about democratic norms. Black Americans, most of all, and also poor people (many of them people of color) were increasingly enfranchised, organized, and active. Part of the reason it had been easy in the past to believe in a perduring American consensus was that many of the people who had the most to complain about were kept far from political power. The end of that more hierarchical world was the beginning of Huntington's crisis.

The 1960s brought a tremendous renewal of democratic energies—in voting rates but also demonstrations, mass movements, and calls for new action from the state. The crux of Huntington's argument was a very Tocquevillean paradox: a more active democracy could produce a weaker, even "ungovernable" polity. New policy demands, coupled with the erosion of authority, "overloaded" the political system by simultaneously increasing expectations of government and weakening its power to enforce solutions. This paradox had a cultural dimension, which expressed itself in polarized self-righteousness and impatience with authority. It also had a fiscal aspect. In common with many observers of the "legitimation crisis" of the early 1970s, Huntington and his coauthors worried that insatiable and accelerating inflationary pressures arose from union demands for regular wage increases, coupled with other interest groups' pressure for public spending. In both fiscal terms and the more ethereal currency of legitimacy and authority, more was being demanded of the state while its real capacities were slipping.[19]

Huntington's analysis was Dahl's with the lighting changed: an account of the American political order as relying on the stabilizing antipolitics of cultural agreement but tragically unable to maintain its necessary consensus. Huntington differed from Dahl in one key respect: his account candidly foregrounded the ways that consensus rested on inequality and effective exclusion of many citizens from the political process. Where Dahl had presented American politics as both relying on and sustaining popular faith that it might in time serve everyone's visions of a better world, Huntington insisted that the country's politics could work only if it did not promise too much—and citizens knew it could not. He recommended a general lowering of expectations, in particular among the new waves of college-educated voters and activists. Although he did not say that the political restiveness and self-assertion of non-white and poor voters had to be contained, the implication was there to draw.

Both Dahl's analysis and Huntington's rested on Tocqueville's style of antipolitics: the reliance on norms to do the work of political decision-making and thus limit the scope and intensity of political conflict. Tellingly, both Dahl and Huntington ended their long and influential careers by giving up on organic political consensus in favor of stronger sources of order. Their two directions still mark major alternatives in the third decade of the twenty-first century. Dahl, toward the end of remarkably long and productive life, asked provocatively, "How democratic is the American Constitution?" and answered: not very democratic at all. It failed, he contended in 2001, to treat citizens equally or to hold government accountable to the people. He fingered familiar culprits—the Senate's distorted majorities, the Electoral College, the constitutional obstacle course of lawmaking, and the Supreme Court's self-appointed role as a constitutional supervisor of all kinds of policy—as nearly insurmountable barriers to a national government that embodied democratic values. Although there was little short-term prospect of change, Dahl urged that Americans should at least stop revering their Constitution as a consummation of justice and democracy and begin recognizing it as a leading source of their frustration with actual, everyday politics. From the optimistic view that broad consensus held together a rickety system, giving it direction and authority, Dahl had moved to a much more critical conclusion: the Constitution stood in the way of democracy, and if Americans were to have a more democratic country, they would need to change the Constitution. Norms and culture could not dissolve this conflict. Dahl had decided that one must choose for or against democracy, and he was for it.[20] The system he had once praised was, unfortunately, against it.[21]

In the same years, Huntington moved from modestly pessimistic conservatism to a stance that presaged the nationalism of Donald Trump's 2016 campaign and the five years that followed. Concluding that the abstract political creed of freedom, equality, and democracy was too weak to hold a country together, Huntington returned to a theme of Tocqueville's that liberal admirers had downplayed: the ethnic and even racial dimension of his picture of cultural consensus. American democracy was rooted, Huntington argued, in Anglo-Protestant culture, Christianity, and the English language, and if Americans disowned these, they would soon find that little held them together. Ideologies could change almost overnight, he argued, pointing to the transformations of political culture in post–Soviet Russia and newly capitalist China: the nation was the thing that held people together, and American liberals were dissolving theirs.

He forecast a reaction to "profound demographic changes," the rise of "white nativism" in "exclusivist sociopolitical movements composed largely but not only of white males, primarily working-class and middle-class, protesting and attempting to stop or reverse those changes and what they believe, accurately or not, to be the diminution of their social and economic status, their loss of jobs to immigrants and foreign countries, the perversion of their culture, the displacement of their language, and the erosion or even evaporation of the historical identity of their country." Huntington tended to see populism as a sign of dysfunction, so he did not celebrate these anticipated Trumpists, but he made clear that he thought many of their worries were reasonable or at least inevitable. In his eyes, liberals who saw the country as postnationalist or multicultural deserved the rude shock of populist insurgency. So where Dahl moved out of political consensus into a stronger commitment to democracy, Huntington followed Tocqueville back to conclude that democracy required cultural unity, with undertones of ethnic unity. The nation was the thing.[22]

When Donald Trump won the presidency in 2016, both Huntington and Dahl had died in the previous decade. Trump's opponents faced a choice, threaded through the many political battles of the years that followed: Did defeating a minority-rule president who led a minority-rule party mean confronting the antidemocratic features of American politics that had brought Trump to power? Did the new "crisis of democracy" show that the country still needed to earn its democratic credentials? Or was the problem fundamentally one of restoration, of returning to a good-enough consensus that had been shaken but, at its core, worked well enough to secure order, stability, and a decent society—if we could only get back to it?

5

NORMS FROM NOWHERE

G alvanized by the shock of Donald Trump's victory in the 2016
presidential election, students of politics, and more casual
observers who followed them, jettisoned the longstanding assumption that "consolidated" democracies like America's tend to
remain democratic. They developed instead a keen interest in democracy's capacity for self-dissolution. For decades, the too-easy
habit had been to assume that emerging democracies were on
their way to resembling the United States of the 1990s: a liberal
market society with regular elections, practicing a basically dis-
enchanted but pragmatic politics. Now strongman populism, left
and right, religious and secular, from Venezuela to Turkey, Russia
to India, Hungary to the Philippines, seemed to contain clues to
the future of the United States. History had returned, personified
in tawdry but dangerous kleptocracies. A flood of opinion and
interpretation sought to understand how things had come to this
pass, producing a new common sense about "what happened" (as
the title of Hillary Clinton's postcampaign memoir had it).

An answer quickly coalesced: norm breaking. Trump was "a serial norm breaker," wrote two Harvard political scientists in *How
Democracies Die*, a book that did more than any other scholarly volume to interpret Trump for liberals and centrists, including Joe

Biden. Trump and the Republican Party had crashed against the "guardrails of democracy" that norms provided: tacit restraints that keep political conflict within constructive bounds—such as not lying about election results, not threatening to jail opponents, not refusing a hearing to a nominee of the opposite party. When norms were pressed past breaking, politics could burst into irresolvable conflict. This was the danger of the age, commentators agreed in a raft of books across the spectrum of respectable anti-Trump opinion.[1]

Being unspoken and often not even present to the minds of those who are following them, norms may be invisible until someone breaks them. You hardly notice that everyone on the highway is taking turns merging until That Guy screams through, splitting lanes and leaning on his horn, perhaps with a set of truck nuts swinging from his trailer hitch. Yet these tacit points of restraint keep political opponents from each other's throats so that a polity can plod along. This story of Trump's dangerous rise brought together longtime commentators on both the left and right, including David Frum, former speechwriter for George W. Bush, who had penned the "Axis of Evil" speech, pitching the invasion of Iraq. In this light, Trump's serial norm breaking became his most salient characteristic. He drew attention to his campaign by behaving unprofessionally and even indecently, mocking audience members (including a disabled reporter), launching personal attacks on judges and bureaucrats, and generally moving fast and breaking things. He refused to release his tax returns, a piece of transparency that had become standard practice after Richard Nixon's scandal-ridden second administration and forced resignation. Once in office, Trump's administration combined nepotism with a nineteenth-century level of dedication to self-enrichment. And it wasn't just Trump. American political elites, especially Republicans, were more and more willing to violate longstanding expectations of how government worked: Use the Senate filibuster to keep a Democratic president from passing popular legislation? Refuse to give a Supreme Court nominee so much as a hearing? Gerrymander states like

Wisconsin and North Carolina to produce strong Republican majorities when voters there were closely divided or even broke Democratic? Just the new business as usual—but also paradigms of norm violation.

Clearly something was happening here that demanded attention. But there was a misleading thinness to the description of the values at stake as "norms." Norms are like statues of dead leaders: to be for or against them, you need to know which values they uphold. The senators and representative who signed the 1956 Southern Manifesto attacking *Brown v. Board of Education* defended segregation on the ground that it had "bec[o]me part of the life of the people of many of the states and confirmed their habits, traditions, and way of life." They denounced the Supreme Court for abandoning "this established legal principle almost a century old," complaining that the justices had "exercise[d] their naked judicial power" in defiance of settled expectations. You didn't have to be a segregationist to think that Jim Crow was a norm: Justices Robert Jackson and Felix Frankfurter politically opposed segregation but also believed that it had become part of the southern way of life and were willing to give that idea enough weight that they had grave doubts about the plaintiff schoolchildren's plea for integration. Complaints of raw, norm-breaking power dogged the New Deal, too: opponents warned that Franklin Roosevelt, with his strong theories of presidential authority and national power, was an American Mussolini who would leave constitutional tradition in tatters.[2]

In the event, Roosevelt did leave the old constitutional tradition in tatters and launched a new one, whose norms included almost unlimited federal lawmaking power, great scope of action for the president, and a vision of government's responsibility to make economic life orderly and secure that seemed to eclipse more laissez-faire ideologies. In turn, some of those new norms about presidential power were set back on their heels in the 1970s, when Congress, responding to the disaster of the Vietnam War and to Richard Nixon's scandals, launched a series of reforms reasserting power over areas the White House had occupied, including public lands, foreign wars, and the intelligence services. In the same episode of reform, Gerald Ford's attorney general, Edward Levi, imposed a new ethical culture on the Department of Justice, ending J. Edgar Hoover's practice of spying on presidents' domestic critics (and, in an abundance of blackmailer's caution, spying on presidents) and establishing the political independence that helped to stop some of Trump's most destructive gambits nearly five decades later.

So the meaning of norms for any particular aspect of democracy is complicated. There is, certainly, something to the image of norms as the guardrails that keep political life from falling into open conflict. In this respect, norms play an indispensable, easy-to-overlook role in all stable forms of politics, not just democracy (nor even democracy in particular). Contests over norms motivated centuries of conflict between the Crown and Parliament in England before the Glorious Revolution of 1688. In China, Xi Jinping broke an important norm in 2018 when he engineered the end of term limits for head of state, party, and military (which three offices he occupies). Xi, Roosevelt, and Edward Levi all stand as reminders that norms do not emerge from some perennial culture outside politics, rising organically to stabilize the fight for power. Quite the contrary, political norms are created by the use of political power. Any set of norms stabilizes a particular kind of regime, and changing them is always part and parcel of changing regimes. The norms that came so vividly into question in 2016–2020 were the products of past political action, even kinds of insurrection: to make norms, you must also break norms. Democracy in particular has been a norm-breaking force. It has broken norms about who can speak in public, who can hold power, and which issues are even considered political, and it has pressed these points from the household and neighborhood to Congress and the White House. In doing so, it has also formed and empowered new norms, including many of those Trump breached.

The norm-centered interpretation of the Trump years managed to avoid paying much attention to the political creation of norms, instead focusing mainly on their degradation. This made it ahistorical, even apolitical, in a way that was convenient for uniting an anti-Trump political center around opposition to bad personalities and egregious behavior. But democratic virtue is not, as norms theorists sometimes implied, just a matter of observing the customs that have been handed down to you by the example of your forebears—or by the previous occupants of whatever office you hold. Instead, it demands the ability to distinguish between norms that need defending and others that need breaking and to see politics as a way to change norms or create new ones.

There are virtues that any democracy needs to function. First among these is willingness to accept majority decisions as binding, even though they are always artificial products of electoral design and could always have gone differently. So, lying about the basic facts of elections, especially by elites and politicians, is a deep kind of norm breaking that really can erode self-rule. Norms theorists were right to raise the alarm when, before the 2016 vote, 84 percent of Republicans told pollsters they believed a "meaningful amount" of fraud occurred in American elections, and almost 60 percent said "illegal" immigrants would "vote in meaningful amounts" in the presidential election. A July 2017 poll showed that 47 percent of Republicans believed that Trump had won the popular vote in 2016, rather than losing it by nearly three million votes. Fifty-two percent of Republicans said they would support the president if he postponed the 2020 elections to "make sure that only eligible American citizens can vote." The conditions of the revolt against democracy that broke out on January 6, 2021, were well prepared more than four years earlier. This is norm breaking of a very particular kind. If it succeeds, it prevents elections from settling political conflicts because agreement over their meaning has been destroyed.[3]

Yet the focus on norms and the search for elite consensus present a selective picture of American political life. Where in this story is the labor conflict that pitted workers against bosses and hired guns from the Gilded Age into the Cold War and did so much to shape the New Deal—and to earn it the acrimony of opponents who called it socialism or American fascism? Where are the Populists who wanted to remake the American fiscal and monetary systems to support small producers and would have broken plenty of eggs to do it? What was Franklin Roosevelt talking about in 1936, when he told a crowd in Madison Square Garden that he "welcome[d] the hatred" of "the old enemies of peace—business and financial monopoly, speculation, reckless banking, class antagonism, sectionalism, war profiteering"? Where is the political revolution of the civil rights movement, which finally put an end to the norm of whites-only democracy—which was never democracy at all?

So the idea of American democracy as bound by a common culture of norms has to be understood as a piece of ideology, recurrently convenient to whichever group adopts it. A focus on norms and consensus shifts the weight of social power away from democratic sovereignty and places it on different, more diffuse foundations. So understood, there is less to hope for from democracy for those who have to put their hopes in it; for those who find it fearsome, there is less to fear. In the past, this culture-first view of politics offered assurance that democratic sovereignty would not disrupt the basic hierarchies of social life—Black and white, man and woman, straight and queer, owner and worker—which it portrayed as being deeper than the ministrations of politics.

Today, an uncritical focus on norms as the real life of democracy obscures how far the system that Donald Trump rode to power was from being a democracy in the first place. The anti-democratic institutions that gave Trump his spurious majorities (once more: the Electoral College, the Senate), pervasive disenfranchisement both of citizens and of others who lead their lives here, and a nearly unchallengeable Supreme Court that protects political spending as a constitutional right, all preexisted his bad behavior and helped translate it into political power. The essential conservatism of norms talk lies in focusing political criticism and interpretation on some recent break with custom, instead of asking whether the political architecture in which that custom was set might need more basic reform. We need to achieve democracy, not just defend it, and defenses of our flawed democracy can stand in the way of a stronger democracy.

Norms theory is right, sometimes urgently so, in insisting that democracy needs a culture and virtues that keep it going through times of conflict, when the temptation to abandon it runs high. It is wrong to the extent that it relies on culture—popular or elite— as a gentle substitute for democracy, the source of an implicit consensus that holds us together.

The emphasis on norms can also distract from asking what kind of political world a norm breaker is trying to create. Just as norms don't come from nowhere, norm breaking is not random or just nihilistic. In the case of Donald Trump, the shattering of political norms was also a way of asserting a piratical version of capitalist norms. Trump was the first president who laid claim to the presidency based not on any record of public service but on an alleged power to make money out of money. His antiethics was that of the salesman for whom marketing becomes an all-consuming form of life: whatever sells is good, and the test of a story is not its truth but whether it raises sales. The distinction between truth and lies is anachronistic moralism; the real difference is between profit and loss. It was standard to say that President Trump was a "bullshitter," someone whose indifference to the truth was more radical and bewildering than a mere liar's. But this was not just a personal vice: it was the translation into politics of a specific capitalist style.

To reckon with democracy's challenges today, we have to be able to see it alongside, and potentially against, the capitalism that shapes so much of our everyday lives and so easily comes to seem natural and obvious—even in its most grotesque extrusions, like the forty-fifth president. This means looking back before Twitter, Fox News, and Trump Tower to an older and very influential idea that markets can substitute for politics. The state may not wither away, but its most important tasks will be technical and not open to the competing judgments of warring majorities. More, the laws of the marketplace bring their own version of what Rousseau promised: to bind people while also leaving them free.

What democracy promised but never achieved, so the story goes, markets can deliver, becoming a kind of sovereign. The work of politics, in this view, is to defend the sovereign market against democracy. Even today, when it may be hard to imagine having such faith in the market, we live with the legacy of that faith in ways that make democracy that much harder to recover. Our all-pervading economic world is our most concrete and everyday antipolitics.

6

THE SOVEREIGN MARKET

B arack Obama entered the White House in 2009 near the height of a global financial crisis. Across the country, millions of mortgagors, especially working-class and Black borrowers, suddenly owed banks more than their homes were worth. Lenders had been eager to extend credit, sometimes on terms fairly described as predatory, and had passed on the built-to-fail loans in complex investment vehicles that produced large fees for investment banks and short-lived windfalls for some of their clients. Fear and outrage roiled the country. In the year following the crisis, the heads of the investment banks JP Morgan and Goldman Sachs took home multimillion-dollar bonuses. Asked about the bonuses, Obama struck a conciliatory note. "I know both these guys," the president said. "They're very savvy businessmen." He continued, "I, like most of the American people, don't begrudge people success or wealth. That is part of the free-market system."[1]

Obama's response showed that, although his presidential win was historic and a great electoral movement had swept him into power, the political world still belonged to Ronald Reagan. In his second inaugural address nearly twenty-five years earlier, Reagan had promised "a new American emancipation." The word *emancipation* pointed back to the end of chattel slavery with the

Emancipation Proclamation of 1863 and the Thirteenth Amendment, ratified in 1865. This time, however, it was the market that would make people free. Reagan aimed to "liberate the spirit of enterprise" and "unleash the drive and entrepreneurial genius that are the core of human progress." Four years earlier Reagan had famously declared that "government is the problem" and that "our present troubles" (in 1981, high unemployment and inflation) "are proportionate to the intervention and intrusion in our lives that result from unnecessary and excessive growth of government." He portrayed a country hemmed in by bureaucracy and high taxes, where hard work didn't pay and dreams grew small. Harking back two centuries to the American founding, he announced: "That system has never failed us, but, for a time, we failed the system." Americans had asked too much of government, handed over too much freedom and too much responsibility.[2]

Reagan sketched the market economy as a realm of organic creativity and cooperation, where people serve one another's needs and wants and, maybe, get rich along the way. Economic life was a kind of national bloodstream. Modern government, with its regulations and distributional policy, was bad cholesterol, slowing and clotting the flow. Reagan was tugging on a very old strand of American politics. In 1834, William Leggett, a Jacksonian newspaper editor, argued that government should protect liberty and property but not "tamper with individual industry a single hair's breadth beyond." Republicans in the Reconstruction era, too, called economic liberty "the noblest principle on earth" and the "foundation of civilization." It seemed to them to be the antithesis of the slave system that they were laboring to uproot, and in their minds, it permitted "free choice and social order" to coexist. Even Thomas Paine, the abolitionist and radical whose writing helped to crystallize the American Revolution, insisted that "society in every state is a blessing, but government even in its best state is but a necessary evil" and announced himself in favor of a simple and minimal government for the Americans. "Our plan is commerce," he wrote of the revolutionaries, and commerce should bring domestic flourishing and international peace.[3]

So Reagan's image of a market society as promising "the warm sunlight of human freedom" chimed with centuries of praise for free exchange.[4] But it was also a watershed. Presidential addresses don't exactly make history, but they are emblems of their times. Deregulation had been rising for a decade, supported by a bipartisan constituency that included many in the administration of centrist Democrat Jimmy Carter (1977–1981). During Reagan's two presidencies, market thinking grew to new dominance. So it was Democrat Bill Clinton who announced in 1996, echoing Reagan, that "the era of big government is over" and signed into law the deregulation of the financial industry that did much to create the crisis of 2008–2009. Clinton defended bringing China into the World Trade Organization by denying there was any real choice in the matter: the globalization of markets was "the economic equivalent of a force of nature, like wind or water." For Reagan, the market had been the standard of a political crusade. For Clinton and Obama, it became a natural limit on moral and political imagination, and so on practical possibility.

Those were decades not just of market policy but of market life. The United States became, even more than before, a reflexively economistic culture. Colleges elevated the cross-hatched supply and demand curves of Economics 101 over history and political thought: ambitious students learned that books were nice and you could buy them by the yard to decorate your den, but both truth and power dwelt in graphs and equations. Even our popular ways of making sense of ourselves took the shape of *Freakonomics*, the best-selling work on "how economics explains nearly everything," and in everyday life it became normal, even pseudosophisticated, to talk about the opportunity cost of a romantic relationship or the return on investment of time with a friend. "I want to test my market value," people would say in a romantic crisis, as they contemplated seeking a new partner—meaning, I want to know what I am worth.

A half century before the Reagan era, the world looked very different. Franklin Delano Roosevelt, entering the second of his four presidential terms, used his 1937 inaugural address to give a picture of government almost the opposite of Reagan's. The country needed, he said, "to find through government the instrument of our united purpose to solve for the individual the ever-rising problems of a complex civilization. Repeated efforts at their solution without the aid of government had left us baffled and bewildered . . . we must find practical controls over blind economic forces and blindly selfish men." Speaking during the Great Depression, when unemployment reached 25 percent, the stock market lost four-fifths of its value, and seven thousand banks failed, Roosevelt rejected the idea of economic life as the healthy and natural play of freedom. To him it seemed nearer a hurricane or a great flood: a force alien to the lives and interests of ordinary women and men, which must be tamed and directed to keep them safe. Markets produced devastating crises. Ignoring that in the 1930s would have been like saying, "Nice weather we're having," during Hurricane Katrina's devastation of New Orleans, and trying to get out of its crises by individual initiative and grit would be like slipping into a breaststroke as the levee broke. Only collective action created the secure ground where people could flourish.

Roosevelt, too, was looking back to an American tradition, though a younger and less dominant one than Reagan's. Two decades before FDR first won the presidency, Woodrow Wilson, political scientist, president of Princeton University, and tribune of the Progressive movement, insisted as he entered the presidency that "there can be no equality or opportunity, the first essential of justice in the body politic, if men and women and children be not shielded in their lives, their very vitality, from the consequences of great industrial processes which they cannot alter, control, or singly cope with"—the same idea as Roosevelt's promise to "solve for the individual the ever-rising problems of a complex civilization." In this new way, Wilson promised, "government may be put at the service of humanity, in safeguarding the health of the Nation." The Virginian Wilson was the face of racist progressivism and as president instituted segregation in federal employment. But on another level, he agreed with his contemporary and fellow social scientist W. E. B. Du Bois that the role of government was to shape an economic order for its citizens. Du Bois called his version of democratic political economy abolition-democracy. As he put it, "two theories of the future of America clashed and blended just after the Civil War" and persisted thereafter: "The one was abolition-democracy based on freedom, intelligence, and power for all men; the other was industry for private profit, directed by an autocracy determined at any price to amass wealth and power." The economy shaped and sometimes crushed human lives, and the counterpower of politics was the way to secure a vision of common life, whether it was Franklin Roosevelt's "permanently safe order of things" or Du Bois's abolition-democracy. These were, broadly, the terms that dominated political life from Roosevelt's New Deal through the 1960s: a premise that citizenship included *economic citizenship*, with elements of security, good work, and the collective power of unionization.[5]

Reagan announced a retreat from this kind of political economy. Although his administration and those that followed used the state as enthusiastically as FDR had—now to break public unions and weaken private ones, authorize banks to enter into new fields, and build legal systems for offshoring and international capital flows—its rhetoricians claimed to be protecting the healthy social circulation of markets against government interference. We can now see the Reagan era in the collective rearview mirror. As I write, both major American parties have moved away from market optimism. (Whether they have moved out of the control of groups that did well in the inequality of the long market era is another question.) Big redistributive and regulatory projects flourish among Democrats, while Republicans have opened a new era of trade conflict that repudiates the assumption of a smooth glide into a global market.

In moving out of an era, there is a risk of misunderstanding what we are leaving behind and so learning the wrong lessons. The risk today is to imagine that the lesson is something relatively modest like, "markets aren't perfect" or "markets need regulation, too." These are true, but they are fragments of a deeper point. The market-first politics of recent decades aimed a blade at democracy itself. Rejecting that politics means once again starting from FDR's and Du Bois's questions: What kinds of lives should democratic citizens be able to live, and what kind of economy supports those lives? If we neglect those questions, we underestimate our challenge.

An influential interpretation treats decades of market domination as the result of an innocent intellectual mistake, in which policy elites took the discipline of economics too seriously and lost sight of important real-world nuance. A *New York Times* writer—one who tends to be quite incisive on issues of political economy—argued in summer 2019 that decades of inequality and insecurity rested substantially on overcrediting economists, who assumed that markets tended to equilibrium and that growth was more important than distribution: "The rise of economics is a primary reason for the rise of inequality."[6] Critics of economics for decades had sounded similar notes, denouncing *Homo economicus*, the "rational agent" of economic method, as a pernicious myth and attacking the alleged belief that markets are natural. People are more complicated—and less rational—than that, the critics insisted, and markets cannot work without a government behind them. Again, these points are true, but they leave out an important part of the picture.

The theory of the market has always been involved with, and often inseparable from, a vision of how diverse people can live together, one that portrays democracy, as FDR and Du Bois understood it, as neither necessary nor desirable. Democratic worldmaking, recall, begins from tragedy. Democracy is a response to the problem of politics: in a world of interdependence and relative scarcity, people must decide who gets what and who gets to do what. We need the same things, including one another's help and forbearance, and there is no possible world in which we all get just what we would like. The tragedy is that we are one another's necessary helpers and also one another's competitors and threats, and no response to this situation will ever dissolve the conflict.

There is no natural harmony among us. What political decisions do is to set terms for living together, creating an artificial order that is nonetheless real. That order may be decent or terrible, equitable or radically hierarchical.

Democracy's moral authority starts from the principle that we should shape our interdependence in a way that gives equal weight to everyone who lives with the outcome and, in class societies, gives decisive weight to middling people or the poor, cutting back domination of politics by the wealthy. Across history, monarchs, aristocrats, and dictators have most often pronounced the law, although they have often called on some version of the people to bolster their right to rule. But it is their will that makes the law. They decide the order in which the rest of us live. What distinguishes democracy is the creation of an artificial will, whose decisions arise from majority voting, that makes the people a real entity, a force that can act to author a common world.

Du Bois defined his vision of democracy by two standards: equal political rights and, just as important, the authority of democratic majorities to set the shape of economic order. Disenfranchisement and the constitutional shielding of racial capitalism (and capitalism per se) were both usurpations of democracy, the first in terms of racial caste, the second in terms of political economy. As he put it,

> The true significance of slavery in the United States to the whole social development of America lay in the ultimate relation of slaves to democracy. What were to be the limits of democratic control in the United States? If all labor, black as well as white, became free—were given schools and the right to vote—what control could or should be set to the power and action of those laborers? Was the rule of the mass of Americans to be unlimited, and the right to rule extended to all men regardless of race and color, or if not, what power of dictatorship and control; and how would property and privilege be protected? This was the great and primary question which was in the minds of the men who wrote the Constitution of the United States and continued in

the minds of thinkers down through the slavery controversy. It still remains with the world as the problem of democracy expands and touches all races and nations.[7]

From its beginnings, economics has been closely involved with a picture of social life that rejects the Du Bois–Roosevelt account of what politics, and specifically democratic politics, adds to the world. The theory of the market is not only a technical, professional methodology; it is also political theory. It offers its own approach to the fundamental political problem, the conflict of human goals, interests, and wills. In rather different ways, thinkers as diverse as Adam Smith and Friedrich Hayek have denied that this conflict is, in fact, an inevitable and necessarily political problem. They claim that a spontaneous harmonization of projects, purposes, identities—wills—can arise but only on market terms. And they deny that politics, and specifically democratic politics, can make a desirable harmony. For them, politics is incorrigibly a domain of conflict, domination, and coercion—and the market is not. If we wish to save ourselves from conflict and coercion, according to this perspective, we must do so not through politics but by escaping from politics. We must escape especially from the myth of democracy, which promises harmony when in fact it empowers some of us to dominate the rest without apology. Binding our politics to the market is the only way to create a decent and harmonious common life.

If a person recalls only two images from the work of Adam Smith, the eighteenth-century Scottish philosopher, jurist, and protoeconomist, they are likely to be the invisible hand and the pin factory. Smith provided the most persistent metaphor for friends of the free market when he wrote that someone pursuing his self-interest in a system of free exchange will act to the benefit of others as if an invisible hand guided him to beneficence. And he opened *The Wealth of Nations*, his landmark 1776 work, with an enduring image of material progress arising through efficiency. He described a workshop in which ten men, of no special talent and with equipment of indifferent quality, divided pin making into eighteen distinct steps, with each workman taking one or two as his own. Each man, working on his own, might have made as many as twenty pins a day by Smith's reckoning. By specializing, they jointly manufactured about forty-eight hundred pins, 240 times more than the ten of them could have made individually.[8]

In a way, it is ironic that Smith's pin factory has become an emblem of progress. The vast increases in productivity and wealth that have remade the world in the nearly 250 years since he published *The Wealth of Nations* are rooted in new technologies more than in the division of labor. James Watt patented his improved steam engine in 1769, prefiguring the Industrial Revolution of the century that followed. Smith, writing at the same time, did not see how compounding innovation could change everything—an idea that would be conventional by the early nineteenth century. Smith thought the limits to economic progress were basically those of specialization. He even thought that Holland in his time might be approaching those limits. (As we shall see a little later, he also harbored a moralist's doubts about whether the division of labor was good for those who experienced it.)[9]

But if the pin factory neither forecasts nor quite celebrates the capitalism of the twenty-first century, it does something else at least as interesting and mostly forgotten. For Smith, the factory's division of labor was the natural expression of a deep human tendency. "A propensity in human nature to truck, barter, and exchange one thing for another," he wrote, "originally gives rise to the division of labor." He proceeded to imagine the primordial life of "savages" as one of incipient specialization and exchange, in which small differences in talent or training make one person useful to others. Soon one person is a carpenter, one a brazier, a third a tanner, and still another a fletcher. This was not the outgrowth of any deep difference among people: "The difference of natural talents in different men is, in reality, much less than we are aware of; and the very different genius which appears to distinguish men of different professions . . . is not upon many occasions so much

the cause, as the effect of the division of labour. The difference between the most dissimilar characters, between a philosopher and
a common street porter, for example, seem to arise not so much
from nature, as from habit, custom, and education." But if our
specialties were not written in our nature, specialization was. The
pin factory was within us, long before it ever came into being.[10]

The brazier and the fletcher seemed content in their modest
mastery. The pin maker, by contrast, might not find his life en-
riched by specialization: "The man whose whole life is spent in
performing a few simple operations, of which the effects too are,
perhaps, always the same, or very nearly the same . . . generally becomes as stupid and ignorant as it is possible for a human creature
to become. . . . His dexterity at his own particular trade seems,
in this manner, to be acquired at the expense of his intellectual,
social, and martial virtues." Smith warned that "the great body of
the people" would suffer this degradation and recommended that
public education might help to expand their minds—a hopeful
gesture, but a somewhat weak cure for those who would spend
most of their lives doing the same thing over and over again.[11]

But why would they stand for it? Could the propensity to truck
and barter, as Smith called it, really reconcile workers to inequity
and tedium? Might pin makers not question whether they really
had to spend their days in the factory? Smith proposed a second
principle of human nature that stabilized the division of labor
and, particularly, the factory owner's place in it: "superior wealth,"
more than any other quality, "contributes to confer authority."
This was not because of any brute economic power the rich could
wield. Human nature simply contained "a strong propensity to
pay them [the rich] respect."[12]

Among the most powerful sources of social cohesion, Smith argued, was sympathy, the tendency to identify with and enter into
the feelings and experiences of others and so to wish them well.
Because of sympathy, people tended naturally to hang together.
Cooperation reinforced cooperation. And it just happened that
"our sympathy with our superiors [is] greater than that with our
equals or inferiors: we admire their happy situation, enter into

it with pleasure, and endeavor to promote it." Social life had a natural form, prepared in our minds and motives: it was hierarchy. For this reason, Smith was being much less subversive than it might have seemed when he told his law students: "Till there be property, there can be no government, the very end of which is to secure wealth, and defend the rich from the poor." The self-defense of the rich was the origin of government, but the need was a moderate one because the principle of sympathy lent the rich authority. The first society of herders naturally deferred to the largest of their great men, and on his death, "his son naturally becomes the chief of the young people, and on the death of his father succeeds to his authority." Hierarchical government was then off to the races. It was worked out through history as a consequence of human nature. "Upon this disposition of mankind to go along with all the passions of the rich and the powerful," Smith wrote in *The Theory of Moral Sentiments*, "is founded the distinction of ranks and the order of society." Understanding social order was not, as for Hobbes and Rousseau, a matter of understanding how authority and inequality could have emerged from the fundamental principle of equality. Rather, the thing to understand was how the tendencies to specialization and hierarchy were braided together across time.[13]

Smith did not claim that hierarchy was good simply because human nature tended that way. His work is full of a moralist's lamentation of the sycophancy and deference that wealth and power attracted. Yet he did not propose curing these maladies with a social order of equality. The result was a complex attitude, in which he both regretted and endorsed hierarchy:

> The disposition to admire, and almost to worship, the rich and powerful, and to despise, or, at least, to neglect, persons of poor and mean condition, *though necessary both to establish and to maintain the distinction of ranks and the order of society*, is, at the same time, *the great and most universal cause of the corruption of our moral sentiments* [italics mine]. That wealth and greatness are often regarded with the respect and admiration which are due only to

wisdom and virtue; and that the contempt, of which vice and folly are the only proper objects, is often most unjustly bestowed upon poverty and weakness, has been the complaint of moralists in all ages.[14]

Smith saw no prospect of overcoming hierarchy, including the deeply inequitable respect and sympathy accorded to rich and poor, which he called necessary to social order. But he thought he saw a way to retune inequality to make it more rational and humane. In a commercial society, where people got their living only if they could sell something (pins, say, or, for the pin makers, their labor in the workshop), the ambition to become great, and so to be esteemed, would be the fuel of usefulness. "It is chiefly from this regard for the sentiments of mankind, that we pursue riches and avoid poverty," Smith held. Because people hungered for the admiration of others, they hungered to grow rich. Where being useful to others was the way to get rich, they would make themselves useful. Then the most ambitious person would act if he were the greatest philanthropist, striving every day to find new and better ways of serving others' needs. This was the point of the invisible hand: with a kind of providential power, it converted egotism into universal beneficence. It promised to work a moral transformation without needing to change the crooked materials of human motive.[15]

There is a hint of utopia here. Rousseau had tried to imagine a polity where order came at no cost to freedom, one designed to take "men as they are and laws as they might be." Smith, too, took men as they were and imagined a market-making policy that reconciled ambition with benevolence. But here the resemblance stops. Smith poured scorn on the idea of a social contract, insisting, "Ask a common porter or day-labourer why he obeys the civil magistrate, he will tell you it is right to do so, that he sees others do it, that he would be punished if he refused to do it, or perhaps that it is a sin against God not to do it. But you will never hear him mention a contract as the foundation of his obedience." The kinds of hierarchies that we find in social life were, for Smith, not wrongs to be overcome but clues to the nature of the human creatures that had created them. It would be pointless, if not mad, to try to evade our own natures, as he thought social contract theory tried to do.[16]

Smith was far from the doctrinaire libertarian that he is still sometimes caricatured as having been. Besides the fundamentally moral, even providential, orientation of his thought, he contended that government should provide what today are called public goods, from infrastructure to education, which markets will not fund spontaneously. (He was, at the same time, *pretty* libertarian by our lights: he liked the idea of toll roads, for example, to minimize public subsidy.) And he certainly understood that the commercial society he recommended required a legal and policy framework, as surely as any social order does. But—at the cost of some anachronism—he could have embraced Ronald Reagan's iconic phrase "government is the problem." It was by getting control of local and national governments and other institutions, such as universities, established churches, and guilds, that people exempted themselves from exposure to the market and so dodged the providential imperative to make themselves useful. Apprentices and guild masters played this trick in towns that regulated their local trades, denying outsiders the chance to compete with them. Manufacturers and farmers did it through protections against imports or by getting monopoly licenses from political patrons. Scholars and priests did it through sinecures in their endowed and subsidized institutions. As a moralist, Smith took aim at aristocratic society, where the ambitious were sycophants to the titled and idle rich. As a critic of policy, he aimed his fire at what today might be called regulatory capture, rent seeking, and special interests. In his mind, government was, by and large, a debased form of commerce, a setting where people pursued ambition and wealth while avoiding the invisible hand's imperative to be useful. Government was where corrupt expressions of ambition took root, producing classes of privileged drones.

By the time of his death in 1790, Adam Smith had become his admirers. Many nineteenth-century Americans, both patricians and Populists, believed commerce was the tendon that joined freedom and order, the system that reconciled selfishness and benevolence. And their world came increasingly to resemble the one Smith described. As trade and manufacture increased, wealth grew more than ever before in human experience, and a world of inherited social roles—guild master, landlord, tenant, servant—gave way to labor contracts among legally free and equal individuals. Smith's ideas, and those his teaching shaped, helped to make sense of a changing social world and to provide blueprints for new change.

Market thinking was never truly against the state. It always had an agenda for government. Much of the populism of Andrew Jackson's Democratic Party was an assault on institutions that were seen to lock up control of the markets to benefit politically connected elites. Jacksonians attacked the elite-controlled national bank and special legislative charters for monopoly businesses, and laid the groundwork for today's widespread market in credit and the right to create a corporation through a little paperwork. In this market populism, universal white male suffrage and general access to the market (for the same people) were two sides of one coin. Democracy, the Jacksonians thought, battered down the doors of economic privilege and set men free in the market.

That market was well provisioned with expropriated land and the products of enslaved labor. Jackson, the market egalitarian, embodied the exclusionary face of market democracy, leading war parties against Indigenous Americans before the presidency and lawlessly expelling the Cherokee from their traditional lands while in the White House. He didn't just "own" enslaved people, as other southern antebellum presidents did, but once personally drove a coffle of chained slaves to market himself. The version of democratic capitalism that grew in the early American republic was a thoroughly racial one, not incidentally but centrally: it didn't simply lock out certain populations but also used the labor and land of the outsiders to produce wealth and opportunity for the insiders. As historian Edmund Morgan documented in 1975, developing an insight that Aziz Rana valuably updated more than a generation later, American slavery and American freedom took shape together.[17]

Adam Smith himself did not regard racial slavery as an aspect of the natural and excusable hierarchy of social life. He took a keen interest in New World slavery and abhorred the tyrannical authority at its core. In his mind, slavery was the antithesis of commercial society. In the marketplace, there was perpetual negotiation: everyone was always trying to persuade others that their interests were aligned. Offering someone a shilling, Smith observed, "is . . . offering an argument to persuade [some]one to do so and so." Smith's vision, in which the market was the opposite of slavery, influenced some of the architects of post–Civil War Reconstruction, for whom freedom meant emancipation into market life. They argued for a version of transracial citizenship that centered on the right to own property, enter contracts, and take commercial disputes to court. The vote was less central in this vision, much less the power of democracy over the market—which was essential, by contrast, to W. E. B. Du Bois's abolition-democracy.

In the wake of northern victory in the Civil War, three constitutional amendments (the Thirteenth, Fourteenth, and Fifteenth) wrote a new conception of citizenship into fundamental law. It was through interpretation of these amendments in the second half of the nineteenth century that American constitutionalism became centrally concerned with the articulation and protection of individual rights (a practice so central to today's constitutional law that it may be surprising to remember that there was a time before it). It naturally occurred to corporate lawyers to define these rights to protect the market from political "interference." In 1872, Supreme Court justice Stephen Field debuted the theory that the Fourteenth Amendment's protection of liberty included the right to enter into certain business relationships unburdened by regulation, and called on Smith for the principle that "the patrimony of the poor man lies in the strength and dexterity of his own hands; and to hinder him from employing this strength and dexterity in what manner he thinks proper, without injury to his neighbor, is a plain violation of this most sacred property. It is a manifest encroachment upon the just liberty both of the workman and of those who might be disposed to employ him." Although Field wrote in dissent, the court soon launched a decades-long era in which it scrutinized labor laws and other burdens on "freedom of contract," striking down minimum wages, limits on daily and weekly hours of work, laws supporting unions, and restrictions on children working in factories, among many others. Although this jurisprudence met resistance on and off the court, it was central to the life of American law until the years 1937–1942, when the Supreme Court was first confronted by and, soon enough, staffed by Franklin Roosevelt's New Dealers, who burned down the doctrine of freedom of contract and ploughed its fields with salt.[18]

It was at about this time that the twentieth century's most influential inheritor of Adam Smith's thinking landed, literally and figuratively, on American shores. The April 1945 edition of *Reader's Digest* contained an abridged version of the Austrian Friedrich Hayek's *The Road to Serfdom*, a warning that well-intentioned regulatory and redistributive policies, such as those of the New Deal, would have terrible unintended consequences. Bit by bit, the progressive state would come to be a new kind of tyranny, managing the economy and, so, the lives of citizens in the finest detail—except that there would be nothing fine about it: the government would weigh down personal freedom and choke off economic growth, leaving American life poor and nasty, if not necessarily brutish or short. Hayek himself was soon promoting the book across the country and remained a prominent figure in American ideas until his death in 1992 (at an enviable ninety-two years old).

The work in which most readers and listeners met Hayek was a popularization of a popularization: *The Road to Serfdom* was the most polemical of his major works. That, and the prominence of the "totalitarianism versus democracy" trope in the popular ideas of the early Cold War, led then, and has often led since, to an understanding of Hayek as an essentially Cold War figure, a tribune of the West against the repressive regimes of communism and fascism. In fact, his intellectual formation was almost entirely elsewhere, in interwar "red Vienna," where the Social Democratic

Workers' Party controlled the city and pursued a municipal version of socialism, including public housing, social services, rent control, medical clinics, and an eight-hour workday. These policies spurred intense theoretical fights over how far democratic politics could go in creating a political economy of freedom and equality.

Hayek became the most visible member of a school of thought that gave this question a curt answer: not much, and the attempt was dangerous. The philosophical architecture of Hayek's response was that of Adam Smith but updated for a time transformed by democratic politics and industrial revolutions that Smith, in 1776, could hardly have imagined. The world had changed, Hayek argued, but markets were still the necessary core of any free and productive social order. Whoever said otherwise was confused or worse.

Hayek's central argument, developed in Vienna and elaborated over decades thereafter, was that the economy was, above all, an information-processing system. It conveyed facts about the supply or scarcity of goods and materials, as well as time and talent. It let those who had these valuable things know who wanted them and how intensely. Any rational decision within economic life—make this or make that, build this or build that—depended on such information. Every choice implies a trade-off, doing one thing rather than something else. If we do not know the implications of that choice, then we are flying blind.

The market's great virtue was that it captured this information in a succinct and usable form: price. The facts that might bear on any given decision are multifarious and beyond the reach of any one mind. But every new bit of information—a drought in Iowa, a shift to meat consumption in urban China, a new European Union regulation, speculation about synthetic substitutes for traditional foods—will show up as a rise or fall in supply or demand and so exert a bit of upward or downward pressure on price. When a buyer looks at a price tag, or an investor at a commodity futures price, it is as if an invisible hand were pointing out these facts that are dispersed around the world and otherwise hidden from view. Price leads people to take account of what they otherwise could not know. It reconciles the individual standpoint with the perspective of humanity.[19]

But unlike Smith, Hayek didn't see the invisible hand's benevolence as the point of his argument. The marker's providential quality was, rather, omniscience. Never mind goodness: prices gathered information and gave it bite. The structure of the argument was still providential, but its mood and motive were no longer religious. Hayek didn't care whether the market made people into better saints than those who set out for sainthood. He did care whether it made them better planners than those who set out to make the economy more rational and humane through democratic politics. Planners were his target. Democrats who hope to turn the economy to popular and egalitarian ends need to replace, or at least recast, some individual decisions in the marketplace with political decisions—perhaps located in an administrative body but ultimately traceable back to a vote. But to be at all rational, such decisions require vast information. No one knows enough to make such decisions, Hayek insisted. But the market knows, which is to say, prices spur us to choose as if we knew. When government moves away from the price system with subsidies, targeted taxes, industrial policy, wage supports, and so forth, it is as if it had spilled ink into clear water.[20]

Adam Smith, writing when the young discipline of political economy was inseparable from moral philosophy, had seen the market's efficiency as essentially moral, a device for marrying self-interest and benevolence. By permitting, even encouraging, people to behave selfishly, it turned them into practical saints or at least humanitarians. Attacking twentieth-century socialists and social democrats who saw economic order as a vital area of political contest, Hayek presented his version of the market as a theory of the necessary limits of politics. If politics meant planning, he would show that there was no better planner than the market. Any other conception of social justice or political legitimacy would defeat itself in practice by trying to manage an economy that, in reality, only the invisible planning of the price system could oversee.

Social and legal order *was* the market. Attempts to overcome the market would fall into a blend of poverty and tyranny.

Hayek's price theory was nested in a broader theory of collective life. There were two kinds of social order (and two kinds of organization more generally), Hayek argued. The first was a planned organization that aimed at a specific purpose. (Think of a corporation or a campaign.) Its operation relied on, and could be captured in, a blueprint, like a corporate charter or, by analogy, the design specifications for a particular tool. The second kind of order was organic and spontaneous. Drawing on the classical Greek, Hayek called the latter a *cosmos*.[21]

The market was a cosmos. It had, Hayek argued (broadly following Smith), arisen piecemeal because people found that it worked, not because it had been imagined in advance. Still more important was that the market, unlike planned orders, was not aimed at any particular goal. Instead, it was neutral with respect to the purposes people pursued within it. Own property, in this vision, and you can broadly do what you wish with it, from reforestation to building a monastery to paving it over as a parking lot. A contract, the basic device of market coordination, is a flexible device that people may use for projects ranging from conservation agreements to establishing a religious order to financing commercial development. Within this order, people's economic obligations to one another are those they have taken on freely. Their projects are their own. The test of success is attracting others as collaborators, investors, or customers. Such a society has personal motivation as its fuel and free choice as its piston rods. Social wealth is its output because the price system drives resources, goods, time, and talent to the most productive uses, as measured by the uses that are most valuable to others. Here we are back, in a roundabout way, to the defense of the market as a system of inadvertent humanitarianism.[22]

Hayek, however, hastened to disown certain moral defenses of the market. The market was not "fair." It didn't reward effort in any reliable way, let alone virtue or excellence. The working of the price system implied that many efforts would fail, many projects come to nothing, just because they did not happen to appeal or because a competitor outdid them. Winners took all. While he surely agreed with Ronald Reagan that government was the problem, Hayek could not in good conscience have signed on to Reagan's glossy image of economic life as the place where honest, hardworking people flourished and got what they deserved. They might or might not.[23]

Hayek didn't care about that and didn't think anyone should. In his view, to talk about what people deserved, about fairness, was a seductive conceptual error. A planned organization, like a charitable project, could allocate resources according to some idea of deservingness; a cosmos could not. It was essential to a dispersed, purpose-neutral order like the market that it had no central node of authority to which a disappointed person could appeal for redress. Hayek held that

> it is meaningless to speak of a right to a condition which nobody has the duty, or perhaps even the power, to bring about. It is equally meaningless to speak of a right in the sense of a claim on a spontaneous order, such as society, unless this is meant to imply that somebody has the duty of transforming that cosmos into an organization and thereby to assume the power of controlling its results. . . . We are not, in this sense, members of an organization called society, because the society which produces the means for the satisfaction of most of our needs is not an organization directed by a conscious will, and could not produce what it does if it were.[24]

The mistake of progressives, according to Hayek, was to imagine that they could mix the efficiency of the price system with interventions to support sympathetic groups, industries, causes, and so forth. This conceit confused purposeful organizations with spontaneous order and, by jamming them together, turned a cosmos into a shoddy tool or badly run organization.

This is the theory of which Reagan's speeches were the folktale. It was the high-church version of perennial opposition to the New

Deal and similar programs around the world. Hayek identified the market as fundamental law, not in the sense that it was somehow implied by the text of the Constitution, let alone prescribed by God, but in the sense that it was the uniquely defensible form of social order in a complex and plural society that must reconcile diverse wills and allocate scarce resources. Its antipolitics was the only adult politics.

In the twentieth (or twenty-first) century, Hayek's claim that market order had arisen spontaneously over time was of purely historical interest. A modern state would have to decide for or against the market, and deciding for it would be, to a considerable degree, a matter of institutional self-restraint, of resisting all the morally charged and often electorally potent calls for social protection and redistribution. If you believe that a free and productive social order is just a market order, you will naturally take an interest in institutional and legal barriers to redistributive democracy. Doing so will seem to be no more than taking the stewardship of collective life seriously.

The fundamental commitment of the tradition we have been examining is to defend markets against the intrusions of politics. This defense, ironically, can be conducted only by means of politics. Smith's was a program of market building, with an agenda for the state that included tearing down restrictions on trade and industry, opening up labor competition, and hanging everyone's ambitions—and survival—on their success at selling and buying. Hayek's was a program for defending and extending the markets Smith had prescribed; his recommendations included establishing a legislature that would be elected for lifetime terms in each generation's middle age, a way of muffling the state's transformative power in the cautious common sense of adulthood. Hayek denounced distributional politics as "agreement by the majority on sharing the booty gained by overwhelming a minority of fellow citizens, or deciding how much is to be taken from them." He warned that "unlimited democracy" was "no better than any other unlimited government." Forced to a choice between economic liberty and democracy, Hayek wrote, the proper choice would be economic liberty; he preferred, however, to move toward a "constitution of liberty" that would inhibit democratic politics from ever forcing the issue. He proposed to redefine democracy as public consent to a set of rules that would encase the market's ostensibly neutral procedures from state intervention. This was a specifically *antipolitical* agenda, one that used both the institutions of the state and the public philosophy of government to minimize the scope of legitimate argument about the distribution of wealth and power and the nature of value.[25]

The story of capitalism is one of ideas as well as factories, laws as well as steam engines and cotton gins, moral argument as well as arithmetic. It came into the world promising a better version of the same themes that have defined modern democracy: the meaning of freedom and equality in a complex world and the right way to use that terrifying institution, the state. Its defenders have understood it as a form of social order, one that replaces coercion with cooperation, command with mutual negotiation. These theories have served as an agenda for the state—it should make and police markets—and, just as important, as a limit on democratic rule. For Smith's followers, and in Hayek's recasting of Smith's thought, the essential problem of modern government is self-restraint, especially abstinence from powerful democratic temptations. The greatest temptation is the democratic impulse to make a world more equal and more secure than markets will allow.

For these reasons, the market version of the democratic state has centered on a separation of powers that cuts across social life. On one side are politics and the state, the domain of collective choice and coercion. On the other side is the market, whose operating principles are its own and which requires support from the state but equally needs the state's self-restraint. If we are going to be free and equal in the market sense, we must police this boundary, keeping politics in its place.

These claims appeal to very basic interests in freedom, prosperity, and sustainable social order. If they were right, they would imply a modest and chastened version of democracy, in which the questions politics should decide would be narrow and the meanings it can give to freedom and equality constrained. But this analysis may be precisely backward. The events of recent decades suggest that, instead of markets needing protection from democratic politics, democracy needs protection from the market—or, at a minimum, both are true.

7

DEMOCRACY AND/OR
CAPITALISM

In 2020, the gamified day-trading app Robinhood announced that its mission was "to democratize finance for all." "Democratize," in this case, meant opening the doors to a stock-market casino. Six years earlier, promoters were talking about crypto-trading as "democratizing Wall Street." Cryptocurrency Bitcoin "seeks to democratize currency and payments." In 2011, the résumé-matching site Monster promised to "democratize recruiting" by letting more kinds of job seekers link up with employers. Start looking, and you will see it everywhere: promises to "democratize" advertising, design, direct marketing, medicine, whatever. Some of these barrier-lowering changes do increase users' powers in real ways. Many just intensify the vulnerability of life in the marketplace, speeding up the already relentless press of speculative bets, pushy ads, and precarious jobs, dressed up to make market vulnerability look like freedom's fun new frontier.[1]

It isn't surprising that touts would debauch a charismatic word. In twenty-first-century America, whatever you care about will be used to try to sell you something. But marketers weren't leading the charge to change the meaning of democracy. In 2010, the

Arbuckle Professor at Harvard Business School explained in the *Harvard Business Review* that Apple cofounder Steve Jobs "set out to democratize computing" by making it "available conveniently to the masses." In the same year, Robert Zoellick, then the president of the World Bank and previously George W. Bush's trade ambassador, promised to democratize development economics by providing open access to the bank's databases, which included loan records and analyses of economic policies throughout the developing world. Already in 2009, the *New York Times* was referring to Robinhood's precursors as "democratiz[ing] investment," and in 2007 the *Times* explained the trend of "democratizing plastic surgery," which meant that people with household incomes under $30,000, who often lacked health insurance, were financing their cosmetic procedures with loans. After all, the paper of record pointed out, earning power follows attractiveness. "I financed my car," the *Times* reported one patient saying in an emblematic reflection. "Why shouldn't I finance my face?"[2]

These are not random abuses of a word. The professional explainers, like the professional marketers, are using democracy in a way that, when you link the points on the scatter plot, adds up to "universal market participation plus some transparency." It's no surprise that Silicon Valley icon Steve Jobs pops up here, along with the Apple empire that he helped to build. The meaning of democracy that these uses trace is basically the one that the internet optimists of the 1990s and early 2000s popularized: universal access and transparency would democratize software (through open, unencrypted code), democratize knowledge (through sites such as Wikipedia, which, it became briefly fashionable to say, was better than *Encyclopaedia Britannica*), democratize the news through blogs and amateur reporting, and democratize democracy itself by enabling citizens to organize online. We now know (and there were warnings at the time, if eyes were open) that actual results would include the largest monopolies in world history, a vile bloom of conspiracy theories and other "alternative" knowledge, and an online Hobbesian dystopia of warring multitudes.

This conflation between democracy and the market is not completely inapposite, but a slippery half truth. The market, like democracy, theoretically (and to a considerable degree in practice) lets everyone in, gives everyone a forum for their convictions or preferences. The market, like democracy, organizes shared life partly by aggregating many dispersed perspectives and values—not by voting, as democracy does, but through purchases. It was partly on the strength of these resemblances that the egalitarian spirit in democracy—"every atom belonging to me as good belongs to you," in Walt Whitman's famous phrase—came to mean the breakdown of barriers to entering markets, of "expert" knowledge, of whatever stood in the way of consumer investors and their plans for their marginal dollars. But a thoroughgoing market order is less a version of democracy than a bizarro democracy, an opposite that, precisely through its resemblances, makes actual democracy ever more unlikely.

What did this new form of political imagination replace, and with what consequences? It grew up within, and in key ways against, the historically unusual period of relative economic equality that coincided with the heart of the Cold War, from the years after World War II until the mid-1970s. Then, as in few other times, high levels of growth were widely shared among the middle classes and many working-class people, including the large portion who were union members or worked in industries where union firms set prevailing wages.[3]

Many prominent commentators assumed that this relative egalitarianism was a new normal. The usual parochialism of the eternal present was assisted in this assumption by the influential research of economist Simon Kuznets, whose study of tax records showed early to mid-twentieth-century inequality rising, then falling. The graphic representation of this trend, dubbed the Kuznets curve, came to be treated as a feature of mature industrial societies: severe early inequality, part of the price of rapid growth, would give way later to moderate inequality. Yes, there were sweatshops and robber barons early on, but the factory worker's daughter would become a secretary, and his son might go to college or join a union. Confidence in this alleged historical law of economic development was strong enough that those who were vividly left out of general prosperity, notably most Black Americans and many Appalachians, were characterized as exceptions, islands that would take just a little longer to be worn away by the currents of history. Liberal economist John Kenneth Galbraith, arguing in *The Affluent Society* for bringing these populations into the order of well-being, treated poverty as the condition of being left out of the social bargain. This was a very different picture from today's inequality, which forms a basic, persistent feature of the American political economy.[4]

The very idea of a social bargain made a different kind of sense then than it does today. World War II had spurred an unprecedented mobilization of labor and industrial capacity, turning countries in real, material ways into platforms of common fate and endeavor. In the United States, war mobilization came just a few years after Democratic supermajorities made the New Deal, an experience confirming as few moments in American history have that the country could recast its terms of cooperation through democratic action. A social bargain, that is, need not be just a metaphor: it might be a concrete agreement among living citizens whose fates were thoroughly entwined. (Galbraith saw this, too. He wasn't a fatalist. Rather, he thought the social bargain of the New Deal and World War II was still strong and needed expansion.)

Economic life, too, confirmed the plausibility of a social bargain. The basic strategy of industrial peace in those decades was collective bargaining between unions and management. The two sides of the negotiation needed each other in part because of the technological nature of production. A factory, and an industry made up of a regional chain of factories, mines, and mills, threw people together in a system that was vulnerable to strikes, which meant each side of the bargain could issue a real threat. Today's dispersed supply chains evade this kind of worker power, at the same time that labor law gives unions fewer opportunities to push for collective bargaining.

At quite a different scale, the global economic architecture that World War II's victors composed at the Bretton Woods conference in 1944 (before they had even won the war) gave national governments considerable scope to set their own levels of spending and debt, stimulate or tamp down growth, and make distributional decisions, while capital remained substantially within national borders. Workers and bosses in a country were, to some meaningful extent, caught together like those in a factory. What was a country, in these decades? Among other things, it was a place where people made things together and so depended on one another, a fact that gave the makers power. Neither that reality nor the World War II mobilization can have been far from the mind of Pacific Theater veteran and eminent political philosopher John Rawls when he described the just society, in his landmark 1971 work *A Theory of Justice*, as a fair scheme of cooperation.[5]

Rawls's theory of justice shaped decades of subsequent political philosophy and came to occupy a place in the broader world of law, politics, and policy that contemporary philosophers very seldom achieve. Rawls famously asked which social world a person would choose if they could not know where they would fall in its hierarchies. He answered that a just economy was one that ensured the greatest possible benefit to the worst off (limited by personal freedoms of the due-process, free-conscience, and free-speech variety). Both the question and the answer gave systematic expression to a robust liberal egalitarianism that was the leading politics of the decades when Rawls developed his thought, enshrined in civil rights law and the program of public investment and social support that President Lyndon Johnson called the Great Society. Rawls described his approach as an update of Immanuel Kant's ethics and an improvement on the social-contract theories of John Locke and Jean-Jacques Rousseau, but intellectual historian and political theorist Katrina Forrester has shown that he also drew pivotally on "ordinary language philosophy," seeking to identify implicit but powerful shared meanings in everyday life. He appealed, that is, to an unspoken consensus about basic ideas of fairness, which could be drawn out systematically, rather as one might turn a few basic points about circles and angles into a system of geometry.[6]

What made this idea of consensus plausible? The answer lay in the world made by the New Deal and World War II, with notes of Cold War patriotism. There were injustices, surely—Rawls denounced segregation, seeing it as too plainly wrong to require much philosophical attention, and later threw his support behind students pushing for an African American studies program at Harvard—but there were also the resources to meet it, in shared principle and in a state that was strong and legitimate enough to seize injustice and bend it straight. In hindsight, this self-confidence is the remarkable thing about the liberalism of the 1950s through the 1970s. This liberalism grew up amid decades of violent labor conflict, economic crisis, a war that killed some eighty-five million people worldwide, the existential shadow of a nuclear-armed Cold War, and the persistence of explicit racial hierarchy as the axiom of American politics in much of the country. Yet its partisans believed the future was theirs.

This wave of twentieth-century liberalism can seem very distant now. In the mid-1970s, economic inequality began a great revival that has lasted nearly fifty years as I write in 2022. The modicum of economic citizenship that the New Deal had granted those whom it reached was now eroded by multiple assaults. Unions, many of them grown complacent and sometimes corrupt, were driven out of the private workforce, leaving workers to bargain individually. That "bargaining" was often a matter of taking what was offered. Companies large and small imposed noncompete agreements to prevent workers from moving to rivals. The rights workers did have were shunted from courts to arbitrators, who worked for employers. Real working-class wages stayed flat for decades, while incomes rose handsomely for professionals and skyrocketed for top executives. The financial industry enjoyed deregulation and loose monetary policy that supported a series of asset bubbles: stock, real estate, stock again. Right-leaning governments slashed taxes on high incomes, which encouraged even higher salaries and bonuses for those who could get them. Liberal and conservative governments alike expanded international trade and investment, which permitted—and then, through the magic of competition, all but required—global arbitrage in search of cheap and vulnerable labor, low tax rates, and weak environmental laws. Workers in industries subject to offshoring took wage cuts rather than lose their jobs. Eventually, many lost their jobs anyway.

The hollowing out of economic citizenship came at a particularly bad time for Black Americans. Although the New Deal made more difference to Black workers than is sometimes remembered, the overall shape of the economy bore the stamp of slavery and Jim Crow. Racist policies had largely kept Black people out of generations of wealth-building programs, especially the boom in federally supported home ownership that followed World War II. Black Americans first achieved notionally equal standing in the economy after the 1964 Civil Rights Act, which barred employment discrimination on the basis of race, and the 1968 Fair Housing Act, which banned discrimination in real estate markets. For all its flaws, the change was a watershed after centuries of explicitly racist policies. But access to wage-earning jobs after roughly 1973 was no longer a clear path to middle-class life. Since the end of World War II, people in the middle and lower ranges of American income distribution had gained significant household wealth. Those gains essentially stopped for all but the prosperous at nearly the same moment that Black Americans had a shot at them. Although quite a few more Black Americans are now middle class than in 1968, middle-class status in a profoundly unequal society isn't what it had been in a society of modest but real economic citizenship. Today's working-class jobs, in which people of color are heavily represented, are seldom steps toward a secure middle class. With wages mostly stagnant, the lion's share of increases in wealth since the 1970s has flowed to those who already have assets, which many Black households were denied the chance to acquire. Today, Black household wealth remains a small fraction of white wealth, bouncing around in the area of 10 percent.[7]

The retreat from the post–World War II settlement had many political sources, from widely shared anxiety about high inflation and unemployment in the early 1970s, which suggested to many voters that the system was not working, to a revolt of investors and bosses. "Revolt" may not seem quite the right image because the ways that capitalism gets out from under political control, or takes control of government, is not generally through anything as dramatic as storming the Capitol. Instead, the constant pressure on money to make more money means that lawyers, lobbyists, and corporate strategists are always looking for cracks in the walls that are supposed to keep them in bounds: a way to cut costs by importing parts from a special enterprise zone in Mexico or China that is exempt from trade restrictions; a way to shed obligations for workers' health care or retirement by reclassifying them from employees to independent contractors—a precursor of the gig economy; a way to avoid taxes by creating shell headquarters in Ireland or some other tax haven; a legal way to punish workers who are trying to organize a union and send a signal that the era of big labor is over. Keeping up profit quarter after quarter is a matter of a thousand tactics, which add up to a world-historical strategy. There were also outright contests of will and force, as owners got more bare-knuckled about moving factories, shutting down union mines and reopening them without a union, and generally grinding down workers' resistance. The 1970s and early 1980s were times of strikes. About 1.8 million Americans were involved in major work stoppages in 1973, some 900,000 in 1983. The comparable number was 12,500 in 2009. This began to change in the late 2010s, and close to half a million workers joined strikes in 2018 and 2019.[8]

In the end, the push for greater tolerance of inequality, which became an embrace of the economy as an inequality machine, won politically. Ronald Reagan carried forty-nine states in 1984, running a campaign in which patriotism and optimism were aligned with skepticism of government and celebration of the principle that some people should be able to get rich. This political victory included control of the Republican Party, which steadily shed its more moderate flanks after the 1970s. It was also a takeover, or at least a rebalancing, of elite attitudes, which increasingly became aligned with market premises. The early 1970s brought new recruits to the worry that American life was turning against "free enterprise," as economist Milton Friedman argued publicly and soon-to-be Supreme Court justice Lewis F. Powell Jr. worried in a private memorandum to the chief counsel of the Chamber of Commerce. Those who shared this worry propagated a network of scholars, think tanks, and advocacy groups that made the market worldview of economics, politics, and society into the argot of smart college students, professionals, commentators, and legislative staffers. Earlier in this book, I mentioned the small but telling tokens of a market culture: talking about the return on investment of learning or friendship, speculating about your value in the marriage market, worrying about your brand. These metaphors are partly spontaneous reflections of how the world works, but they are also fragments of the new common sense that market advocates cultivated.[9]

The new common sense also shaped the worldview of the liberals who inherited the Democratic Party and the network of institutions around it, including elite universities, traditional media, and established think tanks. Concerned not to seem naïve or behind the times, new generations in these institutions accepted that making markets work and treating government work "like a business" were the tasks of smart and humane people. Organized labor became a slightly embarrassing old uncle to liberals. The very rich were not, as the radicals of the late 2010s would later put it, policy failures but rather potential patrons. Deregulation of the workplace, banking, and trade was the coin of the realm. What distinguished the liberal side of that coin was an advertised interest in getting some of the fruits of economic growth back into the hands of ordinary people. But this goal turned out not to be so easy when the main work of government was building legal pathways for capital to roam the world looking for profit and helping employers at home to shed duties to their workers. Democrats coordinated by Bill Clinton's White House helped shepherd welfare reform and cuts to family support through Congress in 1995. Federally sponsored retraining for workers who had lost jobs due to offshoring, a touchstone for protrade liberals, turned out to be useless, a kind of spiritual symbol like the indulgences that late-medieval priests sold to speed souls through purgatory.[10]

In the mid-2000s, I heard a very influential and very prominent Democratic Party policy expert say that, the fact was, no one knew how to fight economic inequality. What that person did not say was that liberals had participated in dismantling the only tools that ever really accomplished that goal: unionization, strong limits on capital flight, and social investment funded partly by high taxes on the rich. These policies were not mysterious, but respectable liberals had helped to build a world in which they seemed anachronistic and, in any case, would be much harder to rebuild than they had been to disassemble.

In the 1990s and 2000s, the world that midcentury liberals inherited and felt entitled to rule was swept away. They were defeated. Yet they and their political heirs seemed not to know it. Or, rather, they were buoyed by the expectation of victory in a wider, indeed global field. The rise of market society in the United States and much of the rich world had been an agenda of the political right, to which liberals had played catch-up, but market-led globalization promised, in liberal minds, to be a liberalizing force. The mystification that surrounded it, however, would have embarrassed even a nineteenth-century devotee of the "natural" marketplace. In 2005, former British prime minister Tony Blair, scolding critics who wanted a debate over the terms of globalization, said, "You might as well debate whether autumn should follow summer." He was echoing former president Bill Clinton, whom we have already seen describing globalization as "the economic equivalent of a force of nature, like wind or water."[11]

The imagination of liberal globalization ran alongside a more hardheaded class politics that was pellucid to many investors, corporate strategists, and lobbyists. The increasingly open flow of goods and investment took place, like any other market, through legal institutions that had required political construction, hard-fought in lobbying and negotiations in Congress and international forums. The Global Agreement on Tariffs and Trade, a multidecade project to open up international movements of manufactured goods, wrapped up in 1995 having transformed offshoring from the exception to the norm. Its changes were absorbed into the World Trade Organization, which continues to enforce liberal trade in goods while also providing a platform for other liberalization agendas, particularly international investment. These changes in international economic architecture, of course, changed economic life at home. Offshoring and tax arbitrage raised businesses' profits and payouts, with a cut going to the financial industries that brokered international transactions. Manufacturing jobs fled high-wage countries. Those jobs had often been the anchors of local and regional economies.

Those hollowed-out regions switched from Barack Obama's Democratic Party to Donald Trump's populist nationalism, markedly and sometimes dramatically. That would not have been a surprise to those who spent the 1930s and 1940s trying to understand how economic dislocation had powered racist nationalist movements in Europe and broken a fragile liberal order. But for the historically amnesiac liberals of the early twentieth century, such setbacks were a shock.[12]

The liberal faith in benign and progressive global markets that pervaded the 1990s and 2000s was an extraordinary thing. It was a peculiarly parochial globalism, anchored in a United States that had tended to stand apart from the world but now stood astride it. There seemed—to many Americans, at least—to be only one human future, which was already the present in the United States. American culture was global culture. American brands and mall architecture were global. Wherever you went, if you happened to leave the country, you met yourself at a McDonald's. All of this seemed natural if you had lived with little comparative sense of the world's complexity, let alone its many entangled histories: being American was just being human, unmodified, what everyone would become once they had shaken off the dust of their local prejudices.[13]

How was this great transformation supposed to happen? There was a theory, more or less, surveyed in a thousand op-eds and political speeches. People everywhere wanted the goods of consumer capitalism and the mobility, self-expression, and other posttraditional privileges that went with them. With these satisfactions came a new kind of personality: the pragmatic, easygoing, tolerant disposition that the Baron de Montesquieu long ago identified with *doux commerce*, the softening, sweetening influence of commercial life. Focused on making and spending money, people would relax about religious and ideological shibboleths. From Coca-Cola, it was a short step to genial and tolerant liberal individualism.

Political liberalism would follow from this change in personality and culture. Market individualists were middle class and would want to have their property and personal freedom protected. This self-interested yet responsible class would press governments toward the rule of law, which meant relatively noncorrupt markets. The market really was natural, the thinking went, not because it didn't depend on politics but because a natural unfolding of history brought about the kind of politics that kept the market safe.

Liberal capitalism would build a world of peace, almost accidentally. The middle classes that it fostered wanted orderly and prosperous lives and had no stomach for war or violence. Governments committed to market-style rule of law would focus on mutually beneficial trade and economic integration, not zero-sum military adventures or trade wars. Any government that interfered too much with markets would become a bad investment and be punished by international capital markets. The middle classes, who needed that capital, would push errant governments back into line. Democracy had no special role in this theory, except as a handsome word for the domestic political pressure that helped maintain market-style rule of law.[14]

The result was perhaps the shallowest worldview ever held by a modern elite, succored in its complacency by the conviction that politics was basically a thing of the past, its work done, the task of social order handed over to market integration under light-touch technical administration. In hindsight, it is arresting that the rout of everything that made twentieth-century liberalism plausible should have been taken as super-empowering twenty-first-century liberalism. The period between roughly 1990 and 2009 was a late, false summer in the short American century. Belonging to that summer was a privilege worn lightly, a confidence that you had been born into universality, with all humanity hurrying to become what you already were. To be American, or a member of that civilization's epigone classes across the globe, was by happy accident to have arrived early at the condition that would become everyone's. The future's lingua franca was economics, its universal means the market.

As the cliché has it, the last thing fish notice is water, and the last thing that the post–Cold War generation noticed was capitalism. In those decades, newly dominant capitalism did what any political economy does: recast social life in its shape and even change the experience of being human. Capitalism is not just the neutral platform for mutually beneficial cooperation that thinkers such as Friedrich Hayek described. It is also a system of power that shapes the feeling, character, and imagination of whoever lives within it.

In a capitalist market, the key to value is profit: for owners, employers, and the managers of more abstract "finance capital" who may launch, sustain, or raid those owners and employers. (Any of these may scatter workers to the winds.) Every market participant faces pressure to show profit, increase margins, and find new sources of wealth. The pressure comes from the fact that everyone and everything is on the market—jobs, food, shelter, education, health care, investment capital itself. Because we have needs, we ourselves are on the market, under pressure to contribute somehow to profit so that we can pay for what we need, contributing to profit yet again.[15]

Under the cultural influence of these pressures, the very rich have become charismatic heroes, even demigods, in a version of what Adam Smith called the instinct to admire wealth and power. Steve Jobs, the founder and mascot of the Apple empire, was long an object of fascination, a person seen to be touched by the universe as kings were once thought to be touched by God. When Hillary Clinton in 2016 wanted to knock down Donald Trump's claims that his business career qualified him for the presidency, she didn't question the premise that billionaires make excellent national leaders. Instead, she reminded listeners that Trump probably wasn't an actual billionaire, just a debt-funded multi-millionaire, and that she in fact knew real billionaires, who supported her.[16]

The adoration of wealth comes partly from Smith's propensity to admire "the great," but also from a fearsome and coarsening result of everything's being on the market and everyone being, therefore, rationally anxious. Whatever comes of misfortune—medical crises, education, relocation, or unemployment—it will have a price tag, and you had better hope your market value can match the price. Both the admiration of wealth and the fear of poverty can inspire dreamy idealization of capitalism. At the start of the twenty-first century, a fifth of Americans told pollsters that they believed they were in the top 1 percent of the country in wealth, while another fifth said they thought they soon would be. (That leaves Occupy Wall Street's "We are the 99%" with only 60 percent of the population.) More recently, nearly 40 percent of Americans still say they expect to become rich. Some of this numeracy-defying fantasy must reflect unwarranted self-confidence: if the market rewards excellence, surely it will reward me! But some of it must also be a way to avoid facing the bleak consequences of not having wealth in a country whose economy is often merciless by design. Not surprisingly, the other side of dreamy idealization is coarse cynicism: consider the eagerness of some of Donald Trump's supporters to agree that if he dodged taxes it was only because he was no fool. Many paths lead to the same injunction: to get what you can get and keep all you can.[17]

Along with all this comes what we might call the capitalist theory of personality. Whatever traits are thought to be advantageous are celebrated (think of flexibility and resilience), and savvy schools and parents will try to inculcate them. Sometimes this involves a recasting of values or more than a little false consciousness. Flexibility, for example, has its good sides but can also mean a lack of attachments or expectations—an attitude likely to be adaptive in an economy in which jobs come and go, and each new one might require a certain reinvention or repackaging of the self. Resilience, similarly, is better than fragility, but it can also amount to a willingness to endure the consequences of structural disadvantage and come up smiling for each new interview. Market virtues, in other words, can be symptoms of the late Lauren Berlant's "cruel optimism" and, not coincidentally, convenient in keeping us flexible in the market for our own labor. It is not surprising that Stoicism, a classical Roman philosophy for those needing to endure suffering without breaking role, found a new millennium of followers in the later 2010s, while mindfulness, a secularized Buddhism that cultivates flexibility and resilience, has become beloved of human resources offices. Caring for oneself is good, of course, but self-care can also be a more or less desperate way of surviving a system that trains others to see your value in your price. Capitalism, like other effective regimes, flourishes by adapting ideals and traditions in ways that serve it.[18]

Why sketch this portrait of the self in capitalist society? Because the colonization of politics by markets is not a mechanical event but one that is inseparable from the attitudes and identities of the people who do—who are—the colonization. Our politics is that of a society shaped by capitalism's pursuit of profit, driven by its all-pervading insecurity, and distorted by the wish to look away from these and imagine that all is well, given that there often seems to be no alternative.[19]

It is in light of all this that we should understand the ways American and global capitalism have shaped American democracy. The country's political life is profoundly divided along class lines. The political values of wealthy Americans are quite different from those of the general public: fewer of the rich support substantial redistribution, national health insurance, affordable college, or a living wage. Elected representatives are mostly professional or wealthy: less than 2 percent of members of the

US Congress entered politics from blue-collar jobs. By the best estimates, at least half of congresspeople are millionaires. If democracy once seemed to threaten the wealthy with the rule of middling people, or of the free poor, we have reconciled mass enfranchisement with basic inequity. The inequity determines whose voice matters, whose anxiety or suffering becomes a matter of public urgency, and who has a part in shaping their own shared world. Recall the conclusions of political scientists Martin Gilens and Benjamin Page: "Under most circumstances, the preferences of the vast majority of Americans appear to have essentially no impact on which policies the government does or doesn't adopt." Most of us, it turns out, just live here.[20]

The influence that wealth exercises over political judgment is not mostly transactional—not a matter of bribes—and doesn't need to be because it is built into the system. (That is, it is structural.) Campaigns need money and must appeal to those who have it. That is how mass democracy recreates oligarchy without denying anyone the vote: by allowing the capitalist inequality of wealth to produce an oligarchic inequality of influence. Those who hold power know, listen to, care about, and identify with those who—like them, mostly—have money. Former officials, in turn, can decorously convert influence into money through a network of corporate board memberships, lucrative lecture circuits, and nominal but remunerative posts at law firms, think tanks, and universities. Our politics is entwined with other elite institutions in what must be this country's most robust and effective expression of class solidarity.[21]

Our oligarchy is not just a de facto conspiracy of the very rich, which is the preferred version of the story on the left. It is also the political access and influence, and the class solidarity, of the richest 10 percent or so of the country, many of them salaried professionals on the blue coasts or in blue cities from Austin to Durham. This is the Democratic Party's financial and cultural base, and it can move the levers of opinion for its preferred tax exemptions— to support college education, for example, and to offset the high local taxes of liberal jurisdictions—as well as its moral priorities.

Wealth is never the whole story in politics. Small political donors can outweigh large ones in theory, and with enough small
donations, a popular candidate can even fight to a draw the effectively unlimited funds that the very rich spend to support their
candidates. But small donations have added up in big ways for
only a few, mostly national figures like Trump and Bernie Sanders. The candidate who raises more money can lose, as Hillary
Clinton did in 2016, when her campaign substantially outspent
Donald Trump's, but money's influence is more pervasive in
thousands of less prominent primary and general races. The exceptions highlight the rule: political success requires cultivating
monied constituencies, which tends to mean listening to and
identifying with them.[22]

So our capitalist economy bends politics to its shape. This
makes it harder to hold economic life to democratic standards.
Doing so requires political choices. As we have seen, those choices
are always artificial. They come from institutions, such as elections
and representative assemblies, that people have created so that we
can act collectively. These institutions, the practical heart of politics, can also be colonized by capitalism. This colonization is partly
practical, the kind of thing that happens when elected representatives are mainly wealthy and mainly listen to other wealthy people,
so that political power just repeats the shape of economic power.
This colonization is also imaginative. It has to do with whether we
believe that we can decide the shape of our shared world.

A pair of examples shows how this colonization works. In the
1980s and afterward, antitrust law, the rules that limit concentration of corporate power, was remade along market lines. Historically, it was a field shaped by the spirit of its founders, such as
Supreme Court justice Louis D. Brandeis, who argued in 1905:
"There is felt today very widely the inconsistency . . . of political
democracy and industrial absolutism. The people are beginning
to doubt whether in the long run democracy and absolutism can
coexist in the same community; beginning to doubt whether
there is a justification for the great inequalities in the distribution of wealth." Brandeis argued that markets are shot through

with economic power, which easily becomes political power, and a democratic political economy requires a state that polices both, keeping companies from growing too strong. The goal was to prevent domination of other citizens, either in the marketplace or in politics. Subsequent antitrust policy tried to put this idea into effect by breaking up companies that had grown too large and powerful and by preventing mergers of the kind that, say, Facebook used in the 2010s to shut down potential competitors by simply buying them.[23]

As Facebook's recent tactics suggest, antitrust doesn't follow Brandeis's playbook anymore. Antitrust law was reshaped in the 1970s and 1980s by the new (and old) idea that markets are almost always open and equitable free spaces where power is inherently dispersed and shifting. It was now assumed that concentration of market share in one company, or a few, indicated that the companies in question must be serving the public well. This meant that a successful antitrust case tended to need to show that a company was using monopoly power to charge artificially high prices. Simply shutting down competitors by keeping prices low tended to be fine, even when it was part of a long-term strategy for market domination. In the bright sun of this market-first theory, Amazon grew strong, along with the rest of the platform economy. (Market concentration was also intense and unchecked in more traditional fields, such as agriculture, where farmers complain that giants like Cargill force them to buy high and sell low.)

It took a new, heterodox generation of scholars and activists to recognize the ways that giant platform companies become the infrastructure of the marketplace and can use their power to shut down competition. Amazon, for example, can negotiate special rates for delivery with companies such as UPS and Federal Express, then offer independent businesses the no-choice choice of working through its platform or getting squeezed out because they can't bargain for the same delivery rates. Now that Amazon has its own delivery fleet, this merger between the company and the market infrastructure is even more straightforward. These platform-based aspects of economic power are new and properly attention getting, but they track more prosaic kinds of domination: once Walmart dominates in-person sales, it can drive down prices by squeezing producers to accept tiny margins. Buyers get low prices, but if they are also farmers or workers, they will see their income, and their control over their workplaces, fall alongside the prices they pay for paper towels and detergent. All of these considerations, the heart of antitrust as Brandeis originally conceived of it, became nearly invisible under the market-first regime.[24]

A second example of how capitalism colonizes law and politics is the transformation of environmental protection in the five decades since 1970. Modern environmental law was created in a wave of legislation between 1970 and 1977, including the Endangered Species Act, the Clean Air Act, and the Clean Water Act. These laws began in arguments over what Americans owed one another and the earth's other life-forms. Addressing a teach-in during the original Earth Day in 1970—a movement-making mobilization in which an estimated ten million people marched, listened to speeches, and joined similar teach-ins across the country— Senator Ed Muskie, the architect of the Clean Air Act, insisted that "man's environment includes more than natural resources. It includes the shape of the communities in which he lives: his home, his schools, his places of work." Ecological awareness implied, for him, "a society that will not tolerate slums for some and decent houses for others, rats for some and playgrounds for others, clean air for some and filth for others." Muskie was speaking in the register of earlier advocates for the human environment, such as the pioneering toxicologist Alice Hamilton, who studied workers' chemical exposures in factories—work that laid the scientific basis for Rachel Carson's pioneering environmentalist book, *Silent Spring.* Muskie was echoing, too, the spirit of the Wilderness Society, an influential movement from the 1930s through the 1960s (and still active today), which had advocated for wilderness as part of a larger remaking of the landscape to create livable and even delightful communities at all scales of density, with the natural and human worlds mutually interwoven. These strands of environmental politics shared the recognition that ecology is inseparable from political economy. Ecology involves questions of justice and distribution (who bears the burden of pollution, and who can enjoy beautiful and restorative landscapes?), of value (which kinds of places and which species should people preserve and prize, and how should we relate to them—in distant reverence, in use, in some kind of community?), and of power (who gets to answer these questions, and who just has to live with the decisions?).[25]

By the 1980s, those questions were in eclipse, and a different approach dominated environmental politics and law. This approach translated environmental values into economic values, weighing extinction and ecological degradation alongside changes in gross domestic product. The environment became essentially an accounting problem: how to balance, say, the loss of habitat from drilling oil against jobs and cheap energy. To work, this approach had to put a price on every living thing and natural system that came into its view and array those prices across spreadsheets (literal or figurative) of alternative future paths of policy and politics. Pricing everything meant turning the most basic question of environmental politics—what is precious about the living world—from a matter for decision into a pseudofact.

There is, of course, a lot of value in trying to make policy decisions rationally through rational techniques. But much can also be lost. It became clear just how much the fiction of objective accounting concealed when environmental accounting turned its attention to global catastrophe. In fall 2006, Nicholas Stern, a British economist, released an influential forecast of the dangers of climate change, urging immediate investment of about 1 percent of global gross domestic product in an energy transition away from fossil fuels. William Nordhaus, a prominent American economist, replied that, according to his calculations, much smaller and slower investments would be enough. The crux of the disagreement was a question of accounting technique: the rate at which to "discount" the "value of future lives." Stern treated the well-being and suffering of future generations as mattering more to present decision-makers than Nordhaus did. Nothing is more important, difficult, or essentially political than the question of our responsibility to those who come after us: that this question was buried in bookkeeping, hardly argued over in its own terms, and only excavated as a kind of hindsight explanation of the difference between Stern and Nordhaus said a lot about the limits of this form of policy rationality.[26]

These examples show what is lost when capitalism colonizes politics and law. Antitrust law began from the idea that no one in a democracy should have too much economic power. When antitrust stops being a tool for political discipline of economic power and becomes a device for making sure that prices stay low, it turns economic power into a problem without a solution, a kind of fate. Similarly, when environmental politics takes shelter in the false objectivity of putting price tags on everything, it obscures what are really its central questions: how we should live, together and with the planet.

Market colonization is most radical when it changes the fundamental law of constitutional democracy itself. Since 1976, the Supreme Court has struck down laws that limit spending and contributions in political campaigns, calling them violations of the First Amendment's guarantee of free speech. The opinions in these cases spell out a picture of democracy that shows how far market logic has penetrated constitutional thinking. One part of that picture is the justices' upbeat assurance that no amount of spending by rich patrons, candidates, or interest groups ever really distorts democracy: spending on advertisements gives voters information, the court has cheerily said, and information lets people make better choices. This argument borrows a very sanguine view of advertising from academic economics—the implausible conceit that ads are just sources of information—and inserts it into the heart of politics. Concepts such as propaganda and manipulation have no place here. Seen in this light, political spending cannot be said to turn unequal wealth into unequal political influence because speech does not "influence" its listeners.

It merely informs them. As so often in market ideology, power is defined out of existence. And the problem of power—that we cannot avoid it and so must give it shape—is why we must have politics. Any view of politics that pretends power isn't there will be confused and confusing. According to a majority of justices, the Constitution commits Americans to just such a view.[27]

While the court portrays economic power in politics as not being power at all, the exercise of *political* power over the terms of politics itself—that is, election law—is always suspect in the justices' eyes. Any law that sets the terms of election spending is seen as a bid to tilt the playing field for one's own party and allies. In decision after decision, from the 1976 case constitutionally protecting campaign spending by wealthy individuals to rulings in the 2010s shielding the spending of corporations and rich candidates, the justices have denounced these laws as efforts to take power away from voters. In this vision, spending is a domain of freedom that makes voting more informed and effective. Lawmaking is a perennial danger to that freedom.[28]

In practice, there is no alternative to letting election law make political decisions about how politics will proceed, from constitution making to local election boards. The best we can hope to do is reach a working agreement on a political process that is reasonably fair, recognizing that no set of rules is ever absolutely neutral and that jockeying for advantage will always be part of the story. The worst thing we can do is follow the Supreme Court in adopting the fantastical idea that a market-style political baseline is neutral, while political "departures" from it are illegitimate. That is how we turn the class power of an unequal society into a form of political fate, when it is precisely what democracy—at once the rule of the free and the rule of the poor—should overcome. The confusion of democracy with capitalism, whose egregious and sometimes grimly funny symptoms we met at the beginning of this chapter, is not just a cultural quirk. It is a deep tendency of a time when a capitalist image of economic order has produced its own versions of freedom and equality and planted them deep in our ideas of politics.

These distortions of political practice, principle, and imagination hobble a polity for some of its most important work: shaping its political economy. Having a political economy is inevitable. That is, we always make rules that shape economic interdependence and power. The question is whether we know it or trick ourselves into imagining that what we do is natural and not political at all. The reasons that a political economy is inevitable are closely tied up with the reasons that politics itself is inevitable. A political economy responds to a few basic facts about us humans, which make us deeply interdependent. First, we need the same things. In a world of finite resources, people need food, energy, and shelter. Because these are not in infinite supply, there have to be some ground rules about who gets what. Other animals address this need by marking and defending territory. So do we, whether through common lands that certain families or groups use for hunting, gathering, or grazing or through laws that mark out certain farmland, pastures, or apartments as one person's property or another's. So, wherever we would like the same things, we are in one another's way. What one of us gets, past a certain point of possible sharing, the rest will not get.

Next, we need one another. Most of what people do, we cannot do alone. Of course, most of us depend on other people's efforts for our food, shelter, and energy, but the interdependence is deeper than that. Our freedom is relative. Whether we want to grow food, write essays, build houses, or make music, we need control of our own time and energy. Most of us also want what we call free time: to read, take walks, watch movies, make new friends, and have long, meandering conversations. Maybe we want to hang out with a baby who isn't doing much except sleeping and grinning.

None of this free time just arises like water from an artesian well. Much of what is called "our" time is doled out in advance: working to live, to service debt, to keep our own houses in order. Any free hour rests in an intricate web of other people's work: those who are keeping you fed, warm, sheltered; those who raised you or are raising your offspring; those who are picking up the garbage today or checking in on your aging parent or making sure the roads are patched and the subways running. Free time is about as spontaneous and random as a cherry tree in Central Park. In a world of finite resources, nothing is more precious than the time of others.

This goes all the more for work, our life in the economy. Building something—a school, a farm, a tech platform, a magazine, a movement with paid organizers, a company—requires other people's time, energy, and ability. Almost nothing happens without many hands and many minds, and those whose plans come true are the ones who can command these. So we develop the practice that fascinated Adam Smith and struck him as the key to progress, the division of labor. And we meet one another in the marketplace.

There have always been ideologies to make labor's division seem a natural form of rank: the European feudal organization of humanity into warriors, priests, and laborers or the Hindu caste system's more complex version of the same. Racism's "scientific" rationalization of slavery is an ideology of this sort that is particularly salient to modern minds, both because its legacy still distorts and breaks lives and because it is so clearly not natural or even plausible. It is harder for us to see the subtler ways that modern political economy generates a division of labor among people who are, in theory, legal and political equals but whose lives run along separate and unequal paths.

There are two basic ways of producing that division of labor: by pretending that the market's ways of sorting people are beyond the reach of politics or through a candid political engagement with the question of what work to value and who will do it. By taking the first path, we deny the political character of our political economy. By taking the second, we ask Rousseau's question: How can we make our freedom and equality the standard for assessing how we manage our interdependence? This is the economic challenge for democracy.

But if confronting economic power is depressing, confronting political power can be terrifying. Confronting one another in the marketplace, we are not equal or very free, but there is still a sense in which our individual choices are our own. Politics hands over some of those choices to the majorities that act on behalf of a polity. When we fear one another, the market's inequities can seem to be the lesser evil. For anyone who hopes to overcome some of its evils through democracy, the challenge is not to show that capitalism is flawed but rather to show that democracy can do better.

8

VOICES AND VOTES

The Perennial Crisis of Representation

W ho speaks for the people? The question has been inescapable as long as anyone has claimed to do so. It is a tricky question because you can't generally ask the whole people directly, and if you ask a representative, then you have already answered the question by picking the representative. This trouble, the problem of representation, is often imagined as a special difficulty of large, diverse, complex societies like ours. Smaller and more ideologically homogeneous groups, the story goes, could act together directly, conjuring a charismatic political unity that is lost to us. This idea, that representation is the political problem of modernity, is owing in good part to the statesman and scholar Benjamin Constant, who, in a lastingly influential discussion of the French Revolution's legacy, contrasted modern, representative institutions with classical democracy, which he envisioned as "20,000 Athenians" spending every day at their city's assembly, governing themselves (while slaves and women did the rest of the work).[1]

Actually, small, homogeneous democracies have the same problems. Consider a constitutional crisis among a few thousand ostensibly like-minded political idealists that took place well past dark on a Friday in 2011. The General Assembly of Occupy Wall Street was meeting on the western edge of Zuccotti Park, across from the Brown Brothers Harriman investment bank and just down the street from the Federal Reserve. The question was the basic one that any political community confronts: how to rule itself.

Like most constitutional reckonings, this one had a practical, even material basis—in the event, the laundry. It had rained for days, and although the sun was back, a sodden hill of clothing and gear loomed just west of the information and press tables, across the path from Sanitation collection of brooms and dustpans and blocking the street from the orthodox Marxist encampment that called itself Class Warfare. Revolution may require patience, but wet laundry does not tolerate delay. According to existing rules, the only way to requisition a couple of thousand dollars in quarters and detergent money was by consent of the whole community or, if that failed after full debate, "modified consent"—a vote of 90 percent. It naturally seemed to the Structure Working Group—a kind of constitutional drafting committee—that this was an apt moment to give say-so over the quarters to some less unwieldy body than the whole people assembled.[2]

Every exchange in the ensuing debate would have made good sense—with a little idiomatic translation—to the propertied white men who drafted the US Constitution in Philadelphia in 1787. If all power lies in the people and they transfer it to a committee to use, how can they control the government they have created? What if the committee becomes corrupt? What happens if the bigger groups use the new center of power to harass smaller groups? (Class Warfare was already grumbling that some of its tents had been "expropriated"—an ideologically awkward point for revolutionary communists but made nonetheless with heartfelt pissiness.) Who will watchdog the committees in winter, when it's too cold to sit through a General Assembly session outside? If we just worked harder and were more radical, couldn't we deal with the laundry ourselves, without creating a bureaucracy?

These debates took place through the community microphone, the no-amplification technology for open-air debate among five hundred or more people: the speaker speaks, a circle around her echoes her phrases in unison, and, when necessary, a second circle repeats the repetition. This was a social fix for a local ban on amplified sound, but ad hoc as its beginnings were, it soon achieved a liturgical quality: the speaker had to pause every ten words or so to match the limits of short-term memory. The crowd intoned together for hours. Every position argued in the assembly was spoken in the voice of everyone participating. People who disagreed sharply and palpably disliked and mistrusted one another nonetheless recited one another's words. Even when the speaker was agitated, an audible care governed the phrasing, as if the anticipated echo of the crowd and the memory of other voices in one's own mouth dissolved some of the ordinary narcissism of oratory.

The geography of Zuccotti Park resembled a Victorian ascent-of-man exhibit. At the eastern fringe, a tree had been designated the community's sacred space, where all gods and sentiments were welcome. Icons, devotional cards, beads, incense, and a poster of John Lennon and Yoko Ono were prominent. Drum circles worked nearby, to the east and northeast, throbbing into the night indifferent to what the General Assembly was debating on the other side of the park. A third or so of the space belonged to long-term campers, unkempt, tired, often sick or asleep during the day. There was some panhandling. At night this part of the park closed up, a faceless field of blue tarps and camping tents.

In the middle, a division of labor had arisen to meet pressing needs. A kitchen ran at nearly all hours, and there was always a line for whatever was on offer. The medical tents and sanitation supplies were also here, and on the edge of this zone, the mound of laundry issued its mute call for constitutional reform. These volunteers, the salt of Zuccotti Park, presented a practical challenge to radical democracy: they were too busy to spend five nights a week in self-government. Yet as long as the place was run by spontaneous action, they were as good as anyone else—indeed, they were leaders, because they were the first to pick up soup pots and brooms when the community needed those. The more decisions got concentrated in an efficient government, the more these volunteers would be carrying out orders and doing someone else's work.

The western end of the park housed Athenian democracy, circa 500 BCE. The General Assembly was not particularly a gathering of the campers, let alone the drummers. Many of the debaters would go home late to apartments in Manhattan and Brooklyn and return to the park the next morning. Many of the campers were under their tarps during the constitutional convention concerning the laundry pile.

The question that the General Assembly took up that long evening has dogged all forms of democratic rule. In 1789, amid the ferment that soon became the French Revolution, a Chartres cleric named Emmanuel Sieyès started down the path that would make him one of the most influential constitutionalists of his turbulent age. "What is the Third Estate?" he asked, meaning, what are the commoners of France, politically speaking? He answered his own question: "*Everything.*" The commoners *were* the people of France. The priests and nobles, the other two "estates" of the nation, Sieyès saw as "foreign" elements. Although the official point of his pamphlet was that the Third Estate should have an equal share in power alongside the other two, it implied something more radical, which Sieyès was not yet ready to face. If the people were everything and the privileged classes foreign, then there was at most a short step to the radical republican view that all power comes from and belongs to the people. Soon this was what much of revolutionary France understood Sieyès—and the revolution—to mean. The claim raised the same problem for France as for Zuccotti Park. If the people are everything and (nearly) everyone, how can the people take action? Everything can't be everyone's job. (Sieyès, incidentally, soon turned to recommending significant property requirements for voting, one way of simplifying the problem and a classic move for those who call on the authority of the people but are content to let the country's owners rule it.)[3]

As we have seen, competing claims to act for the people helped produce a cascade of governments in revolutionary France. Each regime was more radical in its program than the last and smaller in its base of loyal constituents. The first revolutionary constitution distinguished between "active" and "passive" citizens, with only the former, propertied men, voting for legislative deputies. The later Jacobin Constitution made all men theoretically eligible to vote, but that government never presented itself to the people in an election. As mentioned earlier, the parliamentary purge that brought the Jacobin Constitution to power had its social base in the radical artisans of Paris, the *sans-culottes*. The Jacobins regarded their street-fighting allies as, in effect, acting on behalf of the French people, a neat shortcut through the problem of representation, which would later attract both vanguardist parties of the left and movements of the fascist right. Sieyès was marginalized during Jacobin rule, of which he later remarked, simply, "I survived." He played an important part in the counterrevolutionary coup that first brought Napoleon to power late in 1799. It was by now extremely clear that the people did not speak for themselves, that claims to speak for them were always competing claims to power, and that the first task of a politics of popular sovereignty was to set out, with institutional precision, what it meant for the people to speak and act.

So the question of representation became crucial to the modern life of democracy. Those who wished to see the people in charge had to decide who should represent them and how. A canonical statement of this issue, presented as a meditation on the lessons of the French Revolution and its aftermath, came in 1819 from Benjamin Constant, whose lost idyll of twenty thousand self-governing Athenians we have already glimpsed. A Swiss French republican, first a young moderate during the French Revolution and then a parliamentarian in the constitutional monarchies that followed, he presented the violence of the revolution as the fruit of a conceptual mistake between two forms of freedom, "the liberty of the ancients" and "the liberty of the moderns." The problem of representation was the pivot point of the distinction. Modern liberty depended on representation, and the failure to realize this had turned the revolution bloody. Representative government was the key to reconciling political freedom and social peace.

By "the ancients," Constant meant the classical Greeks and Romans. He described their idea of liberty as centering on active political self-rule, what today is often called direct democracy. As he put it, the ancients exercised "collectively" and "directly" the "complete sovereignty," including war and peace, the supervision of public officials, and the pronouncement of guilt, innocence, or ostracism, proscription that sent the condemned into exile by popular vote. For the ancients, being free was not so much a personal condition as a condition of the political community, in which each citizen shared. Freedom centered on the collective power to control the direction of the polity—typically a city-state with a few tens of thousands of citizens, with slaves, women, and foreigners a multiple of that number but not counted in the polity. Sovereign power was almost absolute, as Constant portrayed it, with scant provision for protecting personal interests:

> Thus among the ancients the individual, almost always sovereign in public affairs, was a slave in all his private relations. As a citizen, he decided on peace and war; as a private individual, he was constrained, watched and repressed in all his movements; as a member of the collective body, he interrogated, dismissed, condemned, beggared, exiled, or sentenced to death his magistrates and superiors; as a subject of the collective body, he could himself be deprived of his status, stripped of his privileges, banished, put to death, by the discretionary will of the whole to which he belonged.[4]

Constant assumed that his modern readers and listeners (his argument was first presented as a lecture) would find the situation of the ancient citizen thoroughly alarming. The moderns liked a quiet life. If they had adventures, these were more likely to be in business and investment than in wars or vendettas, and they did not relish mobilized bands of fellow citizens getting into their bank accounts. They cared, too, about their own consciences and religious scruples. Modern liberty, Constant argued, was the assurance of being left alone in these matters, a matter of individual security. It depended on putting politics in its place.[5]

Constant praised representative government as "the only one in the shelter of which we could find some peace and freedom today" and as the preeminent political "discovery of the moderns," which had been "totally unknown" in the ancient world. Under representative government, he contended, "the individual, independent in his private life, is, even in the freest of states, sovereign only in appearance. His sovereignty is restricted and almost always suspended. If, at fixed and rare intervals, in which he is again surrounded by precautions and obstacles, he exercises this sovereignty, it is always only to renounce it." Constant was describing the life of a citizen under a constitutional monarchy or in a republic: ruled by designated representatives, whom he could occasionally vote for or against, under a constitution that just might have been presented to the country's citizens at some point in the past. The essence of modern political power was not the action of direct collective decision but the "right to exercise some *influence* [italics mine] on the administration of government" by voting, petitioning, and argument. Modern political life turned on shaping public opinion, demanding change, swaying minds, not on collective decision-making.[6]

Representation meant delegation. "The representative system," Constant explained, "is nothing but an organization by means of which a nation charges a few individuals to do what it cannot or does not wish to do herself. Poor men look after their own business; rich men hire stewards." The ancients were poor, by modern standards, for commerce had made the moderns rich. And so they hired stewards to run their governments. Karl Marx's famous description of liberal governments as "the executive committee of the bourgeoisie" is simply Constant's with the lighting changed.[7]

Restraint was of the essence for representative governments: they must be more limited in their powers and more modest in their reach than the classical democratic absolutisms. When modern citizens talked about liberty, they meant control of their own property, freedom of opinion and religion, protection from arbitrary arrest or imprisonment, and a modicum of influence on politics. The liberty of the moderns was not just different from ancient political liberty: it positively prohibited it. Classical freedom, with its restless, searching activity and boundless scope of power, would destroy modern freedom. It had almost done so during the French Revolution. Reinventing politics in the form of limited and representative government was the only way for the revival of popular sovereignty to coexist with the kinds of lives that nineteenth-century citizens lived and to shelter rather than ruin what they most prized.[8]

Constant told his listeners that the people who made the French Revolution had failed to understand this. Those revolutionaries had been enchanted by philosophers "who had themselves failed to recognize the changes brought by two thousand years." Rousseau in particular, "by transposing into our modern age an extent of social power, of collective sovereignty, which belonged to other centuries . . . has . . . furnished deadly pretexts for more than one kind of tyranny." The result was an abject failure to reconcile popular self-rule with modern conditions: "free institutions" could have survived, Constant insisted, if only they had reflected a proper understanding of the age. Revolutionary efforts at self-rule collapsed because they attempted a doomed project: trying to revive classical popular sovereignty. Representative government was the free institution that could survive.[9]

Constant was elegiac, rather than dismissive, toward classical democracy. The ancients' civic spirit was admirable and inspiring, he wrote; it properly stirred "an indefinable and special emotion, which nothing modern can possibly arouse." Revolutionaries had been "noble and generous" in trying to reopen those moral and political sources. But they had been terribly mistaken. The politics of modernity must be a chastened politics.[10]

It is not hard to see why Constant's thought entered the liberal canon and seemed particularly salient again in the twentieth century when seductive utopias seemed to license runaway abuse of power. His argument was a historically minded spiritualization of liberal political circumspection: modest collective aims might be uninspiring, but they were the soul of wisdom, and higher goals were siren songs. Constant's frame was essentially that of the most influential liberal essay of the Cold War period, Isaiah Berlin's "Two Concepts of Liberty," which distinguished between "negative liberty," the right to be left alone (not terribly charismatic but morally valuable and—the critical thing—politically achievable) and "positive liberty," the power to follow an ideal form of life (heady but dangerous and probably impossible). As Berlin put it: "No one saw the conflict between the two types of liberty better, or expressed it more clearly, than Benjamin Constant. . . . Democracy may disarm a given oligarchy . . . but it can still crush individuals as mercilessly as any given ruler. An equal right to oppress—or interfere—is not equivalent to liberty." The move to representation was thus part and parcel of a retreat from the classical conception of popular sovereignty, which could play no decent part in the modern world.[11]

Constant's story was charismatic, but was it true? Had the primitive politics of popular sovereignty given way to the skeptical and sophisticated politics of representation? There is a good deal more countervailing evidence than Occupy Wall Street's recourse to representation in the laundry crisis of 2011. Constant's sketch of classical peoples as lacking any concept or practice of representation was—as that anecdote suggests it would have to be—a caricature. The classicist and political theorist Daniela Cammack has emphasized that representation pervaded classical politics, including in the institutions that have been regarded as quintessentially direct, the assemblies of the city-states and the Athenian juries of citizens (which were populated by hundreds of volunteer citizens per jury, often drawn from the poorer classes of the city, and which, unlike today's juries, decided questions of politics and law as well as issues of fact). Although Constant asked his readers to imagine Athens's tens of thousands of citizens spending "every day at the public square in discussion," neither contemporaneous material nor the physical capacity of public spaces suggests this was remotely accurate as a picture of classical politics. The entire free populations of ancient cities could not have fit into the spaces provided for political gathering, not by a long shot. During any given political gathering, most of those who were eligible to attend were off seeing to their own affairs. They were represented by those citizens who did show up.[12]

The difference between classical representation and ours is that the classical kind was what Cammack calls "synecdochal representation"; that is, for the ancients, a part of the *demos* could stand in for the whole. What gave the part this power, or more precisely, what led members of the whole to identify with the part? Some of the answer must lie in the relative homogeneity of classical citizens, members of small societies linked by shared history and intertwined families. But another part of the answer was a form of political imagination, a way of inhabiting the polity that rested on a premise of commonality. In political life, people looked at one another and thought—or assumed so deeply they did not need to think it—"that might as well be me; what he does, in the assembly, on the jury, I have also done."

We moderns, certainly we Americans, do not experience one another that way. All modern political representation must bridge a felt gap between the part and the whole, giving some account of how representatives may act on behalf of the polity in conditions in which no one believes that they are synecdochal parts of a whole. We live not in Athens or Argos but Constant's Paris—or Zuccotti Park in 2011. Philosopher Frank Ankersmit identifies the pervasive modern form of representation as metaphorical rather than synecdochal: the legislative majority, president, or other political representative stands in for the political community, not as a part that can act for the whole but in some more complex fashion, like an employee, as Constant suggested, or because it has a special relationship to some source of authority, like the Supreme Court in its role as final interpreter of the Constitution.[13]

So the real difference between classical and modern democracy was not, as Constant said, that the first was direct and the second was representative. No large society has ever governed itself directly in the rather fantastical sense that all the citizens spend their days together in deliberation. The difference, rather, is that in classical representation it was taken as obvious that some of the citizens, without special selection or qualification, could act as the whole. By contrast, modern democracy is unrelentingly caught in contests over who can act on behalf of the polity and what kind of connection to the whole, or what kind of difference from it, can qualify that representative to do so.

Appreciating that representation is not new points toward an important insight that reverses Constant. Voting in mass elections is not a watered-down substitute for the political grandeur of Greece; it is something much more powerful than that. It is, indeed, a more direct form of democratic action than the ancient world knew. We have surpassed as democrats the inventors of democracy (or at least the people who coined the term).

The history of thinking about representation has obscured this principle in ways that give aid and comfort to antidemocratic attitudes. From Constant forward, modern theories of representation have tended to understate the value of voting. In discussing ancient liberty, Constant insisted that classical citizens had real power: "The share which in antiquity everyone held in national sovereignty was by no means an abstract presumption as it is in our own day. The will of each individual had real influence: the exercise of this will was a vivid and repeated pleasure." By contrast, in modern life, "lost in the multitude, the individual can almost never perceive the influence he exercises." Like Constant's claim that the ancients had no experience of representation, what he says here does not withstand scrutiny. It certainly wasn't true that the typical Athenian citizen had a prospect of persuading his fellows, maybe by giving a great speech: few spoke, most just voted, and, lacking the custom of the human microphone, those who spoke could only make themselves known to a fraction of the citizenry.[14]

Does modern voting do any better at giving citizens power? Political scientists tend to focus on the question of whether one's own vote is the deciding factor in a political decision. Following them, theorists of democracy often say that political equality means having an equal chance to be the decisive voter. If this is the standard, all is lost in the search for democratic power. Three hundred million, thirty million, or thirty thousand citizens will be enough to make anyone's vote a snowflake in a blizzard.[15]

Whether voting gives a voter power is, like the nature of representation, as much about the experience of politics as about its mechanics. Intellectual historian and political theorist Richard Tuck has argued that the dominant understanding of voting across most of its history was not that only the pivotal vote counts as doing something—meaning most votes are wasted effort, "lost in the multitude" in Constant's words—but that a voter could think of himself as having caused the outcome of the vote if he had been part of the total that was necessary to a majority. (Technically, this is called contributing to a sufficient cause of the outcome rather than being a necessary cause of it.) In 2020, Joe Biden defeated Donald Trump in Georgia by about 12,000 votes. Almost 2.5 million people in Georgia voted for Biden. On the older and, it seems to me, more plausible understanding of voting, almost everyone who voted for Biden in Georgia can say that they contributed to his victory. On reflection, this is exactly how we do think about it and a good deal of the reason we bother to vote. It would be a little much to say, "I elected Biden in Georgia!" but I would warrant that most of those voters understand that they are part of a majority in which nearly every bit counted.[16]

A popular vote, then, is more direct than classical democracy because it does not rely on representation. The effect of the vote is not less than that of a classical citizen's voice. We still have the liberty—and the power—of the ancients. This power is what, in part, makes democracy frightening. The question for the theory of representation is not how to function without self-rule but how to make this power compatible with the other features of twenty-first-century life: our diversity and pluralism, the premium we put on our own ways of living, the complexity and frequent opacity of our problems (climate change and financial regulation, to give

just two examples), our persistent and nagging fear of one another, and our mistrust of self-rule itself.

Who represents the voters? To begin with, in modern democracy, voters represent themselves. The questions about which institutions may then act in the name of the people, which I have
discussed in terms of the constitutional design of the United
States and shall return to, are, of course, extremely important.
But as long as voters can form majorities that decide the questions
before them, there is no reason that the people cannot act in a
modern democracy. They can, in fact, act in an inclusive way that
the ancients did not contemplate, without reliance on synecdochal representation by fragments of the polity. Each person can
vote in their own voice, as it were, and in the sum of votes the
community acts.

9

IF DEMOCRACY IS THE ANSWER, WHO ASKS THE QUESTION?

W ho poses the questions that a democracy answers? A polity is represented as much in the issues it presents to itself as in the decisions it makes. The laundry heap in Zuccotti Park presented itself, hulking and beginning to stink, but most political agendas begin with a definition of the problem. Is the question of the hour immigration or workers' rights, a wealth tax or the way public schools teach history, climate change or the price of gasoline, overdose deaths or police killings? And which ways of engaging the question are on the table? What are we deciding *on?* In a perfect world, there might not have to be a choice, but in a world of limited time and attention, a few questions will dominate voters' and policymakers' time and attention. Posing the questions that get taken up is as much an exercise of power as answering them, and it is often harder to see who does it or how it happens.

"A concrete choice had to be presented," wrote Walter Lippmann in his 1922 polemic *Public Opinion,* and so professional politicians "organized the caucus, the nominating convention, and the steering committee, as the means of formulating a definite choice." Lippmann was writing under the influence of Robert

Michels, a German Italian student of politics who formulated what he influentially called "the iron law of oligarchy." Studying the new mass democratic parties of Europe, Michels observed that a small number of people always set the agenda. This was not a corruption of democracy, he argued, but a functional requirement: there was no other way of getting coherent decisions and organized action from a mass organization. "The number of those who govern," Lippmann wrote, summing up the idea, "is a very small percentage of those who are theoretically supposed to govern." Lippmann wrote with serene condescension for the everyday idealism of democrats, but he was not wrong in claiming that we have no clear idea of what it would mean to set the agenda of a democracy democratically, let alone a means of doing it.[1]

Lippmann doubted that democratic decisions could ever be rational enough even to deserve terms such as "posing questions and deciding them." He argued that democratic decisions could take two forms: concealed oligarchic control, on the one hand, or, on the other, emotional, ill-informed, and largely incoherent judgments of yes or no, him or her. In other words, if they were really decisions, they could not be democratic, and if they were democratic, they could not really be decisions. People came to their yes or no by too many different paths for the converging votes to count as a common judgment on a shared question. Because few people have the time or attention to become expert in more than a few domains, we orient ourselves to political disputes in other ways. We rely on what Lippmann called symbols, often phrases, that hold together a large and unspecified set of moral affinities and aversions: "Make America great again," "Black lives matter." As Lippmann put it, "Americanism, Law and Order, Justice, Humanity . . . do not stand for specific ideas, but for a sort of truce or junction between ideas. They are like a strategic railroad center where many roads converge regardless of their ultimate origin or ultimate destination. But he who captures the symbols by which public feeling is for the moment contained, controls by that much the approaches of public policy." Symbols often trade across ideological borders, mobilizing enthusiasm on one side and fear or disdain on the other. The vote may end up as a tally of these responses, telling us little more than that there was more attraction overall, or more aversion, to a set of symbols.[2]

We complement attachment to symbols with deference to those we trust. And in this, too, we are basically helpless, as the people we trust "constitute our means of junction with pretty nearly the whole realm of unknown things," in Lippmann's phrasing—meaning by "unknown" whatever we do not know by first-hand experience. We take the great bulk of the world on faith, from its basic science to the details of policy to what is happening in China or the Arctic. We could not do otherwise. It is all too familiar that, on questions ranging from climate change to whether vaccines work to the effects of policing on public safety, what we believe depends on an amalgam of whom we believe and what symbolic associations the facts have for us: patriotism or justice, optimism or despair, safety or racism. In the 2020s, the phrase "Science is real" has itself become a partisan touchstone.

Democratic self-rule, Lippmann argued, was basically an illusion. The thing to understand was instead "the manufacture of consent" through the management of information and symbols. Who did the manufacturing? Politicians, yes, and also the media, teachers, preachers, and neighbors. For Lippmann, though, the industrial metaphor was telling: managers—whether in parties, on editorial boards, or at universities—made the key judgments, and others followed. Lippmann's proposal to rationalize politics was managerial, too: he called for a new part of government, "an independent, expert organization for making the unseen facts intelligible to those who have to make the decisions." Beyond that, he urged public "re-education" in critical thinking, a sort of pedagogical therapy to encourage people to release their emotional attachment to symbols and moral prejudices and instead come to honor facts, above all, as the only remedy for our otherwise hopeless subjectivism.

There is one ironic comfort in reading Lippmann's attack on the public's (ir)rationality a century later: seeing that the joint crises of representation and reason are not new but perennial.

Recently, Shoshana Zuboff has argued in *The Age of Surveillance Capitalism* that the intensive and refined psychological manipulation built into the architecture of online platforms threatens to undermine the autonomy and deliberative capacity that democracy requires. Writing in the *New York Times* in 2020, she warned of "a new . . . power that works its will through the medium of ubiquitous digital instrumentation to manipulate subliminal cues, psychologically target communications . . . trigger social comparison dynamics and levy rewards and punishments"—and, ultimately, catch people at their most vulnerable to "trigger the inner demons of unsuspecting citizens."[3] A century earlier, in 1922, Lippmann wrote that "as a result of psychological research, coupled with the modern means of communication . . . a revolution is taking place . . . the knowledge of how to create consent will alter every political calculation and modify every political premise. Under the impact of propaganda . . . the old constants of our thinking have become variables"—that is, subject to control.

From that century-old stepping-stone, we can follow the recurring crisis backward. Sixty years before Lippmann, we find John Stuart Mill writing in *On Liberty* that the free mind is under constant threat in mass society:

> Like other tyrannies, the tyranny of the majority was at first, and is still vulgarly, held in dread, chiefly as operating through the acts of the public authorities. But reflecting persons perceived that when society is itself the tyrant—society collectively, over the separate individuals who compose it—its means of tyrannizing are not restricted to the acts which it may do by the hands of its political functionaries. Society can and does execute its own mandates: and if it issues wrong mandates instead of right, or any mandates at all in things with which it ought not to meddle, it practices a social tyranny more formidable than many kinds of political oppression, since, though not usually upheld by such extreme penalties, it leaves fewer means of escape, penetrating much more deeply into the details of life, and enslaving the soul itself.[4]

Mill, in turn, was looking back twenty-five years to an earlier moment in the life of mass democracy when Alexis de Tocqueville had begun to describe "the tyranny of the majority" as the force of opinion rather than the simple exercise of political power:

> Princes made violence a physical thing, but our contemporary democratic republics have turned it into something as intellectual as the human will it is intended to constrain. Under the absolute government of a single man, despotism, to reach the soul, clumsily struck at the body . . . but in democratic republics that is not at all how tyranny behaves; it leaves the body alone and goes straight for the soul. The master no longer says: "Think like me or you die." He does say: "You are free not to think as I do; you can keep your life and property and all; but from this day you are a stranger among us. You can keep your privileges in the township, but they will be useless to you, for if you solicit your fellow citizens' votes, they will not give them to you, and if you only ask for their esteem, they will make excuses for refusing that. You will remain among men, but you will lose your rights to count as one. When you approach your fellows, they will shun you as an impure being, and even those who believe in your innocence will abandon you too, lest they in turn be shunned. Go in peace. I have given you your life, but it is a life worse than death."

Tocqueville was writing about the same problem that Lippmann put at the center of his picture of political irrationality. The conceit of the modern age was self-reliant individualism: people were to reach their conclusions by their own judgment. But most of us know very little at first hand. What we think we know we mostly take on trust. And if we dissolve the kinds of hierarchical authority that stabilized political and moral judgment under the ancien régime (at least as Tocqueville pictured it), then we will inevitably submit to a more horizontal authority, a running average of the opinions of our social world, which will seem obviously true to someone who inhabits that world. Individualism and equality, ironically, brought on subjection to a new kind of authority: opinion, the soft rule of all over each.[5]

About eighty years before Tocqueville, Jean-Jacques Rousseau gave much the same picture of how social life makes us the colonizers of one another's minds: "The man accustomed to the ways of society is always outside himself and knows how to live only by the opinion of others. And it is, as it were, from their judgment alone that he draws the sentiment of his own existence." In such a condition, he continued, "with everything reduced to appearances, everything becomes factitious and bogus: honor, friendship, virtue, and even our vices, about which we eventually find the secret of boasting . . . we, who are always asking others what we are . . . have merely a deceitful and frivolous exterior." It was not yet democratic society that Rousseau addressed but the sort of courtly and salon culture in which he was establishing himself as a (middle-aged) enfant terrible. The problem, in short, was the vain, oscillating, obtuse thing called humanity, trying to make sense of itself in the presence of others. No surveillance capitalism was necessary: social life was itself the architecture of our mutual manipulation, which came down to a kind of incorrigible self-manipulation.[6]

The promise of politics is to create a form of collective rationality, a way of posing and answering questions of how we shall live together. The democratic gamble is that this politics can be built out of, and make a way of reconciling, the wills, perspectives, and judgments of everyone who must live with the results of politics—that equals can cooperate to make their world. But again and again, it has seemed that human judgment is very poorly suited to assembling this kind of collective rationality. It is hard for us to see a common reality or to compose ourselves as a common actor that can grapple with that reality. When we achieve enough unity of feeling to act together, it is often at the cost of a clear grasp on the facts. When we achieve a public sense of the facts stable enough to act together, it is often because we have accepted the kind of expert and elite agenda-setting tutelage that Lippmann recommended. Who are we to govern ourselves, who can barely see one another or the problems before us?

A persistent answer has occurred to those who take these difficulties seriously and are also committed to democracy. This is the turn to civil society, a catchall term that sweeps in many institutions, practices, and habits that fall somewhere between the isolated mind whose gyrations so exercised Lippmann and the vote that contributes to a public decision. Generations of Americans have embraced Tocqueville, in part because he optimistically described local government and "voluntary associations"—clubs, mutual aid societies, and advocacy groups—as the schoolhouses of democracy. These struck him as places where citizens learned to sympathize with and address themselves to the views of others and to see the public interest in ways that went beyond their own hopes and attachments. There citizens practiced living with disagreement, accepting inconvenience, and compromising so that the political community could go on being. Civic involvement modified selfishness into what Tocqueville called "self-interest properly understood," an appreciation that individual flourishing and the community's well-being cannot be kept separate for long.[7]

It was in the same spirit that John Dewey defended democracy against Lippmann's skeptical knives. Dewey and Lippmann were nemeses of a sort in American intellectual life from the Progressive Era into the Cold War. A passionate democrat who accepted the force of Lippmann's criticisms, Dewey adapted Tocqueville's picture to the twentieth century. It was true, he admitted, that there is no "public" in any straightforward sense. There is no collective mind—Lippmann sardonically called it an "oversoul"—that unifies millions of perspectives into one political consciousness that can act. Elections are thoroughly imperfect ways of generating shared decisions: both artificially narrow in the scope of questions the ballot can address and incorrigibly vague in what they reveal because so many motives and perspectives shape our votes.[8]

Nonetheless, if there is not one public, there are many publics. They coalesce in different places and with different purposes. A labor union, a civil rights movement, a mobilization to win a

war abroad or to end it: each of these draws people out of themselves and creates a common purpose that was not there before
it. A union organizing drive creates a public. So does the push
for a piece of legislation—each of the major national acts for racial equality that Congress passed during the 1960s, for example.
These publics get their goals onto the legislative agenda or put
them foremost in voters' minds. They put phrases in the mouths
of political representatives: when Lyndon Baines Johnson intoned
"We shall overcome" during his nationally televised address in
support of the 1965 Voting Rights Act, a speech whose tropes were
those of the civil rights movement, he implicitly granted Dewey's
point. Publics made themselves and, through joint action, remade
political representation. It was all messier, more organic, and less
focused on voting than Lippmann's criticisms supposed. Democracy was less an action (voting) or a decision principle (majority
rule) than a form of life, a fabric woven from many threads.[9]

But civil society is not an organic, spontaneous domain where
people come together to remake themselves and deepen their
understanding of shared principle. Civil society is deeply shaped
by the American political economy. Consider "social movements,"
sometimes a reflexive term of praise among progressives. The
paradigm here is the civil rights movement. But that movement,
deeply rooted in networks of Black churches and the segregated
Black professional classes and actuated by decades of white supremacist repression that coexisted unstably with the civic rhetoric of democracy, has proved both too hard to replicate and all
too easy to imitate. For a case of imitation, take the Tea Party, the
right-wing antitax movement that first emerged in opposition to
the Affordable Care Act, which was on its way through Congress
in 2009. The careful work of liberal political sociologist Theda
Skocpol highlighted that the Tea Party had genuine community
origins, with broad-based support among both conservative activists and tens of thousands of previously quiescent citizens whom
they mobilized. At the same time, its influence depended on intensive investment from wealthy right-wing donors, most famously
Charles and David Koch, who rolled a good deal of Tea Party

energy into the well-staffed Americans for Prosperity, giving the somewhat inchoate movement a set of coherent aims that tracked the Kochs' longstanding antiregulatory and probusiness goals. Partisan media, especially Fox News, did their part to lionize the movement and give it definite shape as a demand by "real Americans" for a political turn to the right.[10]

The comparison of the Tea Party to the civil rights movement may seem inapt, even offensive, but the point is to highlight the differences that the label "movement" can conceal. There are always grievances looking for an audience and—in the telling new term—"political entrepreneurs" looking for a market. Donors cannot create a movement out of whole cloth, but for an incipient effort to turn into a sustained political presence, financial support and media amplification are often critical. With that support, it is not so hard, whatever your grievance, to get one hundred thousand people to march in Washington and claim a million.

As for those who turn out to build these organizations, they are predominantly—according, for instance, to Leah Gose and Skocpol's study of anti-Trump activists—educated, older, white, and prosperous, despite the charismatic images of insurgent youth that emerge from certain marches and electoral campaigns. To paraphrase what political scientist E. E. Schattschneider once wrote about the class composition of advocacy organizations, social movements chant "This is what democracy looks like" in a decidedly upper-class accent, even if that is now the NPR vocal fry rather than the old Ivy League intonations that Schattschneider might have had in mind. Civil society is imagined as ordinary people's way of influencing power, but it emerges from and bears the shape of existing orders of power. That is no surprise. Civic engagement takes time and benefits from money, training, and social standing. People with other advantages are the most likely to start with these as well. In contrast to all this, and despite the ways that privilege makes ballot access easier, voting remains the most egalitarian of our political acts. It should matter more.[11]

Between civil society and elections, students of politics have often looked to political parties as the keys to translating messy and diverse social realities into a clear-enough set of questions on which voters can make a choice. Party platforms, party discipline, and the broader culture of parties—a sense of what partisans think is wrong and how they propose to change it—all give cogency to voters' decisions, making the binary choice that a ballot presents somewhat more articulate. Parties, of course, are oligarchic in all the ways that social movements are, often more so, but whatever their internal hierarchies and processes, they survive only by appealing successfully to the people. No one has to take them at their word.

"Party government," wrote Schattschneider, "is good democratic doctrine because the parties are the special form of political organization adapted to the mobilization of majorities." Parties, according to this hopeful view, do what dispersed voters cannot: provide competing, more or less coherent accounts of the country's interests and values, its challenges and dangers, and a strategy for navigating these. Because "the people are a sovereign whose vocabulary is limited to two words, 'Yes' and 'No,'" party programs offer articulacy and intention that voting alone cannot. But voters, once they are confronted with competing party agendas, can confer legitimacy that the most charismatic movement can never acquire. Majorities, uniquely, can rule, but because they do not make their own platforms, they must find their options somewhere. Parties offer the menu of choices.[12]

Parties are accountable to the public, doubly so. Because their power to keep offering proposals is always at stake in their electoral competitiveness or collapse, they are constantly fighting both to assemble a majority and to stave off, or absorb, alternative and insurgent programs. A party is a long-lasting social movement, or assemblage of movements, but with democratic accountability.

The basic logic of this position is extremely powerful. It makes clear why parties seem to be an inevitable feature of large-scale electoral politics. Whether it also establishes that parties enable the people to rule is less clear. Viewed cynically, parties are organizations devoted to accumulating votes, as corporations are devoted to profit. In articulating its vision of the country, a party does not start with truth as the organizers see it but with an interpretation of the country's divisions that will put a majority on its side. Party platforms, then, are devices for dividing people in ways that are advantageous to the party—and it gets worse because not all divisions are created equal. If the divisions can be anchored in perennial features of voters' identities, then party insiders have more leeway to cultivate other agendas, for which they won't be held accountable because their voters are not going anywhere. When Donald Trump's ostensibly populist Republican Party passed a massive tax cut, mostly for the wealthy, it was relying on the loyalty of a base that had made support for the Republicans (or at least mortal opposition to the Democrats) part of its identity. The Democrats, of course, enjoy a similar flavor of loyalty and have used it in ways that may have tested their supporters, such as imposing work requirements and time limits for family support (welfare reform) in 1995. Parties create their voters by drawing people into ideas of how the country is divided. It is not surprising that the ways of doing this that benefit the parties often do not focus voters on a constructive idea of the common good.

But sometimes they do. Many of the institutions Americans most rely on were hammered out as part of a program of governing, by people whose profession was politics and whose institution was the party. It took the Democratic Party, under President Lyndon Johnson's influence, to create Medicare in 1965 (57–7 support from Democrats in the Senate, with Republicans opposed 17–13). And party politics isn't always partisan in today's sense of all-pervasive and incorrigible division. Bipartisan votes on important legislation, such as Social Security in 1935 or the Fair Housing Act in 1968, were signs of the strength of the party system, not its irrelevance. This is not to lionize the early to mid-twentieth century as a golden age of American democracy now gone, or to deny the many ways that the twentieth-century party system was oligarchic and exclusionary, but the fact that our parties are often machines for producing strategic social division should not obscure the truth that parties can play a constructive, even necessary agenda-setting role in democratic politics.

Party politics is always moving between Henry Adams's "organization of hatreds" and efforts to build better ways of living together. The two are not matter and antimatter but cords in a rope. It is too easy to blame partisanship, hence parties, for political dysfunction, which actually has broader roots. Until recently, our parties, with all their problems, have been the platforms for proposals to combat climate change, improve health care, make the immigration system more humane and equitable, revise the tax code, and otherwise rework our collective life—albeit in line with divergent, not always admirable ideas of what the country's challenges are and how we should meet them. At least one of our parties is still making such proposals, at least some of the time. Even with the distortions of the money-soaked politics the Supreme Court has helped to foist on the country, Americans regularly express majority support for and manage to elect Congresses with majority support for many of these reforms. But constitutional skews in Congress and the Electoral College make these majorities rarer than they would be in a more representative system, and the antilawmaking features of Congress's design—some constitutional, some, like the Senate filibuster, later accretions—mean that even these elected majorities can make reforms only with Herculean labor and rare supermajorities. All this systemic thwarting of constructive politics naturally encourages a switch to more demagogic forms of partisanship, centered on claims that "they" are trying to destroy people like "you." If one of our parties no longer tries to make the system work, we should remember that it is, itself, thoroughly a product of that system and specifically of the system's antidemocratic features.

Parties do essential work, at least when they are not turned into cults of personality or vehicles for conspiracy theories. The clearest lesson of the American politics of 2016–2021 is the reminder that parties are core features of democracy and control of their agendas is one of the most important political battlefields. Was Donald Trump merely a fluke whom the adults in the system could wait out? Not once his stamp was on the Republican Party and loyalty to him and his worldview became an aspect of political identity. More constructively, the reason Bernie Sanders's runs for the presidency in 2016 and 2020 left such a mark is that they were bids to control a party. The sweeping agenda of social support and investment that the lifelong procorporate moderate Joe Biden felt at ease embracing in the presidency was the legacy of Sanders's movement within the party, which changed the Democrats even as his presidential campaign failed.

Reformers have long looked for ways to appeal directly to voters, cutting out the parties. At one time, as Lippmann noted in looking back on Progressive reforms of the late nineteenth and early twentieth centuries, this meant agenda setting through mass democracy, especially through citizens' initiatives and referendums. Lippmann remarked cuttingly that these systems only delayed or concealed the oligarchic activity of party bosses (or wealthy policy patrons, who secured voter signatures and funded advertising for pet initiatives). Today, initiative systems such as California's are widely perceived to bear out Lippmann's criticism, being erratic and readily manipulated, and reformers propose instead that the appeal to the people should take a more orderly form. A favorite model is a randomly selected set of citizens, sometimes called a "citizen assembly," deliberating under closely controlled conditions, who can propose legislation or constitutional provisions, which may then go to referendum or be taken up by the legislature. Although pilot efforts in Iceland, France, British Columbia, and other jurisdictions have not ended very dramatically (interesting proposals have been mostly rejected or quietly shelved), there is clear appeal in getting pressing questions onto an often slow or blocked political agenda. Such reforms, however, are likely to be at best supplemental to others that press parties to do their work better—more responsively, more rationally, with less tendency to devolve into either sclerosis or personality cults.[13]

We can, for example, reform the way that parties translate social sentiment into political power. It is well appreciated now that part of what drives ideological polarization is that candidates are selected in low-turnout primaries, where activists and voters with strong views have extra weight, and then compete in districts that are designed to be safe for one party or the other. The result is that an ideological core of voters picks the candidate who will win the race. We might get very different representation in Congress if a single primary were open to candidates and voters of all parties and the top two vote-getters competed in the general election. In liberal-leaning districts, those candidates might then represent different versions of the Democratic Party. In red districts, they might embody different versions of the Republican Party. A conspiracy theorist who today wins the Republican primary and goes to Congress on the party loyalty of general election voters might have to face a more reality-based Republican who could assemble a coalition of Democrats and nondelusional Republicans. The parties would still stand for competing programs and understandings of national life, but the way of composing them electorally would be a bit less of a radicalization machine. Because parties do so much to shape the outlooks of their supporters, the result might be a virtuous circle of modest deescalation—not away from disagreement but away from the bipartisan strategy of sowing apocalyptic enmity.

The best reform might be to require parties to compete for voters in an uncompromised democracy. The more potential voters are disenfranchised, and the more easily the constitutional system allows a minority party to control the government, the greater the likelihood of a party strategy like that of the Republican Party at the start of the 2020s: holding on to a stable block of support, basically on identity grounds, without even bidding for real majorities. The more easily majority support translates into control of government, and the more widely enfranchised the population, the harder it is to succeed with a defensive, minoritarian strategy. Parties that must win democratically to hold power will do more of the useful work of social interpretation and agenda setting that Schattschneider identified as their necessary work in a democracy. Those that have a chance at implementing policies that majority coalitions support will be held accountable on the merits of the properly political work of governing.

A polity that is more authentically democratic will have a better chance of generating parties that set a serious agenda for its politics. No doubt those parties will interact with social movements, the many strands of public opinion, and perhaps new institutions such as citizen assemblies, but there is still a lot of reason to believe that the parties will do the work of translating these into choices to which voters can reply with yes or no.

10

WHO ARE THE PEOPLE?

"The only important thing is the unification of the people," Donald Trump said about his 2016 presidential campaign, "because the other people don't mean anything." In this vision, politics is a battle to the finish, and the sides are morally unequal. One side—his side, "the people"—belongs here. The other side, "the other people," doesn't belong.[1]

Liberal sentiment during the Trump administration was one long repudiation of this idea. Assertions of human equality crystallized in a series of slogans, ubiquitous on lawn signs, T-shirts, and social media posts: "Black lives matter" was a counterpoint to Trump's "the other people don't mean anything" and an insistence on fundamental equality. "No human being is illegal" was a denial of moral difference between authorized and unauthorized presence in the United States. In the South, where I wrote most of this book, "y'all means all" was a drawling statement of solidarity with trans people.

But the moral sentiment runs up against hard political reality. If you are shut out of power, then others can act like you don't matter. No human being is illegal, but some 10 million lack legal authorization to be in the country, meaning that in the 2020 general election some 1.6 million Texans could not vote, along with 325,000 North Carolinians, 275,000 Virginians, and 210,000 Nevadans. There are also some 12 million authorized noncitizen immigrants who cannot vote.[2] Black lives matter, but state laws disenfranchising people with felony convictions deny the ballot to one out of every sixteen Black citizens of voting age. That figure was recently more than one in seven Black voters in seven states, including Florida and Virginia. (As I write, both of these states are in the midst of contentious efforts to restore the vote to those who have completed their sentences.)

Even among those who could vote, who was it that Trump had to unite for his 2016 victory? As we have seen, it was not a majority of voters but of Electoral College votes. Trump became president in 2016 because, in terms of democratic power, national majorities did not matter and neither did disenfranchised citizens, noncitizen residents, or unauthorized migrants. The politics of the 2010s and 2020s is about who the people are and what it means for them to matter.

A century ago, the far-right French Catholic thinker Charles Maurras distinguished polemically between "the legal people," the abstract sovereign embodied in the political structures of parliament and the presidency, and "the real people," the true French, whose racial, religious, and civilizational identity abided beneath the superficial liberalism of the government. There is some of that invidious spirit in Trump's "the other people don't mean anything." But to understand today's fights over who the people are and how they rule, we need clearer distinctions. Five meanings of the people jostle for primacy in American politics. First is the *sovereign people*, the people who make and remake the country's fundamental law, the Constitution. Second is the *ruling people*, the voters who decide elections. (This means those who get to vote, as opposed to the disenfranchised, but it also means those whose majorities count by conferring control of, among others, the Electoral College and the Senate.) Third is the *legal people*, those who are recognized as having the right to be within the borders of the United States. Last is the *actual people*, everyone who is here, those who are working, raising families, being neighbors—making their lives, regardless of the kind of permission they have to do so. A full democracy would align the first four of these senses of the people: whoever is here would be part of the legal community, jostling to form majorities and joining in the sovereign power to reaffirm or change fundamental law. In reality, they are anything but aligned. And the lines that separate them are haunted by a fifth version of the people: the *historical people*, "real" Americans defined by some blend of race and nationality and never far from mind in talk about "the people" and "the other people."[3]

The sovereign people are the subject of the most portentous sentence in American history, "We the People," which opens the US Constitution. The propertied white men who ratified that document as fundamental law get further away every year, in time, demography, and the everyday sense of what makes a polity legitimate or even decent. At the time of ratification, the constitution-making sovereign people and the ruling people who voted were all but identical: indeed, voting requirements for constitutional conventions were sometimes lower than for ordinary elections. In stark contrast, the men-only politics of a patriarchal republic gave women no part in democratic sovereignty, and even among men, the actual people of the time comprised Black and enslaved majorities in some states. The amendment process set out in Article V of the Constitution all but prevents living generations, let alone living majorities, from revisiting fundamental law, even to reaffirm it. If there is a sovereign people today, it is made up of a majority of Supreme Court justices, who alone can give new meaning to fundamental law, whether to deny Congress the power to expand health care or to require states to enforce marriage equality.

The sovereign people of 1789 left a curious political bequest to today's ruling people. The Senate's representation by state rather than population, which the Electoral College translates into extra power for small states in presidential elections, gives disproportionate political weight to older, white, rural voters. A constitution ratified in a white supremacist society still, though not precisely by design, puts a thumb on the political scale for the kinds of voters who, nearly two hundred and fifty years ago, would have been the only ones permitted to weigh in on it. So it is not surprising that white nationalist Three Percenters and other self-styled militias identify themselves with the founding revolutionaries. Nor is it surprising that the 1956 Southern Manifesto, in which nineteen senators and seventy-seven members of the House of Representatives denounced *Brown v. Board of Education*, opened with an affirmation that "the Founding Fathers gave us a Constitution of checks and balances" to prevent such "unwarranted exercise of power" and "chaos and confusion" as *Brown* supposedly presented. The manifesto asserted that *Brown* lacked "the consent of the governed," and it "reaffirm[ed] our reliance on the Constitution as the fundamental law of the land." By fencing the living out of sovereign power and skewing whose votes count in forming today's ruling majorities, the Constitution encourages the idea that real legitimacy belongs to the historical people. That is, of course, the idea behind "the other people don't matter."[4]

Contests over the contours of the ruling people highlight how much it matters to exercise—or be denied—the vote. The Civil War's end brought substantial enfranchisement of formerly enslaved people across the South, under Reconstruction governments and, after 1870, through the Fifteenth Amendment (although its promise was soon broken with Reconstruction's end). Making up a substantial share of the population of every southern state and, for a time, majorities in Mississippi and South Carolina, Black people potentially held the balance of power in their votes. For some time after the breaking of Reconstruction in 1877, the plutocratic Democrats who took over southern state politics were able to expropriate enough Black votes through force, fraud, and corruption to rule on behalf of railroads, banks, and large property owners. By the early 1890s, however, this arrangement began to shake. In response to postwar decades packed with pro-corporate giveaways and graft, including outright grants of tens of millions of acres of public lands to railroad companies, there arose movements of indebted and exploited small farmers and wage laborers who tried to wrest control of government to serve their own interests. Calling for debt relief, public ownership of railroads and utilities, progressive public education, and other measures to lift up common people and humble their wealthy rulers, the Populists seemed to their enemies "a mighty torrent pouring down the mountain side" or "a prairie fire."[5]

A new majority is a special kind of prairie fire. Uprisings of the downtrodden are as old as inequality itself. John Locke wrote in the 1690s that when laborers faced "some common or great distress, uniting them in one universal ferment . . . sometimes they break in on the rich and sweep all like a deluge." In Locke's telling, these episodes receded like floods, leaving disarray but making no essential change. This was true of peasant revolts across time. But those peasants rose up before mass enfranchisement. In the 1890s, the insurgents had votes. The state could be theirs. Where they took power, as they did in much of the Midwest and Great Plains, the Populists instituted state control of railroads and utilities, raised taxes on the rich, and provided for common education—the kinds of political revolution that were never available to Locke's disenfranchised rioters, who lacked a way of turning revolt into rule.[6]

Suddenly, it mattered very much that, in the South, Black voters held the balance of power. Many rank-and-file Populists were shaped by anti-Black racism, rooted in the Democrats' post–Civil War ideology of white unity and, before that, upland small landholders' resentment of plantation wealth, perversely crystallized in hatred of the enslaved Black people whose labor created that wealth. But the political theory of the bolder Populist leaders was that common interests would unify Black and white laborers and farmers against the common enemy of plutocracy. For a few years in the mid-1890s, Black and white organizers together worked barbecues and revivals across the South. According to historian C. Vann Woodward, when a Black organizer's life was threatened in North Carolina, two thousand white farmers came to stand guard over his home, some of them riding overnight to get there.

Woodward quotes a white Texan Populist voicing the formula of economic interest over racial division in simple language: "They are in the ditch just like we are."[7]

The Democratic bosses, who had been running the former Confederacy as a one-party state with scant electoral accountability, found two ways to break the threat. First, they launched a massive propaganda campaign, linking Populists and their allies to racial insurrection and the familiar Black menaces that white supremacists traded in: rape, theft, murder. Drawing on deep wells of white solidarity and fear, the bosses made gains in the later 1890s, pushing back the radicals. Then, having poisoned the spirit of democracy just as it was waking up, they killed the body with a staggering campaign of disenfranchisement. Following the model of Mississippi's 1890 constitutional amendments, which established poll taxes and easily manipulated literacy tests, states across the South rewrote their constitutions to choke off democracy for decades.

Black political exclusion was almost total: in North Carolina, the number of Black registered voters fell from some three hundred thousand to about three thousand statewide after adoption of the 1900 constitution. Many disenfranchisement measures also swept out the "lower orders" of whites, returning large parts of the South to a pre-Jacksonian condition of racist disenfranchisement and selective disenfranchisement by class, defining the ruling people as both white and propertied. As Woodward recounts, "in Virginia the average votes cast for Congressmen declined about 56 percent between 1892 and 1902, in Alabama the decline was 60 percent; in Mississippi, 69 percent; in Louisiana, 80 percent." It was 75 percent in Arkansas, 69 percent in Florida, and 80 percent in Georgia. Seeing the writing on the wall, many former Populist voters, even whites who had been peeled off by racism, opposed the amendments. But almost none were taken directly to the voters. In this they resembled the Confederate states' decisions to secede forty years earlier. The elite coup remained a vital form of American antidemocracy. As historian Barbara Fields points out, the creation of the white supremacist South, both as a culture and as a political scheme, was always two things at once: a campaign of anti-Blackness and a battle over which group of whites would rule and which would be ruled. Du Bois's abolition-democracy, uncompromised by racial exclusion or class domination and exercising genuine majoritarian control over economic order, was broken even in prospect.[8]

The resonance of that history has provoked comparisons between Jim Crow and today's fights over the boundaries of the ruling people. The scope is different, but the stakes can come to the same thing: whether, contrary to democratic principle, a faction will succeed in crafting an enduring ruling people that substantially excludes a large and distinct portion of the population. The five million people who were ineligible to vote in 2020 because of a current or former felony conviction were more than the total number who voted in the presidential election in forty-one states. If the disenfranchised were the voters of one state, it would be the tenth largest in the country. The rate of felony disenfranchisement for Black Americans is nearly four times that for non-Black citizens. Disenfranchised people are part of the polity, but they can have no part in forming its majorities, no chance to rule.

Fights over state laws that manipulate ballot access have become endemic in American politics. Laws like the one adopted in Texas in 2021 restrict election policies, such as allowing drive-through voting or mailing out absentee ballots automatically, that are thought to give Democrats a slight advantage—and Democrats are overwhelmingly the party of the voters of color who were systematically excluded from Texas politics for generations through a series of creative and invidious devices, including such bizarre measures as a private, whites-only Democratic primary developed to avoid desegregation laws. In closely fought North Carolina, 2 percent of Black voters were registered as Republicans in 2020, and the Republican Party has engineered large majorities in the state legislature through expert gerrymandering and voting laws that a federal court in 2016 described as "laser-targeted" at the Black vote. Disenfranchisement today seeks to make the difficulty of voting a little greater over here, the value of the vote a little lower over there, to support by a thousand props and shims the unsteady body of a minority ruling people.[9]

All these fights over who votes and how the votes are counted, which define the ruling people, mark out marginally different subsets of the actual people, the (as it were) natural body of the democratic polity. As noted earlier, estimates put the number of unauthorized immigrants in the United States between ten and twelve million, and another twelve million legal permanent residents lack citizenship. The permanent residents are "legal" people but cannot rule. The unauthorized do not rule and lack some of the most basic protections of law. They are easily exploited, to the convenience of employers large and small, from the farms of California's Central Valley and the chicken plants of the Southeast to food delivery in Manhattan and housekeeping in San Francisco. Immigration courts, which determine their rights if they are in trouble and fortunate enough to avoid summary deportation, are notoriously inconsistent (to the point of arbitrariness, according to many who go before them) and virtually immune to oversight by regular courts. These participants in American life, who are kept firmly outside the working of American democracy, make up a total population larger than that of any state besides Texas and California.

The democratic response to this situation is to bring the actual people into line with the ruling and sovereign peoples. Whoever is within a national territory, living with the laws of the country, should have the choice of taking political citizenship and a role in shaping or approving those laws. Anything else is caste, and caste is an antithesis of democracy, as much as authoritarianism is. It is an antithesis because it effectively guarantees permanent minority status: those who are excluded from the ruling people are always outside the disposition of power, even if some governments are more sympathetic to them than others. They may, of course, argue, plead, and pronounce in the political conversation that swirls around a democracy, but at the moment of decision, when power takes a definite shape, they have no part. The situation of the disenfranchised toward the ruling people resembles that of the ruling people toward political sovereignty: the latter can vote but cannot reset the Senate or the Electoral College or reclaim from the Supreme Court the effective power to change or reaffirm the country's fundamental law. These powers belong together, in an actual people that is also ruling and sovereign.[10]

But there is more. Forming a majority is only a beginning. For voting to produce legitimacy, it must succeed as a modern version of what the last chapter called synecdochal representation. It must be possible for the losing side to identify enough with the winners to accept that in some sense "we" have made a decision, and it will be our government that rules (all) of us until the next vote. Some of the stability of a democratic system comes from the fact that if it is working well it produces no permanent losers, so a part of quiescence is just rationally biding one's time and working to be part of the next majority. But in the meantime, we losers are being ruled. And there is no persuasive idea of metaphoric representation that can explain the authority of the majority: we who voted the other way are not going to believe that they somehow deliberated differently from us and found a higher wisdom, or that their decision more authentically expresses the community's intrinsic nature. We losers have to be able to accept that the winners' decision counts for the whole.

This might sound like an alarming, or just sentimental, call to sacrifice conscience, but it isn't that at all. It's simply an observation that elections do not produce binding decisions if the losers take shelter in the idea that they have not *really* lost and so the country has not really acted. False stories of election fraud are the most vivid expression of this dysfunction in the United States today, but they are only the cutting edge of something larger: an aversion to democratic results with two very different but complementary roots. One root is the aversive partisanship that sees in the other side a threat to one's own idea of the country. This kind of partisanship posits a gulf so wide and deep that *they* on the other side cannot act on behalf of us. This kind of aversion is driving the Republican mistrust of American elections. The other root is less tribal, to use the popular term for aversive partisanship (we might also say clannish), than hyperindividualistic. Its slogan is "Not my president!" and it treats voting as an expression of personal identity, as subjective as a consumer choice. The car I didn't buy is not my car, and the person I didn't vote for is not my president.

The clannish and the individualist forms of political disaffection are superficially opposite—one is about *us*, the other about *me*—but in fact they have much in common. Modern partisanship is already an oddly individualistic form of collective identity. The political theorist Nadia Urbinati points out that antisystem politicians such as Donald Trump and Mario Salvini of Italy's nationalist Northern League "disfigure" representation by offering supporters the fantasy of direct, personal representation in an imaginary bond with the leader's personality, style, words, and decisions. As long as he is in power, I am in power, and I can identify with the country, which he represents. If he loses power, I have lost power, and the country is no longer mine. This version of "my country" fits perfectly with "(not) my president": if someone else's president takes power, it cannot be my country anymore.[11]

Political representation depends on more than institutional design. No one can represent us if we are steadfastly unwilling to be represented. The willingness is a part of civic virtue: wanting the polity to survive as a political project and being disposed to put that survival ahead of your personal interests or even your partisan convictions. It implies the willingness to accept defeat and the commitment to seek and use power in ways that try to give everyone reasons to uphold future majorities.

A political system must reproduce its own legitimacy, reconcile people to living with the answers it gives, even when they lose and have to give up interests and hopes that they passionately hold. Democracy depends on solidarity and, to survive, must generate solidarity, over and over, in the face of new challenges. It requires what Bernie Sanders and Alexandria Ocasio-Cortez urged at a twenty-six-thousand-strong rally in Queens in October 2019: the willingness to "fight for someone you don't know," to defend the lives and interests of those very different from you, whoever you are.[12]

But this is also too easy. The democratic problem is more specific and harder: to fight not just for someone you don't know—whom you get to imagine in an ideal or at least sympathetic light—but for someone you do know and can't stand, or someone you don't know but suspect would detest you if they knew about you. A democrat must take seriously, recognize as moral facts to be grappled with, the identities of everyone in the polity. These are not fixed points: politics can make us into different people, but the existing identities of people you mistrust, fear, even suspect you might hate, have to be among the materials of democratic life.

Who are the people? It should be everyone who is here, and that means sharing rule with people we may also see as being in some sense enemies. Our "enemies," too, are part of the potential majorities that we, as members of a democratic public, consent to be ruled by and whom we address when we speak politically in public, for common things. If there is no majority for majority rule itself, if members of a polity cannot stomach the idea of being ruled by one another, then democracy is not possible there. "There," of course, is here.

11

DEMOCRATIZING DEMOCRACY
(AND EVERYTHING ELSE)

D emocracy can seem illusory, futile, and dangerous, by turns or even all at once. Many critics have assured us that it is an impossible ideal and also hazardous to pursue, a myth we should outgrow. And it is true that, of all political systems, democracy gives the trickiest answer to the essential question: Who rules here? In a monarchy, the answer is a queen or king, a person you might touch (though at your own risk!). Elsewhere it might be an institution, such as the supreme council of a ruling party or a senate of oligarchs: you could walk into the place where your rulers meet and see them adopt a law or condemn a prisoner. In a democracy, the answer—the people rule—may seem to be no answer at all. Where can you find the people? How do you know when they have spoken?

It is easy—too easy—to suggest that because there is no simple answer, democracy is just a word, a pretty cloth draped over the manufacture of consent, a confusing way of talking about a reality in which small groups do the actual ruling, more or less well. Two prominent political scientists speak for the doubts many of us harbor when they recommend giving up "the folk theory of democracy"—in short, the belief that anything like the people does or could rule.[1]

The difficulty is real, but it is the other side of the coin of democracy's strength. The *demos* of democracy is an artifact, an event, something that we achieve together. The people never speak from a mouth, as a queen, a pope, a dictator, or a friend can do. But it is possible to create institutions, above all elections, that root political power in the choices of those who will live with the results. If these institutions are working, and if those who participate in them can believe in them, then we can say that the people rule. We should not shy from saying that or from trying to make it true.

Democracy pivots on elections in which majorities prevail and in which everyone in the polity has a real and unburdened opportunity to vote. But that is not the whole picture. Democracy must also remain open to the unseating of this majority and the creation of a new one, who can then speak and act as the people. Any permanent version of the people ceases to be democratic because the openness to new versions of the polity is what keeps democracy vital as a form of collective freedom. Our power to decide each new political question maintains an open future, rather than foreclosing it. Rule by elites, an oligarchy, usurps democratic power, and so does the rule of nationalists who claim to speak for the people but refuse to be ruled by new and changing coalitions of their fellow citizens.

Because democracy is open-ended, it depends on competing claims to speak for the people, clashing visions of what our problems are and how we should grapple with them. Struggles over representation require free institutions, above all parties and media, where these competing visions get spelled out. Democracy can become impossible if citizens are absorbed in lies and fantasies so that their political judgment is uprooted from real problems and responses (and often entangled in delusions of conspiracy or apocalypse). By the same token, a certain kind of well-intentioned fact-checking response to political disorder misses the most important fact: political action is not mainly about discerning and enumerating information but about organizing it into pictures of what matters, who we are and what threatens us, what we owe one another and how to honor those obligations. Politics is oriented to action, and although the corruption of facts can rot it out, no exhaustive encyclopedia of facts could ever substitute for political judgment about what we should do.[2]

This is the answer—partial, imperfect, but decisive—to the knotty problem of representation. We, the people, are always deciding who speaks for us, and with each decision we become a somewhat different people. In a democracy, citizens never stop asking, "Who are we?" because every election poses the question again. If it stopped being a question, we wouldn't have a democracy but a permanent governing class. The work of democratic politics is to keep giving answers while also keeping the questions open, staving off both breakdown and usurpation.

The democratic gamble is that the more self-rule becomes a real form of action rather than (just) a form of entertainment or identity-affirming ritual, the more demand will arise for solid facts, actionable agendas, defensible conceptions of who the people are. Responsibility is the virtue of capacity. From great disempowerment comes great irresponsibility. The fact that our politics is often inane means that we need more reasons to uphold democracy—not that adults should take it from our unreliable hands.

Democracy's institutionalized uncertainty fosters anxiety, and political anxiety powers antipolitics. Antipolitics is a constellation of tactics for limiting democracy in advance by setting a limit to collective choice. Market ideologists such as Friedrich Hayek and Milton Friedman, and their many epigones, hold that we cannot decide to organize our division of labor and wealth, our material interdependence and system of economic power, outside a certain formula of economic life, on pain of poverty, tyranny, or both. Cultural conservatives of the Burke and Tocqueville variety, and some norms theorists who follow them, claim that if democracy seems to be real, this is only because people are actually being held together by shared habits, prerational affection or solidarity, and common skeins of political imagination—a shared grammar, you might say, that everyone intuits but only the theorist can really see. Constitutionalism, which arose in modern form as a vessel of democratic power, has become a form of antipolitics that limits democracy in the name of principles that only judges can define. It adds irony to injury that, in the United States, the judges may launch their interpretations in the name of the people themselves—even a long-ago, narrower, and more hierarchical people.[3]

A successful antipolitics generally isn't a simple ideological lie. Simple lies can spark a riot, but they have trouble persisting through challenges and crises. A powerful antipolitics tends to be an overstatement or distortion of some ground truth of political life. Constitutionalism, when it becomes an antipolitics, starts from the ground truths that democracy is possible only with rules and legitimate only with bounding principles. It turns those truths into a shackle, tying democratic self-rule to old, rickety, antidemocratic institutions, such as the Electoral College, and into a general license for judicial supervision of political life.

Market ideology trades on realities: economic life is opaque and complex, price systems are good at aggregating information, trade-offs and conflicting goals mean that we cannot just say the word and have whatever economic order we might like. But it turns these realities into a dogma that denigrates politics, exaggerates the capacity of markets to reconcile conflicting desires and plans without coercion, and denies democracies the power to engage some of the most important questions about what people need and what their economies should prize and reward.

Cultural conservatism recognizes that people will permit others to rule them (if they have a choice at all) only when they feel something more in common than abstract citizenship; they need some trust or identification, a shared feeling about the history and meaning of the politics that binds them. The theory of norms is the wonky modern version of this insight: when abstract political systems come down to the ground, habits and small virtues play a key part in making them work. But it is too easy to conclude from this that norm breaking per se is bad, rather than an essential aspect of politics, or that people cannot act together unless they already more or less agree.

Antipolitics tends to uphold existing patterns and systems of privilege, but this is not its most distinguishing feature: there is a great deal in public life that does that. The deeper and more distinctive harm of antipolitics is that it artificially narrows the scope of self-rule, leaving us with fewer reasons to care about democracy, even lulling us into the thought that it is more trouble, or danger, than it's worth. Limiting the scope of politics and upholding existing privilege can, however, come to the same thing. E. E. Schattschneider once observed that the powerful tend to prefer keeping questions out of politics, where class conflict and racial domination might face demands for freedom and equality and be subjected to democratic judgment. Antipolitics is usually also antiegalitarian.[4]

Each version of antipolitics says, in its own distinctive register, "We can't do that thing, even though we might want to: it is beyond our power *because of how the world is*." On a closer look, though, it often turns out that "how the world is" is itself a political creation. When Bill Clinton and Tony Blair argued that market-led globalization was as inevitable as rising tides and changing seasons, the reality behind that image was decades of international system building that had linked the world's economies in webs of investment and trade. Capital is not water or sunlight but a specific use of money, and despite the best efforts of cryptocurrency alchemists, money can organize social life at a large scale only with the backing of governments. It took a great deal of political work for the world's leading powers to embed themselves, and politically weaker states, in an inevitability strong enough that Clinton and Blair could pass it off as natural.

The same point holds at many scales. Private property is a building block of markets, and the ownership of land, goods, or knowledge ("intellectual property") can always be traced back to an act of government—for instance, granting expropriated land to settlers and railroads and patents to the companies that make new microprocessors and drugs. If it is true that we can't just do whatever we like in economic life, it is equally true that every market that has ever been defended as natural and inevitable was built by political will and effort. We can't be sure in advance what parts of economic life are open to change, but the antipolitics of the market suppresses the question. Yet we need to be asking what kinds of lives to support people in living, what kind of work to reward, and what kind of value an economy should prize and produce.

When Tocqueville called American democracy the fruit of "the social state of the Anglo-Americans," he centered his cultural understanding of democracy on American assumptions about race. He took it that, for political purposes, the American people were the white, English-speaking population of the country, and he argued that long-term coexistence was probably impossible among what he called the "three races" of the continent. Tocqueville did not appreciate, however, how much political and legal work had gone into establishing those racial categories in the two-plus centuries of European settlement before his visit. Legal scholar Cheryl Harris and other students of the history of racial ideology have stressed that colonial and early American statute books are full of laws defining the racial boundary (often but not always by the notorious one-drop rule) and enforcing racial caste in every current and eddy of social life. These included bans on "miscegenation," criminal penalties indexed to the race of the offender and victim, and the laws of slavery.[5]

Politics creates groups: collective-bargaining units, Medicaid recipients, subsidized farmers, land-grant settlers, naturalized (and birthright) citizens and green-card holders, asylum seekers and unauthorized migrants, soldiers and employees and independent contractors, and so on across hundreds of domains and the laws that touch them. With membership comes interests, affinities, vulnerability, and power, as well as the potential to build more power together. Some group making becomes invisible because it does its work so "well" that it fades into the background. The existence of the group and its meaning for those who belong to it come to seem less like open political questions and more like parts of nature, beyond the reach of politics. This was what the American politics of race had created by the time Tocqueville encountered it. (At least it seemed that way to the white citizens whose conversation was a chief source of his judgment.)

As for constitutions, we have already seen that the late Justice Antonin Scalia's poignant inquiry ("who it is that rules me") raises the right question on the way to a confused and confusing answer. A constitution can give a political community a way to author its own fundamental law, not just once but in each generation, so that in basic ways the living have chosen their common world. It can also be a vehicle of mystification, a parchment incense that persuades some of us, some of the time, that an old law we cannot change, adopted by a polity we would not today regard as legitimate, binds us over and above our own democratic will because it is "ours." Instead of a work of collective authorship, a constitution is then an entailed inheritance, a mandatory identity, and a limit on who we can become. Because the American Constitution sharply inhibits its own popular amendment, Scalia's originalism meant celebrating the fact that we the living cannot make our own fundamental law and have to accept very old rules as interpreted by nine rather old lawyers. Scalia's criticism of living constitutionalists for allowing judicial interpretation to make fundamental law is apt, but he does not get out of the problem by objecting to it. We get more clarity from outside the Supreme Court's chambers: "With incantation and abracadabra," wrote W. E. B. Du Bois, "the leaders of a nation tried to peer back into the magic crystal, and out of a bit of paper called the Constitution, find eternal and immutable law laid down for their guidance forever and ever, Amen!" The problem is in "immutable," which can only lead to incantation and abracadabra.[6]

In its idealized form, as a unanimous collective will that makes law for the polity, the rule of the people does not and could not exist. Because its simple form is impossible, democracy's possible form is difficult. There is no guaranteed way to keep the self-rule of free majorities open, effective, and legitimate in the eyes of citizens. That is only to say that democracy is politics, and politics is hard. It offers unavoidably imperfect answers to the problem of making, and remaking, the terms of coexistence for people who are not quite built to cooperate. Because humanity is crooked timber, we can only be joined together in buildings with interesting and surprising shapes. Fortunately, there is a lot to be said for living in such buildings.

So we cannot just prescribe a formula that would make our politics, our economy, or our culture truly democratic. The search for such formulas is a political version of what Evgeny Morozov aptly calls "solutionism," the assumption that every problem has a corresponding fix. Some problems are perennial, and the goal is not to solve them once and for all but to understand them clearly enough that we can live with them. The central problem of politics—finding terms of alliance for people who need one another and are in one another's way—is a problem of this kind.

Rejecting dogmatic solutions doesn't mean we can't steer in democratic directions (toward democratic vistas, Walt Whitman might have said) or away from antidemocratic ones. We can ask whether any element of our politics, our economy, our constitutional law, and our civic culture tends to support or to undercut a democratic common life and try to foster those that support it.

Although no formula can make a polity democratic, there is one that goes a long way toward doing so: the principle that everybody votes. By this strict and clear standard, we are still not much of a democracy, although we are doing a great deal better than we have been for most of the country's history. Still, tens of millions make their lives here and cannot vote, including some ten million immigrant legal residents, more than five million people who have served terms for felony convictions, and about two million who are presently incarcerated. By this standard, too, democracy is even more recent and fragile than self-confident talk about the stability of "consolidated democracies" once suggested. As I write, the country is only about fifty years away from open and massive racial disenfranchisement—about as far as from the

Beatles' arrival in America. From fights over ballot access to conspiracy theories about election fraud, we are still learning about people's willingness to live with the rule of real majorities.

Whatever moves toward universal voting moves closer to democracy. Whoever stands in the way silently concedes how little they believe in the appeal of their political ideas or the resilience of their party. Contrary to naïve demographic determinism, great waves of enfranchisement do not reliably shake politics, let alone shift it to the left: expansions of the British parliamentary vote to many more working people in the nineteenth century ushered in a period of Tory rule, and British women voted disproportionately for Conservative candidates from 1928, when they got the vote, until Margaret Thatcher became party leader and prime minister. What enfranchisement does bring is an imperative for creativity: for everything to stay the same, everything has to change. A conservative platform that can win a truly democratic contest has to rest on something broader than class privilege or a minority-rule strategy like the one that now defines the Republican Party.

So a democratized democracy opens the way to majorities of the whole people, meaning no one is outside the ongoing argument and intermittent decisions about how to live collectively. There are no permanent rulers or permanently ruled. Truly universal suffrage is the first step in this formula. The next is for the institutional circuits of political power to let majorities act. Here the greatest barrier to democratizing American democracy is the Constitution.

What would a democratic relation to the American Constitution look like? In a polity that honored the joint principles of popular authorship and present consent, a basic feature of political life would be each generation's encounter with its fundamental law. A special convention selected for the purpose would review the constitutional text and propose revisions, which would then go on the ballot in a special election. Conventions might proceed in two stages: first, multiple smaller meetings in states or regions and then at a single national convention that would vet proposed amendments and decide which would be sent to referendum. The referendum would be national, unlike the state-by-state procedure specified in the Constitution's current Article V, which both grants disproportional power to small, rural states and makes amendment all but impossible. A constitutional referendum every twenty-seven years would mean that every generation of adults would live under a fundamental law that it had affirmed in its sovereign role. We would be the authors of our political world. This cycle of constitutional politics would set the tempo of political life, much as the four-year presidential election cycle does today.

This proposal will likely strike many readers as utopian and even alarming. The idea of a constitutional convention ranks, in respectable American politics, somewhere in the neighborhood of militias and citizen sheriffs—a reckless and probably right-wing fantasy of personally embodying the law. But this response is a symptom of the troubled condition of our democracy, not a mark of our political maturity. The fact that democratic sovereignty has come to seem unrealistic, and staging a convention as reckless as toying with an atom bomb, is an effect of constitutionalism's descent into ancestor worship and juristocracy. Why on earth should we assume that a harried group of eighteenth-century elites, whose political culture we otherwise self-confidently impugn, had more insight into our political times than we do? The question answers itself. Very few who fear constitutional politics actually believe this. Rather, they—we—fear one another and distrust the democratic capacities of the living generation too much to risk authoring our own basic law. Instead, we hope judges' constitutional interpretation will sync up with other institutions, norms, and movements to keep things both stable and (if these are our lights) modestly progressive. This is our version of the ancien régime, our consultative empire, whose distinctive incantation is praise of the Constitution, coupled with terror that "we the people" could ever again be the subject of a new constitutional utterance.

Radical as they may sound, regularly scheduled conventions could be quite conservative—or, more precisely, preservative—in their results. If Americans think as highly of the Constitution as they tend to profess, there should not be much to change. And although the prospect of a convention and potential referendum would itself change constitutional culture, probably eroding passive adoration of the Constitution and quickening the sense of real, live popular sovereignty, it might be a sign of a healthy polity to be able to approach the Constitution in this spirit and come away saying, "Everything's fine here." It would become an essential task of civic education to prepare people for the responsibility of the generational convention. "Now we must educate our masters," urged Robert Lowe, an antidemocratic British political leader of the nineteenth century, after the Reform Act of 1867 substantially expanded the franchise. The same imperative holds in a system of popular sovereignty, in which citizens must educate one another in preparation for ruling and being ruled in turn.[7]

Maunderings about separation of powers and the wisdom of the founders would not do for people who found themselves in the same position as the founders. Defenses of the Constitution as it stands would need to be more precise and powerful than today's make-weight apologies for something that is not expected to change anyway. (Who *really* needs to understand why the sky looks blue, since nothing turns on it besides being able to give curious children an adequate answer?) At the same time, radical disaffection of the "just try something" or "burn it all down" variety should have less appeal to people who know they will be living with the results of what they decide. To give some weight to the worries, it is plausible to imagine a supermajority requirement for amendments: a proposal might need 55 percent support, or 60 percent, to reduce the potential for false positives, that is, votes embracing what the majority would not, on reflection, want as fundamental law.

Imagining conventions is a chance to think creatively about democratic agenda setting. It is all too easy, in today's politics, to imagine competing campaigns for convention delegates, drumming up partisan bases with a mix of questionable proposals (for example, a balanced budget amendment, the official goal of an actual effort to call a convention that has won the support of more than half the state legislatures at the time of writing) and dire warnings that the other side will destroy the constitutional order. This, after all, is the tone of our ordinary elections. Fundamental lawmaking can't make popular sovereignty real if it is simply drawn into the maelstroms of existing party politics, formed as they are around the antidemocratic distortions in the constitutional order. At the same time, as we've seen, simply junking the parties' role in spelling out visions and agendas is likely to leave self-rule adrift, not purified. A convention that bridged these considerations might include delegates selected by a mix of techniques. For instance, some delegates might be elected in contests where party affiliations were permitted and weren't restricted to Democrats and Republicans, so that candidates who could demonstrate a certain amount of support could affiliate themselves with, say, green, libertarian, or socialist platforms. Other delegates might have occupied high positions of public trust, such as congressional leadership or the federal appeals courts (judges get too much authority in our system, but they do often have worthwhile thoughts about constitutional order). And enough delegates would be ordinary citizens selected by lottery that their support would control whether any proposed amendment went before the public. This sketch is not intended as an exercise in solutionism, but it does suggest that we could design a system of constitutional representation that could both connect with existing lines of loyalty and authority in the political order and break out of its self-replicating constraints.

A revival of democratic sovereignty might bring major changes to the Constitution. Polls show overwhelming majorities supporting a hypothetical constitutional amendment to make it easier to control campaign donations and spending. The Supreme Court's decisions defending money in politics might well fall in the first generational convention. At the same time, polls are only initial mood-reads, and the argument would get considerably more intense as actual decisions approached. Recent supermajority support for stricter gun control, which has not been translated into political action, just might junk the Second Amendment's "right of the people to keep and bear arms," which the Supreme Court first affirmed and enforced as an individual right in 2008; but public attitudes about gun control have shifted from decade to decade, and the Second Amendment (which anyway does less than ordinary political barriers to block gun control) might well survive a sustained campaign. There would certainly be efforts to reverse the Supreme Court's decisions identifying rights to choose abortion and same-sex marriage, but with popular support approaching two-thirds, those liberties would likely be secure. (In fact, they might be more so than in the hands of the current court.)

But the most important changes would be ones that shifted the structure of government to empower majorities to rule between constitutional conventions. As we have seen, the three branches of national government that the US Constitution establishes now block majority rule and authorize minority rule. (Recall the senators who voted to confirm Justice Brett Kavanaugh in 2018, who represented a historic low of 44 percent of the country, and the Electoral College win with a minority of the popular vote that put President Trump in place to nominate Kavanaugh.) More often, the many barriers to passing legislation simply smother initiatives such as a clean-energy transition, deep infrastructure investment, universal health care, and other measures that majorities recognize as desirable, even imperative, if only there were a way to them. The democratic sovereign that is now constitutionally blocked could use constitution making to clear the way for everyday democracy.

For more than a century, reformers have argued that the United States needs a political system more closely resembling the British Parliament, in which elections produce a clear majority and the resulting government has the power to pass laws and put its program to the test (or to stand pat if its position is that things are fine). This is basically right. Praise for our inherited scheme of separated powers is mostly obscurantism today. Constitutional bias against political action, and particularly against lawmaking, was always a specifically elite version of political prudence, expected to block populist movements for debt relief and other redistribution. (James Madison is quite explicit about this in his famous explanation of how the constitutional structure will choke off "faction" in *Federalist* No. 10.) But be that as it may, origin is not essence, a lesson Americans are always forgetting in our moralized attitude to national history. It is much harder to rationalize sand in the political gears as grains of prudence when social, economic, and ecological crises are accelerating without political response. We tend to forget that the political thought of the late eighteenth century, which informed the Constitution's design, owed much to a cyclical conception of political time: polities were thought to run from liberty to tyranny and back again in a foreseeable circle of passions and institutional shifts. At best, a constitutional order could hope to slow the cycle, at least for some centuries, and drop anchor in good harbor until the next season of storms. In the twenty-first century, when the climate changes faster than politics, we don't need institutions that are designed to slow down political time. We need, rather, the constitutional means to change those institutions.

The Senate and the Electoral College (whose distortions are, in good part, a corollary of the Senate's apportionment) are very basic barriers to majority rule. Trends in geographic and partisan polarization make it likely that they will continue to be for decades. Together, they represent a feature of the US Constitution that needs a reckoning: the refraction of national sovereignty through the so-called sovereignty of the states. When the people elect a president, shape legislation through the Senate, or decide on a proposed constitutional amendment, they must act in political forms that channel their sovereign power through the diminishing (New York, Texas) or magnifying (Wyoming, Delaware) bodies of the states, then add up the results as a sum of states, not as the body of a national majority. Here the Constitution's origin as a successor to the Articles of Confederation, which was essentially a treaty among the newly independent states, persists and constrains democracy. "No political dreamer was ever wild enough to think of breaking down the lines which separate the States, and of compounding the American people into one common mass," Chief Justice John Marshall wrote in 1819, but more than two centuries later, that is just what we need to do. The United States has struggled on for too long as a constitutional hybrid: part nation, part confederation.[8]

These changes would require reopening the constitutional text and authorizing new fundamental law. The changes would be as basic as any since the Reconstruction amendments made the Constitution a charter of national citizenship. There is no politically straightforward way to do this—that is the problem. The natural place to start is with James Madison's insistence, in the *Federalist Papers*, that the authority of the people to revise their basic law sometimes requires changes to come from outside the approved constitutional channels, coupled with his observation that, if the Constitution created a nation rather than a confederation, then national votes would obviously be the way to approve (or change) it. If constitutional law is not the law of the living, it is no law: sober Madison, when pressed, expressed this as clearly as the giddy Rousseau.

Firm majorities in favor of majority rule itself can find a way. Although the Constitution erects high barriers to amendment, and the last significant amendment was adopted in 1962, citizens have taken the constitutional citadel before. In 1913, reformers drove the Seventeenth Amendment, which stripped state legislatures of the power to appoint US senators, through the very legislatures that were surrendering that large and sometimes lucrative power. A mobilized supermajority in favor of a more democratic constitution is not beyond imagining.

If necessary, constitutional reform could also pass through what Madison called an "irregular" change, as long as it were done in a consistently democratic way, such as a congressional proposal to be ratified by a national majority. Recall James Wilson's insistence that the power to make such a change is one of which the people can never be legitimately deprived, and (again) Madison's concession that, if the Constitution were a national charter rather than a document of confederation among states, national majorities would naturally have the power to approve or disapprove it. In the minds of most Americans, the Constitution has become just such a national charter, and we would not be outside our rights in asserting—in line with the basic principle of twenty-first-century democracy and also with the original conception of constitution-alism—that the people who live together in a polity should be the authors of their own law.[9]

An advantage of treating constitutional change as a democratic project rather than a judicial one is that a movement for reform might achieve some of its goals in subconstitutional ways, even if the Constitution's text didn't change. It is technically straight-forward to legislate around the Electoral College for a national popular presidential vote, and an effort to do it is well underway as I write. (State legislatures simply have to pass laws indicating that their states' electoral votes will go to the winner of the na-tional popular vote.) The Senate can adopt voting rules that ad-just different members' power according to the populations of their states. ("One senator, one vote" is not actually a democratic principle, although it resembles one.) Congress can pass laws creating voting rules for the Supreme Court, such as requiring a unanimous decision for rulings that undercut democratic prerog-atives. Again, these brief suggestions do not add up to a solution-ist agenda, but they are glimmerings of the politics that a more self-assertive democracy might create.[10]

A stronger democracy would also create, and rely on, a more democratic economy. An economy that supports democracy treats people as equals in our everyday relationships. It presents us to one another as people who would and should seek one another's help in making a world. Part of the meaning of Abraham Lincoln's definition of democracy—no slavery and no masters—is that a so-cial world that trains some to obey and others to give orders will undercut democracy because it will train nobody to regard their fellows as corulers. If political democracy cannot go some way to-ward securing this kind of economic democracy, then the econ-omy will undercut democratic politics at every point. This is why making the economy more egalitarian and secure makes it more democratic, not just by enforcing majority preferences but also by helping to make the kind of society in which majorities can rule.

A democratic economy also ratifies political democracy by showing that majorities can make a world that fits their idea of a good life. For example: most people say that they think lasting relationships, caregiving, and family are the most important parts of life, distinctly more important than most jobs. If they mean it, then the ways that this economy makes such caregiving costly and inconvenient are badly out of line with the world we would choose. Caregiving, maintenance, and other kinds of work were praised as essential during the COVID-19 pandemic but were never honored with a guarantee of a living wage, health care, or other bases of dignity and security. An economy that supports such work tells us that we can actually give our lives the shape of our moral priorities. An economy that neglects and exploits these kinds of work mocks that hope.

A democratic economy is also one that citizens can understand to the greatest extent possible, so that making political decisions within it does not feel like voting on issues in theoretical physics. It's too late (and in some cases would make no sense) to avoid complexity and the need for expertise that complexity demands in many domains, from climate policy to the monetary system. But there are also political choices to make about the degree of complexity in many important areas. For instance, it is perfectly possible in principle to make banking extremely boring, treating the management of the money supply as a kind of public utility and separating it from investment services and other financial industries. The latter, in turn, could be made much simpler by regulations prohibiting many "sophisticated" instruments and directing finance into relatively simple services. Ever-more-complex financial vehicles for the wealthy solve none of the world's present problems. The economy does not have to be as mysterious and susceptible to technocratic antipolitics as it is. The more institutions citizens actually have a chance of understanding, the more of the world might belong within the ambit of democratic politics.[11]

A similar point applies to the geographic reach of economic life. Globalization, contrary to certain antipolitical stories, is as much a political creation as a technological fate. Everyone knows its standard lesson for politics: nation-states have much less power now than some of them (the big, rich ones) once did because the economies they seek to govern sprawl beyond their borders, making them susceptible to capital flight, labor and regulatory arbitrage, and crises that may begin anywhere. But the global economy is built of legal and political blocks. Rather like the American Constitution, it is a political structure that serves to hobble and baffle democratic politics. Once we see that, we can begin trying to remake it. The democratic principle for economic life should always have been that political control must expand with and set the pace of economic expansion. Having got this backward for more than a half century creates a democratic crisis but not an irreversible one. A simple example of reversal: imposing tariffs on imports to reflect the carbon pollution allowed in the country or countries where they were made would undercut a key part of global regulatory arbitrage and reassert political control over the future of the planet. Naturally, these tariffs would be more effective to the degree that they were coordinated among countries imposing them and even more so if they were linked to an internationalist politics in which some forces pushed for an equitable global regime that, as the phrase goes, levels up. Similar policies are easy to imagine for labor rights and systems of social support. Pursued intelligently, they could both reassert political control against labor arbitrage and link up organically with an internationalist politics of labor rights.[12]

Economic life also touches us intimately, in ways that can undercut democracy as effectively as capital flows. One of the cruelest and most alienating features of our social life is the ideology of meritocracy. Americans are about twice as likely as residents of most rich countries to say that they believe people get what they deserve and that both wealth and poverty come from hard work and talent, not luck or social structure.[13] The ideology of merit is transpartisan but in a way that fits a polarized society: it has both right-wing and liberal-centrist versions, which are at odds but also share basic features. The affluent wing of American liberalism—professionals, academics, progressive technology and financial types—lives in thrall to a lifelong regime of assessment and sorting, a dystopia of big tests and high-stakes applications. Accordingly, they specialize in producing measurable merit. Exams seeking out certain kinds of verbal and analytic ability, as our standardized tests do, produce cottage industries and soon enough factory-scale industries in which those who can afford it will pay to acquire those forms of "merit." Sometimes the payment is in the form of $350-an-hour tutoring for middle-school entrance exams. (I wish I were inventing this example. Many of the people making the payment are rigorously egalitarian in their politics, but purity is too much to ask of parents.) Sometimes it takes the form of living in an area with expensive homes and property taxes high enough to support good public schools. Sometimes the payment is simply private school tuition. The result? More than half of Harvard students come from families in the top 10 percent of income and under 5 percent from families in the bottom 20 percent. Other elite colleges do worse. The reason is not that poor, working-class, or just middle-class people are born without aptitude. It is that they lack the resources and sometimes the parental obsession to spend decades shaping their lives for the production of measurable "merit."[14]

The products of this meritocracy staff Democratic administrations, write the scripts for Hollywood and "quality" TV, document it all in the *New York Times* and *New Yorker*, and teach at the colleges and universities that prepare the next generation to take their places. But for all their prominence, they most definitely do not enjoy the general admiration of their fellow citizens. Instead, they are the target of the populist wing of the Republican Party, which resents their control of cultural institutions, despises their conceits, and doubts they are, in reality, good at much or good for much. Never mind disdaining the *New York Times*. (That disdain is practically a legacy institution in itself.) The contempt is much broader. Between 2012 and 2019, the share of Republicans who said that colleges and universities have a negative effect on the country went from 35 percent to 59 percent. (Democrats took the opposite view all along, with only about 20 percent thinking ill of higher education.) That is a dramatic turn against the most visible institutions of meritocracy. These attitudes support, and take fuel from, the Republican attacks on flagship state universities in places such as North Carolina, where one of the country's great schools, the University of North Carolina at Chapel Hill, has been besieged since 2012 by hostile politicians and their appointees. In the same spirit of tearing down whatever is seen to give shelter to enemies, the Trump tax legislation enacted at the end of 2017 used federal fiscal policy as a tool of partisan class war, slashing a deduction for local income taxes that mainly benefits high earners in liberal states and cities—the meritocratic base. It also imposed a 1.4 percent tax on investment income from the endowments of wealthy colleges and universities, turning culture war into tax law.[15]

For all its hostility to the mainly liberal meritocracy, the right has its own meritocratic ideology, which centers on the market. Conservatives may despise the gatekeeping institutions of the liberal meritocrats, but capitalism's winners are often conservatives' heroes. One of many perverse things about Donald Trump's populism was that he did not attack inequality but claimed that American inequality had the wrong basis. He attacked the winners of a "rigged system" as an incompetent, self-serving, corrupt elite, but presented himself (ironically enough) as a winner on the right kind of testing ground, the struggle for dominance in the marketplace. He stocked his administration not with professionals of the institutional-meritocrat type but with moneybags of the market-meritocrat variety. Partisans of the two meritocracies don't think much of one another, but they agree that the citizens who really count are the ones who prevail in systems of relentless, hierarchical pressure. The systems vary, but key conceits are the same.[16]

Apologists for both meritocracies tend to ignore that being a "winner" often depends on inherited wealth. This may be literal capital like Donald Trump's inheritance. It may also be what is tellingly called "cultural capital"—the effect of schools, camps, and everyday social life in elite enclaves, which prepare people for high test scores and, just as important, a certain air of merit. (Liberal meritocrats are more vocally aware of this difficulty than conservative ones, but this has not helped them to find a way around it.) Both meritocracies produce classes of successful people who are prepared at every stage to believe they deserve what has come to them; after all, it came through rigorous sorting, or so everything conspires to tell them. The sorting logic is so powerful that the liberal meritocrats' privilege check, meant to call the whole system into at least momentary question, is a piece of cultural capital itself. Its fluent use is as much a class marker as a good tennis serve might once have been. If you were already inclined to dislike liberal meritocrats, you might not be surprised that even their self-criticism turned out to be a way of showing their superiority to you.

Both meritocratic systems are powered psychologically as much by fear as by entitlement. This is fear of being thrown or, worse, seeing one's children thrown into one of the ever-shifting American demimondes of social neglect, with ever-present threats from untreated illnesses and unsafe neighborhoods, and a daily barrage of small indignities at work or in joblessness. Adam Smith opened the era of capitalism by remarking that the poor were socially invisible, but the prospect of being socially left behind is forever in the backs of the minds of our striving classes. Both kinds of American competition put their prizes—wealth and esteem for the right, esteem and wealth for the liberals—in the spotlight, but the prospect of indignity and invisibility does just as much to keep the contests going.

All this meritocratic dysfunction cuts a gap into social feeling and political imagination. How can those who do not deserve as much as we do, who lack merit, be entitled to rule us? Lifelong practices of sorting and ranking get under the skin and all but immunize us to Walt Whitman's democratic credo: "Every atom belonging to me as good belongs to you." We may say we believe it, may want to believe, but most of us are, in key ways, structurally unable to live as if we believed it: on pain of our children's happiness, the Achilles' heel of anyone who has a basic disagreement with the social order of things. It is how we live that shapes what we believe, more than the other way around. Meritocracy is a mortal enemy of democracy because it tells us, in a thousand large and small ways, that people have unequal value and that the lives we live prove this. It undercuts the willingness, even the capacity, to see one another as genuinely part of a joint project of self-rule. It is no small thing to say that you rule me, and I rule you, and to mean it. Our social life erodes democracy by training us not to meet one another as equals.[17]

The classical Athenians considered a hallmark of citizenship to be *isonomia*, equality of the laws, and that ideal echoes through modern democracies, not least in the Constitution's guarantee of "equal protection of the laws." But what does equality mean in the sharing out of benefits and burdens, power and vulnerability? One of today's key terms for arguing over this question is *privilege*. Although its root is Latin rather than Greek, privilege is a semantic opposite of *isonomia*: it literally means "private law." It sets you apart by giving you power that others lack or making you safe where they are not. Understood in this way, privilege deserves to be anathema to a democracy.

The word *privilege* is, however, often used imprecisely so that it can seem to be an indiscriminate complaint against any power or protection, at least if these can be associated with the privileged person's membership in a traditionally high-status group. (This lack of precision is most often observed in meritocrats' catechisms of their own privileges, recited before going back, suitably shriven, to enjoying them.) To democratize society, a polity needs a picture of how benefits and burdens, power and vulnerability should be shared to produce a sense of one another as equals. Privilege needs to be anchored to an idea of how we should live together.

Privilege names three kinds of problems, which need to be teased apart. First, it names advantages that should not exist at all and that need to be razed and replaced. Paradigms of these are what it means to be male in a patriarchy or white in a white supremacist society. These are forms of power that depend essentially on contrasts with, and domination over, other people. The second kind of problem that privilege names is an advantage that is not illegitimate per se but is tainted by the fact that it is denied to some people. Every democratic citizen should be able to expect that bureaucrats and public safety officers will treat them with a modicum of respect and care. The fact that many cannot and that their doubt and fear track race, class, and gender make this most basic civic self-assurance a kind of privilege. An advantage of this sort needs to be relentlessly extended, not eliminated, to move closer to a democratic social order. The third kind of problem that privilege names is an advantage that can probably never be identical for everyone but that is now distributed on an illegitimate basis. Not everyone who wants to will hold certain positions of power and responsibility, such as judgeships or political office. Not everyone who wants to will be a doctor, a marine biologist, a scriptwriter, or the editor of an influential magazine. The task in assessing these kinds of advantages is to ask two questions. First, are they being distributed on the right basis or for the wrong reasons? Second, do they bring along other advantages that they should not?

Take an example from the earlier discussion of liberal meritocracy: seats at Harvard College and similar institutions, now dominated by the children of the country's (and world's) wealthy and high-professional classes. The ways that wealth and other social advantages help to produce the "merit" that selective colleges measure are prime instances of the wrong basis for advantage. So are the notorious roles of family connections (politely, legacy status) and donations (politely, development prospects) in admissions.

But the even more basic problem is that elite college and university admissions matter as much as they do. This has to do with the second question, whether one advantage brings along other advantages that it should not. Fighting one's way into or—more likely in our stratified reality—holding on to a place in the upper-middle or professional classes should not be a precondition of expecting that you and your family can count on decent schools, good infrastructure, safe neighborhoods, or reliable health care. Nor should the class status that school admissions can confer be a precondition of social standing and respect. These problems with meritocracy need responses that are not about reconfiguring the narrow doorway into a specific elite but rather softening the contrast between the lives of people who pass through those doorways and the lives of others. It might be fine for Harvard and the University of North Carolina at Chapel Hill to train more doctors and editors than most schools, especially if their admissions became more equitable, but it is not fine that so many kinds of lives are so vulnerable. To address this kind of privilege, we need to draw back our lens from gatekeeping institutions to the broader political economy of citizenship. We need to return to one of the basic ideas in democratizing the economy: that economic life should give us less to fear and more ways to do good work and to spread broadly the expectation of basic security and the respect of others.

A country that could offer that kind of life to everyone would deserve patriotism. The Trump administration's flag-waving nationalism gave a boost to the perennial belief that patriotism is a parochial attachment, even a form of bigotry. Patriotism does have affinities with moral clannishness, the belief that your fellow citizens matter more than other people, and with American exceptionalism, the conceit that the United States doesn't have the problems and weaknesses that every country has. This pairing was hardly new in the Trump years: George W. Bush responded to the attacks of September 11, 2001, by leading a crowd in chanting "USA! USA!" and then launched a pair of wars and nation-building projects that only a nation exempt from the usual forces of history could have expected to succeed. (They failed, with terrible human consequences.) But this sort of blinkered self-assurance is not the only thing patriotism might mean.[18]

It might also mean an attitude we could call the patriotism of responsibility—not a license for favoritism and recklessness but a way of owning up to your place in the world and doing your best by it. This identification with the country means carrying a moral burden: it means accepting that your country's wrongs, harms, and inequities are your responsibility as a citizen, regardless of whether you personally caused them or benefit from them. It also means cultivating an attachment to those elements of the country's institutions and history that have the potential to repair its harms and make a fairer future. In practice, this attachment means not giving up on the country but gambling on the premise that your fellow citizens, with whom you are trapped together, can make something better of what you have in common.

In one of his most radical speeches, a 1967 denunciation of the Vietnam War, Martin Luther King Jr. reminded his audience that the Southern Christian Leadership Conference had taken as its motto "To save the soul of America." He explained that "no one who has any concern for the integrity and life of America" could ignore the ties between violence and injustice at home and wrongs abroad. King didn't mean that he cared only about Americans or saw the war mainly through the lens of their spiritual condition: as a Christian, he claimed a more universal ministry, "bound by allegiances and loyalties which are broader and deeper than nationalism and which go beyond our nation's self-defined goals and positions." But the country was where he could act politically, calling on other citizens "to recapture the revolutionary spirit" and "make democracy real." If his ministry was for all humanity, it was as part of his half-democratic country that he affirmed the Harlem poet Langston Hughes's iconic lines: "America never was America to me," but King swore with the poet that "America will be!" A polity is the place where we can act democratically, the place that we can try to make democratic.[19]

In *Black Reconstruction*, W. E. B. Du Bois is a patriot of this sort, keenly interested in the inheritance of what he called abolition-democracy, a tradition that took universal suffrage as the tool to create a just political economy. Du Bois explained this political stance in words borrowed from a Black abolitionist minister, J. W. C. Pennington. The Black "population of the United States has no destiny separate from that of the nation in which they form an integral part. . . . Her ship is ours; her storms are ours . . . if she breaks upon a rock, we break with her." Du Bois was describing, from the perspective of those communities most beaten down and shut out in American life, the general situation of humanity: we are, with a few wealthy and privileged exceptions, caught together in countries whose politics are simultaneously oppressive threats and our chief means of calling one another to account. Democracy is how equals make that accounting, and what Du Bois called abolition-democracy was democracy unmodified for a country where equality was not yet real: a democracy fully open to all its members and able to shape economic as well as political life. The basis of responsible patriotism is appreciating the unique power a polity creates: to remake the shared world in line with an idea of justice, to turn an ideal of how we should live together into a model for how we will live together. As long as politics is the singularly powerful lever for making these changes, our polities are our main settings for practical responsibility taking.[20]

Democracy is not the whole of politics. It does not begin to answer all questions, though it provides a way to answer them. Nor is it morally neutral. It is defined by cornerstone commitments to equality and political rights and the rejection of caste and exclusionary partisanship. But all of that leaves a great deal open in the conception of a just and good society that people can pursue democratically. It isn't mine, or anyone's, to say what that should be, but the ideas in this book sketch one direction: a stronger commitment to majority rule and democratic sovereignty, coupled with a deepened equality in economic and social life. Together, these would make a polity in which the terms of our shared lives are set by the people who live by them, that is, a place where we could say the people rule. That goal has an unsettling meaning: that we are one another's rulers, ruling and being ruled by turn. The alternative is not a life free from power but the incursion of other forms of power, less shared, equitable, or transparent than democracy. Either we make our politics our own, or we knuckle under to some form of antipolitics, and our common lives are shaped by the market, by inherited and undemocratic political institutions, by atavistic loyalties and fears.

A goal of this book has been to learn from the traditions of antipolitics—not just to criticize or condemn them but to draw from their cautions about politics, and particularly about democracy, precisely to make the commitment to democracy more mature and stable. Much of the appeal of constitutionalism is anchored in liberal values of individual freedom, self-definition, and self-expression. In judicial decisions elaborating the meaning of these values, some liberals and progressives have, quite understandably, found a higher set of principles, which they treat as hard boundaries on democratic decisions. To them it seems foolish, and maybe callous, to put majority rule ahead of right and wrong, and personal freedom seems to be at the core of what is right. (So violating personal freedom seems at the core of what is wrong.) The moral appeal of the market, too, is tied to the value of personal autonomy. A market society, argued capitalism's great modern publicists Friedrich Hayek and Milton Friedman, is a society of free people who set their own goals and choose their obligations. Progressives may resonate to the morality of personal freedom but doubt that the market has much to do with it, while some conservatives and libertarians affirm that the market protects freedom but suspect broader theories of personal autonomy are idealistic and impractical. All may agree, though, that freedom is too essential to be left to democracy.

The democratic response starts with the market. The virtues that foster a culture of individuality, such as curiosity, tolerance, and the everyday courage to try something new, are just as precious as liberals say. And like any other virtues, they need an institutional ecology, a material life in which they flourish. But this is not uniquely the market, which can undercut them as easily as support them. Liberal virtues thrive when people are not afraid of one another in their daily lives or constantly anxious about the damage a piece of bad luck or the whim of a boss might do to them and their loved ones. Somehow in the triumphalism of the late Cold War and its aftermath, it became easy to think of yourself as a liberal without giving much thought to what has been, over the centuries, the central problem of modern life: how far it is possible to achieve a society of free equals in an economic order that concentrates wealth and turns energy and creativity relentlessly to profit.

Ordinary people understand the ways power works in economic life, however much economic thinking tends to conceal it. If you care about the freedom and development of the individual, then you care about the power to make a living, to be free from abuse at work, to enjoy basic security in your own life, and to have the chance to learn and change. Thoughtful liberals follow John Stuart Mill in being committed to individuality, self-development, and self-expression. They understand these not as static or abstract values but as the fruits of experiment and discovery, the learning that happens when people can approach one another as free equals, undistorted by dependence or oppression. People knew as much about their potential, Mill wrote in 1869 in "The Subjection of Women" (with the uncredited Harriet Taylor), as we know about that of plants that are kept in greenhouses or cut and bent into topiaries. Mill knew that nothing limited people more than poverty and the petty tyrannies of the household, the workplace, and the neighborhood. Our twenty-first century versions include vulnerable jobs, poverty and joblessness, rule by the rich, structural racism, and mass incarceration. If you are horrified by cruelty, as liberals are often said to be, you will be horrified by these. Truly universal health care, free higher education, increased power for workers, and deep criminal justice reform are all ways of mobilizing politics against cruelty. The class politics of democracy—once more, the rule of the poor or of the broad middle—gives the power to make the world to the people who carry its everyday weight. As long as that everyday weight is the great threat to personal freedom and development, rough-hewn democracy will be a better vehicle for personal freedom than the crystalline lines of market principles.[21]

Beyond any affinity with the market, the liberal emphasis on personal freedom is a trenchant reminder that democrats should reject the caricature of majority rule as an amoral form of arbitrary power, a mere act of collective will. It is an act of collective will but not an amoral one. It rests on a profound respect for the moral importance of others: this is the basis of the foundational democratic willingness to be corulers with one another. And the point of the democratic power to decide how we will live together is a moral one: to make a world that respects and fosters human freedom and equality. A commitment to democracy is not a rejection of these values but a judgment about where we should turn to give them life: not to the economic machine of the market, not to wise philosopher-kings and queens, but to one another.

Why to one another? Partly out of respect. Partly because we need one another's help to make a world where personal freedom really can flourish. In the business-as-usual default settings of our economy, ecology, and society, the libertarian wish to be left alone cannot secure the liberal ideal of real autonomy. We need democratic action to change those settings, not once and for all but over and over.

A democrat can also learn from the antipolitics of culture and tradition. Apart from its appeals to exclusionary visions of the country, which a democrat should reject, this conservative strand of thinking starts from a feeling for continuity, belonging, a sense of home. Conservatives often claim these as their special values and promise to protect them from democratic intrusion. This description may be hard to recognize in the contemporary right, which tends to combine nationalism or half-coded racial appeal with almost unstinting support for existing economic power. In the face of this kind of politics, democracy should be a radical turn toward the future, a pronouncement that we do not have to be what some of us have previously been. But although democracy is always partly a declaration of independence from the past, it does not need to be a politics of amnesia or ingratitude. None of us did much to make the world, and none of us choose the time in which we are born. The very institutions, practices, and ideas that give us the democratic power to remake our world are legacies from the past.

The conservative attachment to what is familiar is emotional and resonates to symbols, touchstones of a common world. These are the everyday images, phrases, and sensations that conjure a whole form of life, what George Orwell famously described in "England, Your England" as being "*your* civilization, it is *you* . . . the old maids biking to Holy Communion through the mists of the autumn morning . . . the suet puddings and the red pillar boxes have entered into your soul." In a rapidly changing country, whose citizens are much more diverse than just a generation ago, those sentimental attachments can become nostalgic and even get in the way of seeing *this* country *now* as the one we share. But there is no need to forgo symbols and feelings that have, as Orwell wrote, entered many of our souls.[22]

The key is that democratic political symbols do not just recall what some of us have been. They are also ways of calling one another to become something more. They do not only tie the present to the past; they also show how different futures can grow from a history we did not and could not choose. Since first reading it in 2015, I have been moved by a passage in a family memoir written by Pauli Murray, a lawyer, scholar, activist, and priest. Murray writes of growing up in Durham, North Carolina, during some of the most oppressive decades of Jim Crow: "It is little wonder . . . that I was strongly anti-American at six, that I hated George Washington, mumbled the oath of allegiance to the American flag."[23]

Murray's beloved grandfather died at about that time, and "as a Union veteran"—one of the Black troops who played a critical role in the late stages of the Civil War—he "was entitled to a United States flag for his grave." So Murray walked every Memorial Day through a field of Confederate flags in the white portion of Durham's segregated cemetery to plant a flag

> at the head of Grandfather's grave. . . . There was little identity in my mind between the Union flag which waved over my

grandfather's grave and the United States flag on which I looked with so much skepticism at West End School. It would be a while yet before I realized that the two were the same. I spent many hours digging up weeds, cutting grass, and tending the family plot. It was only a few feet from the main highway between Durham and Chapel Hill. I wanted the white people who drove by to see this banner and me standing by it.[24]

We may love what is familiar because it is us, what makes the world a home in these fleeting lives. We may rage against it for what it does to the people and places we love. If we are reflective, many of us will do both. The common action of democracy can only take place within these fraught and uneven inheritances. It puts them in the realm of *doing together*, not just feeling or remembering. But feeling and remembering are vital tissues in the lives we bring to politics, the lives that are also the reason politics matters in the first place.

Conservatism also claims some practical values that are exiled from modern capitalism. One is stability: economic security is important because "the economy" is a place where people live. Uprooting jobs and industries, submitting people to the whims of the market, is often a false and socially destructive version of progress. Another such value is pluralism: it is critical to preserve institutions and parts of life where nonmarket values of affection, craft, and, yes, utopian radicalism can flourish. Wendell Berry, a rare American agrarian conservative, writes of the forces of "progress," from land-jobbing colonists to coal corporations: "These conquerors have fragmented and demolished traditional communities. . . . They have always said that what they destroyed was outdated, provincial, and contemptible."

If conservatism has any relevance to twenty-first-century politics besides protecting private hierarchies from democratic pressure, it should be to press warnings like Berry's against self-assured devotees of modern homogeneity. These values won't come to life on today's political right, which wants to privatize every level of education and defer to global capital markets. It won't do much better with a meritocratic liberalism that grades life chances by tests, sorts us into jobs that will eventually let us pay off our student loans, and otherwise treats us as human capital, just with a somewhat different accounting system from that of the promarket right.

In recent years, challenging an often inhumane and antidemocratic economy has been the work of new political forces that are also revivals of old political visions. These forces include a progressivism that aims to limit inequality and cut back on the economic power of giant companies and the very rich, and a social democratic movement, whose candidates and activists sometimes call themselves democratic socialists, that works to make daily life safer and more dignified and humane. Though critics call these movements radical and utopian, they are, ironically, the most realistic about what it takes to build a world in which the best liberal and conservative values can have a home. They depend on recognizing that no one—notably no boss or investor—should have unquestioned power over other lives, that the market has no special claim to wisdom or morality, and that we need social investment in caregiving and education so that affection, play, and learning for its own sake can all persist. There are many human values, by no means all or even mainly political, but for better or worse the survival of many of the most important nonpolitical values depends on the world-making power of politics. With this in mind, a democrat can embody enough fruitful self-contradiction to count as a liberal-conservative-socialist, with various emphases among the strands of those different traditions, and still put democracy first.[25]

We have seen that the political scientist Samuel Huntington made some dangerous misjudgments about American life, but a trenchant observation of his about what he called "modernizing" societies applies well to the United States: "The truly helpless society is not one threatened by revolution, but one incapable of it." A vital democracy weaves political revolution into the more ordinary rhythms of life: voting in elections but also reflecting about parenthood or one's religious tradition, engaging in strikes and rallies but also having conversations with family and friends about the country's history or the mood of the neighborhood. In a healthy democracy, the preservative work of being together and keeping institutions up and renewing them is continuous with the revolutionary work of shifting our common ground, changing the terms on which we come together—starting the world again, not in the sense of uprooting what is already there but in the spirit of a sunrise in a changing season. The failure of democracy would mean the loss of this capacity for peaceful revolution. This has never been more important than now, when ecological and economic crises require two things at once: urgent preservation of fragile systems and ultimate transformation toward a form of life that can sustain both the planet and a just and peaceful human life.[26]

If we lose democracy, it may be out of fear of one another or disgust with the tricks and machinations of politics and with other citizens' prejudices and lack of sense. We may find ruling and being ruled in turn to be intolerable. But in losing democracy, we would not escape one another. In leaving democracy behind, we would only hand over power to the economic, ecological, and racial fate that determines who does which work, whose sickness goes untreated, who may go where and who is fenced out, and, in the end, who lives. We would give up our only way to take those decisions into the hands of all of us who must live with the results. We cannot escape power or the politics that shapes it. We can only decide whether we will try to take responsibility for it. Democracy is the name for the responsibility of equals.

Democracy is by turns gray, slow, and frustrating and then rapid and scary. It is a myth we recount to one another and also a vulnerable but durable reality, still imperfect, achieved over centuries of struggle. It brings recurrent betrayal of its own principles of freedom and equality, but it is also, in Langston Hughes's phrase, "True anyhow no matter how many/Liars use those words." Living with its contradictions is a way of living with our own.[27]

It is also how we can become, sometimes, another people. "I give the sign of democracy," pronounced Walt Whitman, promising,

"I will accept nothing which all cannot have their counterpart of on the same terms." This radical equality seemed to Whitman to be the key to an exhilarating change, "quivering me to a new identity." This is the poetry of which political thought is the prose and history the record. We are the species that remakes itself in line with new forms of imagination. But we do not do this however we like. To make our changes deep and lasting, we must enlist one another and make the change together, in ourselves and in the world we share. This is how we make real and learn to believe Whitman's often betrayed democratic creed that "every atom belonging to me as good belongs to you." So far as we do believe it, we will not be too afraid to cross the next horizon together. We are not too late to seek a newer world.[28]

ACKNOWLEDGMENTS

M any people's generosity made this book possible. Several read the full manuscript. What I have written doesn't do justice to the richness of their comments. It was, at least, an opportunity to learn from Alyssa Battistoni, Christopher Elmendorf, Katrina Forrester, Jonathan Gould, David Grewal, Matt Karp, Madhav Khosla, Lev Menand, and Nadia Urbinati. Other readers gave me incisive comments on portions of the manuscript. Particular thanks go to Seyla Benhabib, Katherine Franke, Jamal Greene, Bernard Harcourt, Jeremy Kessler, Kerrel Murray, David Pozen, Chuck Sabel, Susan Sturm, and other participants in the faculty workshops at Columbia Law School, the University of Pittsburgh Law School, and Pace Law School.

I have been fortunate to discuss these issues with many people over the years. Of those not named above, this book is owing especially to Michelle Wilde Anderson, Olatunde Johnson, Amy Kapczynski, Jack Knight, Joe Landau, Sabeel Rahman, Aziz Rana, Kendall Thomas, and Isaac Villegas. I learned particularly from forums at New York Humanities with David Bromwich, Leah Wright Rigeur, and Brandon Terry, and from several public exchanges with Katrina Forrester. I'm sure I have accidentally omitted some people from these lists, and I thank them, too.

I am grateful to my agent, Kim Witherspoon, and her office. Emma Berry, who edited the manuscript at Basic Books, is beyond splendid. Her skill and intelligence deserve the credit for much of what is good in this book. I am also grateful to everyone else at the publishing house who helped to turn these words into a book.

My biggest thanks go to my family. I would not have finished the manuscript without the partnership of my wife, Laura Britton. She also took on a disproportionate share of household management in the last months of writing, and I hope I can reciprocate adequately. Her parents, Edward and Kathryn Britton, often cared for our son, James, in spring and summer 2021. So did the wonderful caregivers at the Tompkins Hall daycare in fall 2021. James gave me reason not to waste time while working so that I could spend more hours with him afterward. I dedicate the book to our family, in gratitude.

NOTES

INTRODUCTION

1. Michael Dimock and Richard Wike, "America Is Exceptional in the Nature of Its Political Divide," Pew Research Center, Nov. 13, 2020 (available at https://www.pewresearch.org/fact-tank/2020/11/13/america-is-exceptional-in-the-nature-of-its-political-divide/).

2. Stacey Abrams, "Our Democracy Faced a Near-Death Experience: Here's How to Revive It," *Washington Post*, Feb. 7, 2021 (available at https://www.washingtonpost.com/opinions/2021/02/07/stacey-abrams-democracy-test-future/); Susan E. Rice, "Our Democracy's Near-Death Experience," *New York Times*, Dec. 1, 2020 (available at https://www.nytimes.com/2020/12/01/opinion/trump-biden-democracy.html); Daniel A. Cox, "After the Ballots Are Counted: Conspiracies, Political Violence, and American Exceptionalism," Survey Center on American Life, Feb. 11, 2021 (available at https://www.americansurveycenter.org/research/after-the-ballots-are-counted-conspiracies-political-violence-and-american-exceptionalism/); and Lilliana Mason and Nathan P. Kalmoe, "What You Need to Know About How Many Americans Condone Political Violence—and Why," *Washington Post*, Jan. 11, 2021 (available at https://www.washingtonpost.com/politics/2021/01/11/what-you-need-know-about-how-many-americans-condone-political-violence-why/). Some of the high estimates of support for political violence reported in these sources have been subject to telling methodological criticisms, and it seems all but certain that they overstate willingness to condone violence. My text reflects these adjusted estimates. The sources of the titles quoted in this paragraph are, in order, Steven Levitsky and Daniel Ziblatt, *How Democracies Die* (Cambridge, MA: Harvard

University Press, 2018); David Runciman, *How Democracy Ends* (New York: Basic Books, 2018); Yascha Mounk, *The People v. Democracy: Why Our Freedom Is in Danger and How to Save It* (Cambridge, MA: Harvard University Press, 2018); and Jill Lepore, "The Last Time Democracy Almost Died: Learning from the Upheaval of the Nineteen-Thirties," *New Yorker*, Jan. 27, 2020.

3. Fred Lewsey, *Global Dissatisfaction with Democracy at a Record High*, Centre for the Future of Democracy, Bennett Institute for Public Policy at Cambridge University, Jan. 2020 (available at https://www.cam.ac.uk /stories/dissatisfactiondemocracy).

4. Pew Research Center, "Public Trust in Government: 1958–2021," May 17, 2021 (available at https://www.pewresearch.org/politics/2021 /05/17/public-trust-in-government-1958-2021/).

5. Sen. Christopher Murphy, "In Order for Our Democracy to Survive, America Cannot Condone the Actions Trump Took," speech, University of Connecticut, Feb. 7, 2020 (available at https://www.murphy.senate.gov /newsroom/press-releases/murphy-in-order-for-our-democracy-to -survive-america-cannot-condone-the-actions-trump-took); and David Marchese, "Senator Chris Murphy Is Worried We're Seeing Democracy's Last Stand," *New York Times*, Aug. 28, 2020 (available at https://www.nytimes .com/interactive/2020/08/24/magazine/chris-murphy-interview.html).

6. Zia Qureshi, "Tackling the Inequality Pandemic," Brookings Institution, Nov. 17, 2020 (available at https://www.brookings.edu/research /tackling-the-inequality-pandemic-is-there-a-cure/); and Francisco H. G. Ferreira, "Inequality in the Time of COVID-19," International Monetary Fund, summer 2021 (available at https://www.imf.org/external/pubs /ft/fandd/2021/06/inequality-and-covid-19-ferreira.htm).

7. Vaclav Smil, *Grand Transitions: How the Modern World Was Made* (New York: Oxford University Press, 2021).

8. Pew Research Center, "Trust and Distrust in America: The State of Personal Trust," July 22, 2019 (available at https://www.pewresearch .org/politics/2019/07/22/the-state-of-personal-trust/); Anne Case and Angus Deaton, *Deaths of Despair and the Future of Capitalism* (Princeton, NJ: Princeton University Press, 2020); and Robert D. Putnam, *Our Kids: The American Dream in Crisis* (New York: Simon and Schuster, 2015).

9. Martin Gilens and Benjamin I. Page, "Testing Theories of American Politics: Elites, Interest Groups, and Average Citizens," *Perspectives on Politics*, vol. 12, no. 3, Sept. 2014, p. 572.

10. Of course, there is disagreement about how to spell out these principles. Does the right to vote mean the right to automatic registration and automatic receipt of a mail-in ballot? If a state imposes very serious limits on abortion, is it enforcing an undemocratic system of gender

caste? If Election Day is not a national holiday, how marred is the resulting democracy by economic caste (and, considering who does what kinds of work in a country like the United States, racial caste)? Taking democracy seriously should mean a strong premise of more equality and easier voting, but trying to answer each of these questions in detail is not the aim of this book.

11. *Federalist* No. 51 (James Madison); *Federalist* No. 63 (Madison; note, however, that there is some question about whether Madison or his collaborator, Alexander Hamilton, drafted this installment, which makes little difference for understanding the early influence of the perspective it expresses); and Alexis de Tocqueville, *Democracy in America*, trans. George Lawrence, ed. J. P. Mayer (New York: Harper and Row, 1969), p. 292.

12. Walter Lippmann, *The Phantom Public* (New York: Macmillan, 1930), pp. 38 ("dogma"); 43 ("intensification"); 55 ("We must assume").

13. Angus Burgin, *The Great Persuasion: Reinventing Free Markets Since the Depression* (Cambridge, MA: Harvard University Press, 2012), pp. 65–67.

14. Richard A. Posner, *Law, Pragmatism, and Democracy* (Cambridge, MA: Harvard University Press, 2004), p. 163.

CHAPTER 1: A POLITICAL HISTORY OF THE PRESENT

1. Karl Polanyi, *The Great Transformation: The Political and Economic Origins of Our Time* (New York: Farrar and Rinehart, 1944); Derek Fraser, *The Evolution of the British Welfare State*, 4th ed. (London: Palgrave Macmillan, 2009), pp. 245–304; and James Chappel, *Catholic Modern: The Challenge of Totalitarianism and the Remaking of the Church* (Cambridge, MA: Harvard University Press, 2018), pp. 144–226 (on Christian Democratic parties and the building of the postwar European state).

2. Newt Gingrich and Richard Keith Armey, "Contract with America," 1994.

3. Václav Havel, "The Power of the Powerless," in ed. Paul Wilson, *Open Letters: Selected Prose, 1965–1990* (Boston: Faber and Faber, 1991), pp. 125–214. In an interesting passage, Havel highlighted how much the idea of "living in truth" was an alternative to politics in the democratic sense of seeking and using power, not a version of it: "The more thoroughly the post-totalitarian system frustrates any rival alternative on the level of real power, as well as any form of politics independent of its own automatism, the more definitively the center of gravity of any political threat shifts to the area of the existential and the pre-political: usually without any conscious effort, living within the truth becomes one natural point of departure for all activities that work against the automatism of the system" (p. 152).

4. Marx's remark is perhaps the only widely remembered bit of his book *The Eighteenth Brumaire of Louis Bonaparte,* a remarkable study of the political and cultural dynamics of reaction, which appeared in 1852. Martin Matishak, "Haines Pledges to 'Speak Truth to Power' if Confirmed as Biden's Intel Chief," *Politico,* Jan. 19, 2021 (available at https://www.politico.com/news/2021/01/19/avril-haines-confirmation-hearing-domestic-terrorism-460373).

5. Barack Obama, *Dreams from My Father: A Story of Race and Inheritance* (New York: Crown, 1995).

6. Barack Obama, speech against the Iraq War, Chicago, Illinois, Oct. 2, 2002 (transcript available at https://www.npr.org/templates/story/story.php?storyId=99591469).

7. Martin Luther King Jr., "I Have a Dream" speech, Washington, DC, Aug. 28, 1963 (transcript available at https://www.americanrhetoric.com/speeches/mlkihaveadream.htm); and Lyndon Johnson, speech before Congress on voting rights, March 15, 1965 (transcript available at https://millercenter.org/the-presidency/presidential-speeches/march-15-1965-speech-congress-voting-rights). I'm not sure of the right way to cite a cartoon, but I can affirm that it was prominently displayed on my parents' refrigerator for at least a decade after Obama's 2008 victory.

8. Barack Obama, keynote address at the Democratic National Convention, Boston, Massachusetts, July 27, 2004 (transcript available at https://www.nytimes.com/2004/07/27/politics/campaign/barack-obamas-remarks-to-the-democratic-national.html); and Obama, "Remarks by the President at Memorial Service for Fallen Dallas Police Officers," Dallas, Texas, July 12, 2016 (transcript available at https://obamawhitehouse.archives.gov/the-press-office/2016/07/12/remarks-president-memorial-service-fallen-dallas-police-officers).

9. Paul Krugman, "Hate Springs Eternal," *New York Times,* Feb. 11, 2008 (available at https://www.nytimes.com/2008/02/11/opinion/11krugman.html); and Alexandra Schwartz, "Should Millennials Get Over Bernie Sanders?" *New Yorker,* Feb. 2, 2016 (available at https://www.newyorker.com/culture/cultural-comment/should-millennials-get-over-bernie-sanders). These comments are emblematic of the mood of the time, and I don't intend any specific or personal criticism of Schwartz, a thoughtful critic with whom I subsequently had valuable exchanges about these questions and whose essay attracted ungenerous hostility from some Sanders loyalists.

10. David Brooks, "The Anti-Party Men: Trump, Carson, Sanders, and Corbyn," *New York Times,* Sept. 8, 2015 (available at https://www.nytimes.com/2015/09/08/opinion/the-anti-party-men-trump-carson-sanders-and-corbyn.html).

CHAPTER 2: MAKING DEMOCRACY UP,
MAKING DEMOCRACY REAL

1. This characterization comes from John Aubrey's *Brief Lives*, a collection of biographical materials assembled during Aubrey's life (a contemporary and friend of Hobbes, Aubrey died in 1697) but first published in the nineteenth century. For "Crowe," see John Aubrey, *Brief Lives*, vol. 1, ed. Andrew Clark (Oxford: Clarendon Press, 1898), p. 329. The references to exercise habits and taste in boots are at pp. 351–352.

2. Aubrey, *Brief Lives*, p. 339.

3. My reading list is undeniably old and European. I take seriously the dynamics of imperialism and racial hierarchy that contributed to the making of the "traditional" syllabus in political thought. In fact, it is because the world's fate is being decided in terms of institutions and systems that emerged and were first rationalized in Europe's "early modernity" and "modernity"—the state, capitalism, and mass democracy—that I look to founding accounts of the nature of these, their relations, and their potential. I do believe and hope that this book demonstrates that certain early accounts of these systems captured key features of their logic and possibility in ways that were both revealing and influential. What began in one set of places, where it was both made up and made real, is now everyone's problem and remains in key ways the template with which we all confront our problems.

4. Sven Beckert, *Empire of Cotton: A Global History* (New York: Knopf, 2015). David Stasavage argues in *The Decline and Rise of Democracy* (Princeton, NJ: Princeton University Press, 2020) that "early democracy was widespread" and gives examples from Mesopotamia, India, Indigenous North America, and Africa. He establishes this claim, though, with a definition that considerably cuts back on the meaning of democracy: "those who ruled needed to obtain consent for their decisions from a council or assembly," and frequently, although not always, "rulers did not simply inherit their position: there was some way in which rising to leadership required the consent of others" (p. 29). In other words, what Stasavage is claiming is that many societies have not been autocratic. His examples show councils of elders, family leaders, and wealthy "big men" negotiating decisions with one another, sometimes with input from more lowly members of their villages or clan groupings. (The evidence, as he notes, is often very thin and requires speculative reconstruction.) It is encouraging, though not exactly surprising, that autocrats can't simply dominate people willy-nilly, particularly where (as Stasavage notes) agricultural practices and ecological features favor dispersed, small-scale production and other activity in which it is hard to establish the kinds

of surplus wealth and enslaved populations that characterized early cities and subsequent empires. This idea of negotiated consent among local elites as "democracy" disregards what is at stake in democracy: not diffuse consent, not a modicum of social mobility, but *rule* by the people who will live with the decisions. *Accepting* a basically stable form of rule is a much more modest standard than *constituting* the ruling power, which democracy enables majorities to do. Moreover, all of Stasavage's examples involve control of actual decision-making by a small number of prominent individuals who are also atop whatever social or economic hierarchies their small societies create. There is no hint here of the Greek recognition that democracy is a form of class rule, the rule of the poor or the ordinary people.

I think roughly the same about the arguments of Benjamin Isakhan and Stephen Stockwell, the authors of *The Secret History of Democracy* (New York: Palgrave Macmillan, 2011) and *The Edinburgh Companion to the History of Democracy* (Edinburgh, Scotland: Edinburgh University Press, 2012), both of whom seek to establish that "at various times and in various ways, people all over the world have come close to the democratic ideal" (*Edinburgh Companion*, p. 8), which they define as including some version of "citizenship" or political membership, a system of rights and rule of law, and a political process characterized by a mix of "contestation, cooperation, and participation" (*Edinburgh Companion*, pp. 6–7). Their examples, like Stasavage's, mainly describe consultative practices in relatively egalitarian and small-scale societies, consultation by monarchs, and oligarchic republics such as that of late-medieval Venice. Once again, it is encouraging to be spared the recurrent stereotype of world history as a parade of autocracy, but the material that Isakhan and Stockwell marshal highlights, against their intention, the distinctiveness of the democratic form derived from the Athenian model via revolutionary developments in Europe and its colonies. Putting the majority vote at the center of a mode of rule locates political power in a very different place, institutionally and socially, from elite consultation.

It is illuminating to consider what it would mean to give full institutional life to the "democratic" modes that these scholars identify across history. It would *not* mean majority rule but consultative oligarchy—a kind of social negotiation among groups, mediated by influential representatives, along with a general governmental practice of information gathering and "listening tours" of the populace. This is perhaps what democracy means to quite a few people today or might simply be what some would prefer.

5. Thomas Hobbes, *Leviathan*, chap. 13. With this and some other frequently reprinted works originally in English, I use chapters and other

internal divisions rather than a page reference specific to one edition. In this case, however, I have used the 1991 Cambridge University Press edition edited by Richard Tuck, in which Hobbes's famous line appears on p. 86. *Leviathan* was first published in London in 1651.

6. Hobbes's arguments are abstract, but anthropological and archaeological evidence suggests that interpersonal violence and intermittent massacres in small-scale warfare do plague small-scale communities with little of what we might think of as formal government. In any case, Hobbes was already writing in the seventeenth century for readers who, like us, lived in large, complex, and diverse societies and would have no way back to organic and small-scale community, even if they wanted it.

7. Hobbes observes that what he calls a commonwealth may be created by "institution," the process I have been describing, or "acquisition," that is, conquest. Chap. 20 in *Leviathan*, ed. Richard Tuck (Cambridge, UK: Cambridge University Press, 1991), pp. 138–145.

8. Thomas Hobbes, *On the Citizen*, chap. VI, sec. 2 ("each member"); chap. VII, sec. 5 ("When men"). I have relied on Richard Tuck's 1998 translation, the first into English in more than three hundred years of the Latin *De Cive*, which Hobbes first published in London in 1642. Hobbes also wrote in *Leviathan*, discussing the creation of political community from a multitude, "if the Representative consist of many men, the voice of the great number must be considered as the voice of them all." Chap. 16 in *Leviathan*, ed. Tuck, p. 114.

9. Hobbes, "Introduction," in *Leviathan*: "The Pacts and Covenants, by which the parts of this Body Politique were at first made, set together, and united, resemble that *Fiat*, or the *Let us make man*, pronounced by God in the Creation" (ed. Tuck, *Leviathan*, pp. 9–10); and Hobbes, *On the Citizen*, chap. VI, sec. 1.

10. Jean-Jacques Rousseau, *The Social Contract*, chap. I, sec. 6. With this frequently translated and republished classic, I refer to these consistent divisions of the text, rather than the pagination of a particular edition. My translations are those of Donald A. Cress, ed., contained in the Hackett edition of *The Basic Political Writings* (Indianapolis, IN: Hackett, 2011). The book was first published in 1762.

11. John Locke, *Second Treatise of Government* (1689).

12. Rousseau, *The Social Contract*, chap. I, sec. 1.

13. Rousseau, chap. I, sec. 6 ("total alienation"); chap. I, sec. 7 ("each individual"); chap. II, section 1 ("if the populace").

14. Rousseau, chap. III, sec. 15.

15. Rousseau, chap. I, sec. 9 ("it substitutes"); chap. I, sec. 8 ("obedience," "obeys only," "a moral quality").

16. Rousseau, chap. I, sec. 7.

17. Rousseau, *The Social Contract*, chap. I, sec. 7; and Bertrand Russell, *The History of Western Philosophy* (London: George Allen & Unwin, 1961), p. 671.

18. This idea can obviously go too far, and soon the sophistical policeman does appear. Do we force someone to be free by imprisoning him? Every time we imprison someone? I don't think so. An adequate standard of democratic citizenship should probably involve much less incarceration than the United States now practices and with much less of a skew by race and class. See Dorothy Roberts, "Abolition Constitutionalism," *Harvard Law Review*, vol. 133, no. 1, 2019, p. 1.

19. *U.S. Term Limits, Inc., v. Thornton*, 514 U.S. 779, 838 (1995); and *Federalist* Nos. 47–51.

20. Hobbes, *Leviathan*, chaps. 2–4, 12.

21. Not long after writing this chapter, I was pleased to see that Michael Oakeshott makes a similar point about the deeply imaginative character of Hobbes's work in his "Introduction" to *Leviathan*, reprinted in Oakeshott, *Rationalism in Politics and Other Essays* (Indianapolis, IN: Liberty Press, 1991; first printed in Blackwell Press ed. of *Leviathan*, 1946), pp. 221–294.

22. Benedict Anderson, *Imagined Communities: Reflections on the Origin and Spread of Nationalism* (New York: Verso, 1983).

CHAPTER 3: THE CONSTITUTION VERSUS DEMOCRACY

1. Inaugural address of Joseph R. Biden, Washington, DC, Jan. 20, 2021 (available at https://www.whitehouse.gov/briefing-room/speeches -remarks/2021/01/20/inaugural-address-by-president-joseph -r-biden-jr/); inaugural address of Barack H. Obama, Washington, DC, Jan. 20, 2009 (available at https://obamawhitehouse.archives.gov/blog/2009 /01/21/president-Barack-obamas-inaugural-address); inaugural address of George W. Bush, Washington, DC, Jan. 20, 2001 (available at https:// georgewbush-whitehouse.archives.gov/news/inaugural-address.html); inaugural address of George H. W. Bush, Washington, DC, Jan. 20, 1989 (available at https://avalon.law.yale.edu/20th_century/bush.asp); and inaugural address of Barack H. Obama, Washington, DC, Jan. 21, 2013 (available at https://obamawhitehouse.archives.gov/the-press-office /2013/01/21/inaugural-address-president-barack-obama).

2. In this situation, each state delegation has one vote, and Republican representatives dominated a majority of state delegations.

3. Joshua P. Zoffer and David Singh Grewal, "The Counter-Majoritarian Difficulty of a Minoritarian Judiciary," *California Law Review Online*, Oct. 2020 (available at https://www.californialawreview.org /counter-majoritarian-minoritarian-judiciary/).

4. See John Rees, *The Leveller Revolution: Radical Political Organization in England, 1640–1650* (London: Verso, 2016), pp. 209–210.

5. In the historical details and argument of this portion, I have drawn on and am strongly influenced by Richard Tuck's argument in *The Sleeping Sovereign: The Invention of Modern Democracy* (Cambridge, UK: Cambridge University Press, 2016). In previous work, David Grewal and I have explored the place of sovereignty in the American Constitution. See David Singh Grewal and Jedediah Purdy, "The Original Theory of Constitutionalism," *Yale Law Journal*, vol. 127, no. 3, Jan. 2018, pp. 664–705.

6. Michael Klarman, *The Founders' Coup: The Making of the United States Constitution* (New York: Oxford University Press, 2016). Klarman also makes a powerful case for the oligarchic roots of the Constitution. He writes: "The Antifederalists were not far off base when they charged the Framers with seeking to establish an aristocracy of sorts" (p. 607), and notes that the framers' mistrust of popular political judgment and preference to keep power in the hands of the "better sort" were constrained by the needs of ratification. Klarman also emphasizes that creditor interests were important in motivating the constitutional convention and that both the Constitution's structure and its specific provisions were designed to prevent inflationary policy and debt relief. The Constitution's architects assumed they were writing a document for a much less democratic society than later emerged. It was, for instance, a matter of historical chance that the framers, most of whom favored property requirements for voting, did not write those into the Constitution (p. 608). Madison's quote comes from *Federalist* No. 40.

7. *Federalist* No. 22 (Hamilton).

8. *Federalist* No. 22 (Hamilton) ("contradicts the fundamental"); No. 20 (Hamilton) ("a sovereignty over sovereigns").

9. I have learned a lot about the trade links of economic and political elites along the Atlantic coast of the colonies from legal historian Maeve Glass, whose 2016 doctoral dissertation in the Princeton history department, *These United States: A History of the Fracturing of America*, is the basis of an anticipated book.

10. It is also possible for amendments to be proposed by a convention requested by two-thirds of state legislatures, although Congress must act to call the convention, and for amendments once proposed to be approved by conventions called by their state legislatures. The first has never happened, the second only once (for the Twenty-first Amendment, repealing Prohibition).

11. *Federalist* No. 39 (Madison). In an important argument, Akhil Amar has argued that the principle of popular authorship implies that it should be possible to amend the Constitution outside the constraints of Article V. See Akhil Reed Amar, "The Consent of the Governed:

Constitutional Amendment Outside Article V," *Columbia Law Review*, vol. 94, 1994, p. 456.

An influential strand of constitutional theory (and political theory more generally) rejects the idea of popular sovereignty altogether and in particular the ambition of connecting popular sovereignty with constitutional authority. See Andrew Arato, *The Adventures of the Constituent Power* (New York: Oxford University Press, 2016). One objection to popular sovereignty is based in worry that it presents extremists and opportunists with an opportunity to seize the banner of "the people" and claim unlimited authority. I agree that the danger is real and explore it in my discussion of the Jacobin constitution during the French Revolution. I insist, and these critics of popular sovereignty agree, that what they call the constituent power—the power to make constitutional law—is incoherent if imagined as the free-floating possession of a whole people and must be embodied in an institutional decision procedure. Here, the critics argue that no decision procedure can claim a special relationship to "popular sovereignty" because in deeply plural societies any institution or set of decision-makers will represent only a fragment of the populace. Relatedly, they claim that an unbounded lawmaking power, such as popular sovereignty is often imagined to have, is—even with the best of intentions—the power of a potential dictator and that any power of some members of a plural society over others must be limited in a rational way. As Arato argues, then, popular sovereignty must become a "negative" principle, a reservation of social power to refuse or resist certain acts of the state in the name of the people who would suffer from them. Actual constituent power should be a "post-sovereign" deliberative process that seeks widespread support but does claim the special status of a sovereign. I suppose it is pretty clear that I disagree. Popular sovereignty, expressed in majority decisions on basic questions about the shape and limits of government power, seems to me a cogent and useful way of understanding the original and continuing role of the whole polity (which does not, of course, mean a unanimous or unitary polity) in setting the basic terms of its own law and collective life.

The democratic understanding of sovereignty solves, or at least suggests solutions to, some problems that are supposed to be fatal to the very idea of sovereignty. H. L. A. Hart famously argued that the idea of an omnipotent sovereign was incoherent because if today's sovereign could act in a way that bound tomorrow's sovereign, then tomorrow's sovereign would not be omnipotent; but if today's sovereign could not bind tomorrow's, then *it* would not be omnipotent. This is basically a theological point about the paradox supposed to attach to a certain conception of God, borrowed to claim that fundamental law is not illuminated by the addition of an idea of sovereignty. The democratic idea of popular sovereignty that I have been arguing for dissolves the paradox. The question has nothing to do with omnipotence over time because part of popular sovereignty is the consent of the living. A sovereign that could prevent future citizens from democratically changing their fundamental law would not be a popular sovereign in the democratic sense because it would have choked off the consent of future generations (as the US Constitution does, I argue).

As for the worry about sovereignty implying unlimited power, I have been clear that democratic rule is constrained by limitations that inhere in and protect democracy itself, including equal political rights, related rights (such as speech and organizing) that uphold political criticism and mobilization, and the repudiation of caste and of any politics that denies that some members of the polity are fully legitimate constituents of a potential ruling majority. When we come down to it, there is no a priori guarantee that any government will not hurt us or politics will not drive us mad. If such a guarantee were possible, it would not be by censuring certain uses of the concept of popular sovereignty. These dangers inhere in collective rule over the solutions to the inescapably shared questions that arise from our interdependence. We can't define them away, only set the *political* terms in which we will confront them.

I am also at odds with a position that understands popular sovereignty as a fluid principle of legitimacy that inheres organically in the people dispersed into what Hobbes called a multitude, with no specific institutional expression or decision procedure. See Andreas Kalyvas, "Constituent Power," in *Political Concepts: A Critical Lexicon*, ed. J. M. Bernstein (New York: Fordham University Press, 2018). While it is certainly true that people *do* mobilize in these terms, it is not true that there is reason to credit any particular claim to stand for the people. This means that I reject both the Romantic-radical image of free-running popular sovereignty that I have just described and also a much more politically temperate version of "democratic constitutionalism" that understands social movements as formulating constitutional claims that courts may then validly adopt as fundamental law. See Robert Post and Reva Siegel, "*Roe* Rage: Democratic Constitutionalism and Backlash," *Harvard Civil Rights-Civil Liberties Law Review*, vol. 42, 2007, p. 373. While in some registers this approach does no more than describe such mobilization in the spirit of political sociology, it readily becomes a normative apologia, in which decentered and open-ended mobilization is how "we" make constitutional law into "our law." See Jack M. Balkin, *Living Originalism* (Cambridge, MA: Harvard University Press, 2011). In my view, there is one uniquely democratic way to express popular sovereignty, which is through majoritarian procedures duly established as the vehicle of constituent power.

12. St. George Tucker, "Appendix," in *Blackstone's Commentaries, with Notes of Reference to the Constitution and Laws of the Federal Government of the United States and of the Commonwealth of Virginia*, vol. 1 (Philadelphia: William Young Birch and Abraham Small, 1803), pp. 172–173.

13. Thomas Paine, *The Rights of Man*, ed. Mark Philip (New York: Oxford University Press, 1995), p. 94; and James Wilson, *Works*, vol. 1, ed. Kermit L. Hall and Mark David Hall (Indianapolis, IN: Liberty Fund, 2007), p. 191.

14. My arguments about the undemocratic character of the Constitution have much in common with those that Sanford Levinson has developed for years. See Levinson, *Our Undemocratic Constitution* (New York: Oxford University Press, 2008). Another powerful recent statement of the antidemocratic role of the Supreme Court is in Nikolas Bowie, "The Contemporary Debate over Supreme Court Reform: Origins and Perspectives," testimony before the Presidential Commission on the Supreme Court of the United States, June 30, 2021.

15. *Prigg v. Pennsylvania*, 41 U.S. 536 (1842); The Civil Rights Cases, 109 U.S. 3 (1883); *Hammer v. Dagenhart*, 247 U.S. 251 (1918); *National Federation of Independent Business v. Sebelius*, 567 U.S. 519 (2012); and *Shelby County, Alabama v. Holder*, 133 S. Ct. 2612 (2013).

16. Scholars of constitutional law try to navigate this difficulty, not always self-consciously, in a variety of ways. Some argue that the Supreme Court's role in judicial review can be legitimate only if it restricts itself to facilitating democracy, with a focus on its institutional workings (voting rights, free speech) and some supplemental protection of the interests of groups that are systematically disserved by majoritarian institutions. See John Hart Ely, *Democracy and Distrust: A Theory of Judicial Review* (Cambridge, MA: Harvard University Press, 1980). Others essentially transform the definition of democracy from a majoritarian decision procedure to a system of political morality, in which judges are the ultimate interpreters of the principles of equal concern and respect for cocitizens. See Ronald Dworkin, *Law's Empire* (Cambridge, MA: Harvard University Press, 1986). Still others argue that judicial reinterpretation of fundamental law is authorized by an informal amendment process comprising political mobilization of particular focus, intensity, persistence, and scale but falls outside the formal requirements of the Constitution's Article V. See Bruce Ackerman, *We the People*, vol. 1 (Cambridge, MA: Harvard University Press, 1991). Taking the bull by the horns, Jeremy Waldron argues that, on the minimal democratic criterion that everyone's views should be accorded equal weight in resolving questions of political controversy, judicial review cannot be justified. See Waldron, "The Core of the Case Against Judicial Review," *Yale Law Journal*, vol. 115, 2005, p. 1346. All of

these approaches seem to me to be basically symptoms of the dilemma posed by a constitution that posits but quashes popular sovereignty.

17. Al Gore, On 2000 Election and Supreme Court Decision, interview with Charlie Rose, 92nd Street Y, Jan. 29, 2013 (available at https://www.92y.org/archives/former-vice-president-al-gore-on-2000-election-no-intermediate-step-between-a-final-supreme-court-decision-and-violent-revolution).

18. *Obergefell v. Hodges,* 576 U.S. 644 (2015).

19. *Brown v. Board of Education,* 347 U.S. 483 (1954).

20. *Obergefell v. Hodges,* 576 U.S. 644 (2015).

21. Aldo Schiavone, *The Invention of Law in the West* (Cambridge, MA: Harvard University Press, 2012), especially pp. 64–73, 105–130, 285–306.

22. *National Federation of Independent Business v. Sebelius,* 567 U.S. 519 (2012); and *Wickard v. Filburn,* 317 U.S. 111 (1942).

23. *Shelby County, Alabama v. Holder,* 133 S. Ct. 2612 (2013).

CHAPTER 4: CULTURE AND CONSENSUS

1. Edmund Burke, "On Conciliation with America," speech delivered in Parliament, March 22, 1775.

2. Alexis de Tocqueville, *Democracy in America,* trans. George Lawrence, ed. J. P. Mayer (New York: Harper and Row, 1969), pp. 250–251.

3. Tocqueville, *Democracy in America,* pp. 262–276, 531–572.

4. Henry Reeve, "Translator's Preface," in Tocqueville, *Democracy in America,* vol. 1, 3rd ed. (London: Saunders & Otley, 1838), pp. v–vi ("the book"); vi ("the necessity"); vii ("the democratic element").

5. John Canfield Spencer, "Preface," in Tocqueville, *Democracy in America,* vol. 1 (New York: Henry G. Langley, 1845), pp. ix ("in the manners," "the means of preventing"); x ("manners, habits, and opinions").

6. Spencer, "Preface," p. vii.

7. *Dred Scott v. Sandford,* 60 U.S. 393 (1857); John Morgan, "Introduction" to Alexis de Tocqueville, *Democracy in America* (New York: Colonial Press, 1899), p. vii.

8. Morgan, "Introduction," p. vi.

9. The Civil Rights Cases, 109 U.S. 3 (1883); *Plessy v. Ferguson,* 163 U.S. 537 (1896).

10. Francis Lieber, *On Civil Liberty and Self-Government,* 3rd ed., ed. Theodore D. Woolsey (Philadelphia: J. B. Lippincott, 1874), pp. 18 ("the idol"); 248 ("without local"); 249–250 ("it consists in"); 250 ("the people-despot").

11. Lieber, *Civil Liberty and Self-Government,* pp. 21 ("We belong"); 261 ("means our own"). On Lieber's nationalism, see Frank Friedel, *Francis*

Lieber: Nineteenth-Century Liberal, one of the few studies of Lieber (Baton Rouge: Louisiana State University Press, 1947), pp. 161, 203, 389. On the role of nationalism in the liberalism of Lieber's German formation, see James Q. Whitman, *The Legacy of Roman Law in the German Romantic Era: Historical Vision and Legal Change* (Princeton, NJ: Princeton University Press, 1990), pp. 67–150.

12. Aldo Schiavone, *The Invention of Law in the West* (Cambridge, MA: Harvard University Press, 2012), pp. 85–98.

13. Robert A. Dahl, *Pluralist Democracy in the United States: Conflict and Consent* (Chicago: Rand, McNally, 1967), pp. 326 ("in the United States"); 329–334 (beliefs about personal prospects and national institutions); 331–333 (identification as middle class, beliefs about the economy).

14. Dahl, *Pluralist Democracy,* p. 329.

15. Dahl, p. 428.

16. See Michel J. Crozier, Samuel P. Huntington, and Joji Watanuki, *The Crisis of Democracy: Report on the Governability of Democracies to the Trilateral Commission* (New York: New York University Press, 1975).

17. Crozier, Huntington, and Watanuki, *Crisis of Democracy,* p. 7.

18. Crozier et al., p. 7.

19. For a discussion of the "legitimation crisis" of the early 1970s, see Wolfgang Streeck, *Buying Time: The Delayed Crisis of Democratic Capitalism* (New York: Verso, 2014).

20. Robert Dahl, *How Democratic Is the American Constitution?* (New Haven, CT: Yale University Press, 2001).

21. Dahl tended to see proportional systems as fairer.

22. Samuel P. Huntington, *Who Are We? America's Great Debate* (New York: Free Press, 2004), p. 314.

CHAPTER 5: NORMS FROM NOWHERE

1. Steven Levitsky and Daniel Ziblatt, *How Democracies Die* (New York: Crown, 2018), p. 195.

2. The "Declaration of Constitutional Principles," better known as the Southern Manifesto, was memorialized in the *Congressional Record,* 84th Congress, 2nd Session, vol. 102, part 4 (Washington, DC: Governmental Printing Office, 1956). On the place of custom and norms in the desegregation arguments even among liberals, see David M. O'Brien, *Justice Robert H. Jackson's Unpublished Opinion in* Brown v. Board: *Conflict, Compromise, and Constitutional Interpretation* (Lawrence: University Press of Kansas, 2017). On the constitutional norm breaking of the New Deal and the ways its opponents used it to try to delegitimate Roosevelt's programs, see Kim Phillips-Fein, *Invisible Hands: The Businessmen's Crusade Against the New Deal* (New York: W. W. Norton, 2011).

3. Levitsky and Ziblatt rightly highlighted these alarming portents in *How Democracies Die*, pp. 195–197.

CHAPTER 6: THE SOVEREIGN MARKET

1. "Obama Doesn't 'Begrudge' Dimon, Blankfein, over Pay," Reuters, Feb. 10, 2010 (available at https://www.reuters.com/article/us-obama-financial-bonuses/obama-doesnt-begrudge-dimon-blankfein-over-pay-id USTRE6193EP20100211).

2. Ronald Reagan, second inaugural address, Washington, DC, Jan. 21, 1985 (available at https://avalon.law.yale.edu/20th_century/reagan2.asp); and Reagan, first inaugural address, Washington, DC, Jan. 21, 1981 (available at https://avalon.law.yale.edu/20th_century/reagan1.asp).

3. William Leggett, "True Functions of Government," *Evening Post*, Nov. 21, 1834; and Eric Foner, *Reconstruction: American's Unfinished Revolution, 1863–1877* (New York: HarperCollins, 1988), pp. 155, 164.

4. Reagan, second inaugural address.

5. Woodrow Wilson, first inaugural address, Washington, DC, March 4, 1913; Franklin Delano Roosevelt, speech at the Commonwealth Club, San Francisco, Sept. 23, 1932; and W. E. B. Du Bois, *Black Reconstruction* (New York: Russell and Russell, 1962), p. 182.

6. Binyamin Appelbaum, "Blame Economists for the Mess We're In," *New York Times*, Aug. 24, 2019.

7. Du Bois, *Black Reconstruction*, p. 14.

8. Adam Smith, *The Wealth of Nations*, book I, chap. 1. Although, as indicated earlier, I use Smith's internal organization rather than page numbers in citing his oft-reprinted books, I have drawn on the Liberty Fund editions (Indianapolis, IN, 1982) for all quotes from *The Wealth of Nations, Lectures on Jurisprudence*, and *The Theory of Moral Sentiments*. These are widely available in inexpensive, high-quality editions, and the volumes' text is also available for free online.

9. Ralph Waldo Emerson's "Nature," first published in 1836, is a splendid example of how the world came to expect continuing and revolutionary technological transformation in the sixty years after Smith wrote: "He no longer waits for favoring gales, but by means of steam, he realizes the fable of Aeolus's bag, and carries the two and thirty winds in the boiler of his boat. To diminish friction, he paves the road with iron bars, and mounting a coach with a ship-load of men, animals, and merchandise behind him, he darts through the country, from town to town, like an eagle or a swallow through the air. By the aggregate of these aids, how is the face of the world changed, from the era of Noah to that of Napoleon!" Ralph Waldo Emerson, *Works*, vol. 1 (Boston and New York: Houghton

Mifflin, 1883), p. 19. By these technological landmarks, Smith's world was closer to Noah's than to Napoleon's.

10. Smith, *The Wealth of Nations,* book I, chap. 2.

11. Smith, book V, chap. 1.

12. Adam Smith, *Lectures on Jurisprudence* (first published 1763), book I, chap. 1.

13. Smith, *Lectures on Jurisprudence,* book I, chap. 1 ("our sympathy"); book I, chap. 2 ("Till there be property," "his son naturally"); and Smith, *The Theory of Moral Sentiments* (first published 1759), book III, chap. 2 ("Upon this disposition").

14. Smith, *The Theory of Moral Sentiments,* book II, chap. 3.

15. Smith, book II, chap. 2.

16. Smith, *Lectures on Jurisprudence,* book I, chap. 1.

17. Edmund S. Morgan, *American Slavery, American Freedom: The Ordeal of Colonial Virginia* (New York: W. W. Norton, 1975); and Aziz Rana, *The Two Faces of American Freedom* (Cambridge, MA: Harvard University Press, 2010).

18. The Slaughterhouse Cases, 83 U.S. 38 (1872).

19. See Friedrich Hayek, "Competition as a Discovery Procedure," in *The Essence of Hayek,* ed. Chiaki Nishiyama and Kurt Leube (Stanford, CA: Hoover Institution Press, 1984), pp. 254–264; and Hayek, "The Use of Knowledge in Society," in *The Essence of Hayek,* pp. 211–223.

20. Hayek, "The Use of Knowledge in Society," in *The Essence of Hayek,* pp. 211–223.

21. Hayek, "Principles of a Liberal Social Order," pp. 363–381.

22. Hayek, *Law, Legislation, and Liberty,* vol. 1 (Chicago: University of Chicago Press, 1973), pp. 35–123.

23. See Hayek, "Equality, Value, and Merit," in *The Essence of Hayek,* pp. 331–348.

24. Hayek, "'Social' or Distributive Justice," p. 101.

25. Hayek, "Whither Democracy?" pp. 357–358; and Hayek, *The Constitution of Liberty* (Chicago: University of Chicago Press, 1960). The image of "encasement" is borrowed from Quinn Slobodian's invaluable study, *The Globalists: The End of Empire and the Birth of Neoliberalism* (Cambridge, MA: Harvard University Press, 2018). The one thing I think Slobodian does not always state clearly is that the program of Hayek and his allies was not just to create market institutions "insulated from democratic decision making" (p. 12) but to redefine democracy in a way that incorporated these limitations as part of the functional and moral logic of self-governance.

CHAPTER 7: DEMOCRACY AND/OR CAPITALISM

1. Isabella Kiminska, "Mythbusting Finance 2.0," *Financial Times*, Oct. 7, 2014 (available at https://ftalphaville.ft.com/2014/10/07/1998142 /mythbusting-finance-2-0/); and April Dembosky, "Monster Comes to Facebook," *Financial Times*, June 26, 2011 (available at https://www.ft .com/content/970ea188-4f1e-35fc-89b0-917597a4f227).

2. Rosabeth Moss Kanter, "Apple and the Leadership Pause," *Harvard Business Review*, April 5, 2010 (available at https://hbr.org/2010/04/ apple-and-the-leadership-pause.html); The FT View, "A Fresh Approach: The World Bank is Right to Swap Dogma for Data," *Financial Times*, opin-ion, Oct. 3, 2010 (available at https://www.ft.com/content/eccc6794-cf1c -11df-9be2-00144feab49a); Claire Cain Miller, "Another Start-Up Wants to Democratize Investing," *New York Times*, Dec. 9, 2009 (available at https:// bits.blogs.nytimes.com/2009/12/09/another-startup-wants-to-democ ratize-investing/); and Natasha Singer, "The Democratization of Plastic Surgery," *New York Times*, Aug. 17, 2007 (available at https://www.nytimes .com/2007/08/17/business/worldbusiness/17iht-surgery.4.7159164 .html?searchResultPosition=3).

3. Thomas Piketty, *Capital in the 21st Century*, trans. Arthur Goldham-mer (Cambridge, MA: Harvard University Press, 2014); and Jefferson Cowie, *The Great Exception: The New Deal and the Limits of American Politics* (Princeton, NJ: Princeton University Press, 2016).

4. Simon Kuznets, "Economic Growth and Income Inequality," *Ameri-can Economic Review*, vol. 45, 1955, p. 1; Piketty, *Capital in the 21st Century*, pp. 13–15 (discussing importance of Kuznets); and John Kenneth Gal-braith, *The Affluent Society* (Boston: Houghton Mifflin, 1958).

5. See John Rawls, *A Theory of Justice* (Cambridge, MA: Harvard Uni-versity Press, 1971), pp. 3–17.

6. Katrina Forrester, *In the Shadow of Justice: Postwar Liberalism and the Remaking of Political Philosophy* (Princeton, NJ: Princeton University Press, 2019). The characterization of Rawls's self-presentation can be traced through his work, as Forrester notes. Indeed, he informed readers in his preface: "What I have attempted to do is to generalize and carry to a higher order of abstraction the traditional theory of the social contract as represented by Locke, Rousseau, and Kant. . . . The theory that results is highly Kantian in nature." Rawls, *A Theory of Justice*, p. viii. It was also a major theme of Philosophy 171, the final lecture course he taught at Harvard in the spring of 1994.

7. Many New Deal programs were, notoriously, crafted to accommo-date that region's racial caste economy by excluding areas in which Black workers were concentrated, such as agricultural and household work. See Ira Katznelson, *Fear Itself: The New Deal and the Origins of Our Time* (New

York: W. W. Norton, 2013). Nonetheless, Black workers in the North, including the many who migrated after World War II, drove increases in Black incomes over the decades in which the New Deal's legacy shaped the economy. See Thomas N. Maloney, "African Americans in the Twentieth Century," in *Encyclopedia of Economic and Business History*, ed. Robert Whaples, Economic History Association, EH.net (available at https://eh.net/encyclopedia/african-americans-in-the-twentieth-century/). For a recent review of the racial wealth gap in the United States, see Kriston McIntosh et al., "Examining the Black-White Wealth Gap," Brookings Institution, Feb. 27, 2020 (available at https://www.brookings.edu/blog/up-front/2020/02/27/examining-the-black-white-wealth-gap/). For recent examinations of the ways racial hierarchy and effective segregation are maintained even in formally "color-blind" regimes, see Keeanga-Yamahtta Taylor, *Race for Profit: How Banks and the Real Estate Industry Undermined Black Homeownership* (Chapel Hill: University of North Carolina Press, 2019); and Monica C. Bell, "Anti-Segregation Policing," *New York University Law Review*, vol. 95, no. 3, June 2020, pp. 650–765 (available at https://www.nyulawreview.org/wp-content/uploads/2020/06/NYULawReview-Volume-95-Issue-3-Bell.pdf).

8. These figures come from the Bureau of Labor Statistics and may be found in Heidi Shierholz and Margaret Poydock, "Continued Surge in Strike Activity Signals Worker Dissatisfaction with Wage Growth," Economic Policy Institute, Feb. 11, 2020 (available at https://www.epi.org/publication/continued-surge-in-strike-activity/).

9. Lewis Powell, "Attack on American Free Enterprise System," confidential memorandum to Eugene B. Sydnor, Chamber of Commerce, Aug. 23, 1971 (available at https://scholarlycommons.law.wlu.edu/powellmemo/1/). For a discussion of some of the institutions and networks that were important to this development, see Steven M. Teles, *The Rise of the Conservative Legal Movement* (Princeton, NJ: Princeton University Press, 2008).

10. See Ramya M. Vijaya, "Broken Buffer: How Trade Adjustment Assistance Fails American Workers," Demos, 2010 (available at https://paperzz.com/doc/8836138/document).

11. Blair made these remarks at the British Labour Party Conference in September 2005 (transcript available at https://www.theguardian.com/uk/2005/sep/27/labourconference.speeches).

12. David Autor et al., "Importing Political Polarization? The Electoral Consequences of Rising Trade Exposure," *American Economic Review*, vol. 110, no. 10, 2020, pp. 3139–3183. Every wave of financial crisis has brought in reformers, such as the influential economists Joseph Stiglitz and Jeffrey Sachs, who emerged in the late 1990s as scourges of the International Monetary Fund and the broader vision of global marketization.

13. This paragraph essentially summarizes the argument of *Being America*, a study of American sensibility and "global culture" that I published in 2003. Jedediah Purdy, *Being America: Liberty, Commerce, and Violence in an American World* (New York: Knopf, 2003).

14. Many voices echoed aspects of the rough-and-ready modernization theory distilled in this paragraph and the previous two. The source for one-stop shoppers is Thomas Friedman, *The Lexus and the Olive Tree: Understanding Globalization* (New York: Picador, 1999). Although Friedman presented globalization as inspiring traditionalist forms of resistance, "the olive tree," the dominant story, is about the logic of its forward march.

15. This definition of capitalism is associated with the late Ellen Meiksins Wood and Robert Brenner, among others. Wood stated it with particular clarity in a 2002 exchange with Adolph Reed Jr., Steven Gregory, and Maurice Zeitlin, an exchange whose broader issues about the intersection of race and capitalism are not my immediate topic here: "Capitalism is a system in which economic actors . . . depend on the market for the most basic conditions of their self-reproduction" (available at https://advancethestruggle.wordpress.com/2009/06/11/how-does-race-relate-to-class-a-debate/).

16. See Jim Zarroli, "Clinton Highlights Billionaires' Support as a Way to Try to Undermine Trump," *All Things Considered*, Aug. 3, 2016 (available at https://www.npr.org/2016/08/03/488568418/hillary-clinton-uses-billionaire-supporters-to-undermine-donald-trump). An ABC News Politics tweet from October 26, 2016, quotes Clinton as saying, "I love having the support of real billionaires," but it does not have a live link, and the quote otherwise lives only on highly partisan sites. See https://twitter.com/abcpolitics/status/791317075503353856?lang=en.

17. Statistic from a *Time* magazine 2000 survey, cited in David Brooks, "The Triumph of Hope over Self-Interest," *New York Times*, Jan. 13, 2003.

18. See Lauren Berlant, *Cruel Optimism* (Durham, NC: Duke University Press, 2011). On Stoicism, see Nellie Bowles, "Why Is Silicon Valley So Obsessed with the Virtue of Suffering?" *New York Times*, March 26, 2019 (available at https://www.nytimes.com/2019/03/26/style/silicon-valley-stoics.html). I won't belabor the corporate adoption of mindfulness, which, if readers haven't encountered it, they can get acquainted with in a few keystrokes.

19. Major works on the self under capitalism and the colonization of nonmarket domains by market imperatives and concepts include Daniel Bell, *The Cultural Contradictions of Capitalism* (New York: Basic Books, 1976); Fred Hirsch, *Social Limits to Growth* (Cambridge, MA: Harvard University Press, 1976); and, more popularly, Thomas Frank, *One Market Under God* (New York: Anchor Books, 2000).

20. On the political attitudes of the rich, see Benjamin I. Page, Larry M. Bartels, and Jason Seawright, "Democracy and the Policy Preferences of Wealthy Americans," *Perspectives on Politics*, vol. 11, 2013, pp. 57–64. Based on interviews with eighty-three wealthy individuals in the Chicago area, this finding cannot really be considered authoritative, but this is a question where data are scarce. On the class composition of Congress, see Nicholas Carnes, *White-Collar Government: The Hidden Role of Class in Economic Policy-Making* (Chicago: University of Chicago Press, 2013), pp. 7–20. On whose views have political impact, see Martin Gilens and Benjamin I. Page, "Testing Theories of American Politics: Elites, Interest Groups, and Average Citizens," *Perspectives on Politics*, vol. 12, 2014, p. 572. A great deal more disheartening material is available in Larry M. Bartels, *Unequal Democracy: The Political Economy of the New Gilded Age*, 2nd ed. (Princeton, NJ: Princeton University Press, 2016).

21. Many people have made this observation over the years, saliently by those who have had experience in turn as practicing politicians, scholars, and activists, notably Robert Reich, Lawrence Lessig, and Zephyr Teachout. Particularly illuminating is Teachout's discussion of structural corruption in Teachout, *Corruption in America* (Cambridge, MA: Harvard University Press, 2014).

22. Numbers of this sort are reliably available at the campaign finance data site Open Secrets; see https://www.opensecrets.org/pres16.

23. Louis. D. Brandeis, "The Opportunity in the Law," *American Law Review*, vol. 39, 1905, p. 562.

24. See David Singh Grewal, *Network Power: The Social Dynamics of Globalization* (New Haven, CT: Yale University Press, 2008). For the new antitrust scholarship, see Lina M. Khan, "Amazon's Antitrust Paradox," *Yale Law Journal*, vol. 126, 2017, p. 710; and Tim Wu, *The Curse of Bigness: Antitrust in the New Gilded Age* (New York: Columbia Global Reports, 2018). Brandeis argued in a 1933 Supreme Court opinion that "only through participation by the many in the responsibilities and determinations of business can Americans secure the moral and intellectual development which is essential to the maintenance of liberty," *Louis K. Liggett Co. v. Lee*, 288 U.S. 517, 580 (1933). The most thorough and telling treatment of how law creates and protects capital as a special form of value and power is Katharina Pistor, *The Code of Capital: How the Law Creates Wealth and Inequality* (Princeton, NJ: Princeton University Press, 2019).

25. See Sen. Edmund Muskie, "A Whole Society," speech, Fairmount Park, Philadelphia, April 22, 1970, in *Congressional Record*, 93rd Congress, 2nd Session, vol. 120, part 11 (Washington, DC: Governmental Printing Office, 1974), pp. 324–325. I have detailed some of these connections in Jedediah Purdy, "The Long Environmental Justice Movement,"

Ecology Law Quarterly, vol. 44, 2018, p. 809. Of course, not all versions of the political economy of nature were what we would think of today as ecologically minded: more exploitative and development-oriented ideas about the natural world were central to the American civic culture of the nineteenth century, and these too were about political economy. The manifest destiny of an expansive capitalist republic and empire was closely tied up with the imperative to timber, plough, mine, and build. These competing ideological visions of the natural world, and the human place in it, were not just battles of words but also had the grip and bite of power because they were written into laws that handed land off to settlers or railroads, dedicated it to timbering or parks or wilderness, and threaded it with roads and canals or left it open as habitat. These laws made landscapes and remade ecosystems. I have addressed these themes in Jedediah Purdy, *After Nature: A Politics for the Anthropocene* (Cambridge, MA: Harvard University Press, 2015). I also recommend to readers Dorceta Taylor, *The Rise of the American Conservation Movement* (Durham, NC: Duke University Press, 2016).

26. See David Leonhardt, "A Battle over the Costs of Global Warming," *New York Times*, Feb. 21, 2007.

27. This idea finds its clearest expression in Justice Anthony Kennedy's opinion in *Citizens United v. Federal Election Commission*, 568 U.S. 310 (2010).

28. This idea is, remarkably enough, *also* present in *Citizens United*, and is also clearly expressed in *Arizona Free Enterprise Club v. Bennett*, 564 U.S. 721 (2011); and *McCutcheon v. Federal Election Commission*, 572 U.S. 185 (2014). I have gone into this ideational structure in more textual detail in Jedediah Purdy, "Beyond the Bosses' Constitution: The First Amendment and Class Entrenchment," *Columbia Law Review*, vol. 118, 2018, p. 2161.

CHAPTER 8: VOICES AND VOTES

1. Benjamin Constant, "The Liberty of the Ancients Compared with That of the Moderns," speech, Athenee Royal, Paris, 1819, in *Constant: Political Writings*, ed. and trans. Biancamaria Fontana (Cambridge, UK: Cambridge University Press, 1988), p. 314.

2. I was in the park at the time, participating in the community microphone. Afterward, I wrote up detailed notes, which is the basis of this description.

3. Emmanuel Sieyès, "What Is the Third Estate?" (first published Jan. 1789), chap. 1.

4. Constant, "The Liberty of the Ancients," in *Constant*, pp. 311–312.

5. Constant, pp. 314–316.

6. Constant, pp. 309 ("the only one," "totally unknown"); 310 ("discovery of the moderns"); 311 ("right to exercise"); 312 ("the individual").

7. Constant, pp. 325–326 ("The representative system").

8. Recent scholarship has suggested there was more protection of private interests for Greek citizens than Constant imagined, but this is not really the issue here.

9. Constant, pp. 317 ("who had themselves failed"); 318 ("by transposing"); 320 ("Free institutions").

10. Constant, p. 317 ("an indefinable" and "noble and generous").

11. Isaiah Berlin, "Two Concepts of Liberty," in *The Property Study of Mankind: An Anthology of Essays*, ed. Henry Hardy (New York: Farrar, Straus, and Giroux, 1997), p. 234. Berlin makes more of an antipolitical liberal of Constant than the text itself supports: Constant presents his goal as a new synthesis of ancient and modern spirits of politics, including active engagement by citizens.

12. Daniela Cammack, "Representation in Ancient Greek Democracy" (under review at the time of writing, available at https://www.daniela cammack.com/papers).

13. Frank Ankersmit, "Synecdochal and Metaphorical Political Representation: Then and Now," in *Creating Political Presence: The New Politics of Democratic Representation,* ed. Dario Castiglione and Johannes Pollak (Chicago: University of Chicago Press, 2019), pp. 236–237.

14. Constant, *Constant,* p. 316.

15. This definition of political equality shows up, for instance, in James Fishkin, *When the People Speak: Deliberative Democracy and Public Consultation* (New York: Oxford University Press, 2011), p. 43: "The root notion of political equality is the equal consideration of political preferences. . . . A key metric is captured by the notion of equal voting power. The basic idea is that if we imagine that each citizen has an equal likelihood of supporting each alternative . . . then the system ought to give each citizen an equal likelihood of being the decisive voter"; and Niko Kolodny, "Rule Over None II: Social Equality and the Justification of Democracy," *Philosophy and Public Affairs,* vol. 42, 2014, pp. 320–321 (defining political equality as "equal a priori chances of being decisive over the decision"). My problem with this definition is what Kolodny regards as its strength: although it implies one person, one vote, it doesn't imply a majoritarian decision procedure in any particular decision, much less majority rule. An equal a priori chance at decisive influence (generally almost zero in real life, as Kolodny notes) can be achieved in various ways of translating votes into decisions and, indeed, via lottery.

16. See Richard Tuck, *Free Riding* (Cambridge, MA: Harvard University Press, 2008).

CHAPTER 9: IF DEMOCRACY IS THE ANSWER, WHO ASKS THE QUESTION?

1. Walter Lippmann, *Public Opinion* (New York: Harcourt, Brace, 1927), pp. 228 ("The number"); 231–232 ("A concrete"); and Robert Michels, *Political Parties*, trans. Eden and Cedar Papul (Glencoe, IL: Free Press, 1915).

2. Lippmann, *Public Opinion*, pp. 206–207.

3. Shoshana Zuboff, "You Are Now Remotely Controlled," *New York Times*, Jan. 24, 2020 (available at https://www.nytimes.com/2020/01/24 /opinion/sunday/surveillance-capitalism.html); and Lippmann, *Public Opinion*, p. 248.

4. John Stuart Mill, "On Liberty," in *On Liberty and Other Essays*, ed. John Gray (New York: Oxford University Press, 1991), pp. 8–9.

5. Alexis de Tocqueville, *Democracy in America*, ed. J. P. Mayer, trans. George Lawrence (New York: Harper and Row, 1969), pp. 255–256.

6. Jean-Jacques Rousseau, "Discourse on Inequality," in *Basic Political Writings*, 2nd ed., trans. and ed. Donald A. Cress (Indianapolis, IN: Hackett, 2011), p. 91.

7. Tocqueville, *Democracy in America*, pp. 509–528.

8. Lippmann, *Public Opinion*, p. 197 ("oversoul").

9. John Dewey, *The Public and Its Problems* (New York: Henry Holt, 1927).

10. Theda Skocpol and Vanessa Williamson, *The Tea Party and the Remaking of Republican Conservatism* (New York: Oxford University Press, 2016).

11. Leah Gose and Theda Skocpol, "Resist, Persist, and Transform: The Emergence and Impact of Grassroots Resistance Groups Opposing the Trump Presidency," *Mobilization: An International Journal*, vol. 2, no. 3, 2019, pp. 293–317; and E. E. Schattschneider, *The Semisovereign People: A Realist's View of Democracy in America* (Hinsdale, IL: Dryden Press, 1975), pp. 34–35.

12. E. E. Schattschneider, *Party Government: American Government in Action* (New York: Routledge, 2017), pp. 52 ("the people are"); 208 ("Party government").

13. See Helene Landemore, *Open Democracy: Reinventing Popular Rule for the Twenty-First Century* (Princeton, NJ: Princeton University Press, 2020).

CHAPTER 10: WHO ARE THE PEOPLE?

1. See Jan-Werner Müller, *What Is Populism?* (Philadelphia: University of Pennsylvania Press, 2016), chap. 22.

2. See Pew Research Center, "U.S. Unauthorized Immigrant Population Estimates, by State, 2016" (available at https://www.pewresearch .org/hispanic/interactives/u-s-unauthorized-immigrants-by-state/). These numbers are from 2016 and are for the total population, including children, so they somewhat overstate the number of people excluded from voting. Authorized immigrant totals: Bryan Baker, "Estimates of the Lawful Permanent Resident Population of the United States and the Subpopulation Eligible to Naturalize," Department of Homeland Security, Sept. 2019 (available at https://www.dhs.gov/sites/default/files /publications/immigration-statistics/Pop_Estimate/LPR/lpr_population _estimates_2015_-_2019.pdf.pdf).

3. The salience of Maurras's ideas in a new era of political nationalism has struck some observers, both those more and those less sympathetic to his thought. See Emma-Kate Symons, "Steve Bannon Loves France," *Politico*, March 22, 2017 (available at https://www.politico.eu/article/steve -bannons-french-marine-le-pen-front-national-donald-trump-far-right -populism-inspiration/); and Nathan Pinkoski, "The Revenge of Maurras," *First Things*, Nov. 2019 (available at https://www.firstthings.com /article/2019/11/the-revenge-of-maurras). Here I don't mean to engage Maurras in any serious way but to use his notorious phrase to capture a *way* of claiming the authority of the people, one that Jan-Werner Müller limns in his valuable *What Is Populism?* (Philadelphia: University of Pennsylvania Press, 2016): an appeal to an idea that some part of the actual people is in fact the "whole" or "real" people for purposes of political authority and moral standing.

4. *Congressional Record*, 84th Congress, 2nd Session, vol. 102, part 4 (March 12, 1956).

5. C. Vann Woodward, *Origins of the New South* (Baton Rouge: Louisiana State University Press, 1951), p. 349.

6. John Locke, "Some Considerations of the Consequences of Lowering of Interest" (1692), quoted in Peter Laslett, *The World We Have Lost* (London: Metheun, 1965), p. 51.

7. C. Vann Woodward, *The Strange Career of Jim Crow* (New York: Oxford University Press, 1965), p. 44 (two thousand white farmers); and Woodward, *Origins of the New South*, p. 257 ("They are in the ditch"). Woodward used the same quote in his *Strange Career of Jim Crow* (p. 43), illustrating the populist "equalitarianism of want and poverty" (p. 42).

8. Woodward, *Origins of the New South*, p. 345 (fall in voting numbers); and Barbara J. Fields, "'Origins of the New South' and the Negro Question," *Journal of Southern History*, vol. 74, no. 4, 2001, pp. 811–826, 815.

9. See Michael Wines and Alan Blinder, "Federal Appeals Court Strikes Down North Carolina Voter ID Requirement," *New York Times*, July 29, 2016 (available at https://www.nytimes.com/2016/07/30/us

/federal-appeals-court-strikes-down-north-carolina-voter-id-provision
.html).

10. In *Neither Settler nor Native: The Making and Unmaking of Permanent
Minorities* (Cambridge, MA: Harvard University Press, 2020), Mahmood
Mamdani urges a project he calls "decolonizing the political," which for
him means "upsetting the permanent majority and minority identities
that define the contours of the nation-state" and "discarding [political
modernity's] divisive identities" (pp. 20–21). I agree with him. It seems
to me that the democratic promise rests on the prospect of there being
no permanent majorities or permanent minorities, almost as surely as it
meant, for Lincoln, "no slaves and no masters." We may part company in
our views of the actual democratic legacy of the United States. Mamdani
defines "colonization as the making of permanent minorities and their
maintenance through the polarization of identity" and states that "the
political is colonized in North America. . . . The United States emerges
as the model modern colony from which the others—the Nazis, white
power in South Africa, the British in Sudan, and Zionists—learned"
(p. 4). I agree instead with Aziz Rana who sees the exclusionary and
subordinating aspects of the American polity as one-half of a dialectic, in
which hierarchy has always been at odds with the principle and potential
of universal citizenship, and states in *The Two Faces of American Freedom*
(Cambridge, MA: Harvard University Press, 2010): "In emphasizing how
settlerism set the ideological and structural parameters for collective life,
my point is decidedly not to demean or reject the past. Our accounts of
liberty may well have emerged precisely in the context of slavery and native expropriation. These contexts were the living antithesis of freedom's
antithesis: bondage and servitude. However, any one-sided rejection of
settlerism, due to its brand of Anglo supremacy and social subordina-
tion, would necessarily ignore how such circumstances gave birth to a
liberating vision of collective possibility . . . a new, universal, and non-
imperial American polity. In a sense, they suggested the real exceptionalism of the American project: the effort to strip republican ideals of
their oppressive roots and to make free citizenship broadly accessible to
all" (p. 14).

Rana is developing here a dialectical view that Edmund S. Morgan
propounded in 1975 in *American Slavery, American Freedom: The Ordeal of
Colonial Virginia* (New York: W. W. Norton): "Racism made it possible
for white Virginians to develop a devotion to the equality that English
republicans had declared to be the soul of liberty . . . by lumping Indi-
ans, mulattoes, and Negroes into a single pariah class, Virginians had
paved the way for a similar lumping of small and large planters in a single master class" (p. 386). As Morgan puts it, the fused history raises the
question: "Is America still colonial Virginia writ large?" I agree with Rana

that the question is as much political as empirical, a paradigm of the challenge of democracy.

11. Nadia Urbinati, *Democracy Disfigured: Opinion, Truth, and the People* (Cambridge, MA: Harvard University Press, 2014).

12. Reader, I was there.

CHAPTER 11: DEMOCRATIZING DEMOCRACY (AND EVERYTHING ELSE)

1. Christopher Achen and Larry Bartels, *Democracy for Realists: Why Elections Do Not Produce Responsive Government* (Princeton, NJ: Princeton University Press, 2016).

2. See Jan-Werner Müller, *Democracy Rules* (New York: Farrar, Straus and Giroux, 2021).

3. The comparison to grammar isn't an opaque thought: much of grammar is tacit but binding. But politics isn't really like language in this way: we don't necessarily produce shared codes just by rubbing against each other long enough.

4. See Schattschneider, *The Semi-Sovereign People* (Hinsdale, IL: Dryden Press, 1975), pp. 113–125.

5. See Tocqueville, *Democracy in America*, trans. George Lawrence, ed. J. P. Mayer (New York: Harper and Row, 1969), pp. 317–407. It is worth highlighting the strength of Tocqueville's own denunciation of slavery. He called the situation in the South "the order of nature overthrown" and wrote "all my hatred is concentrated against those who, after a thousand years of equality, introduced slavery into the world again" (p. 363). Having said that, his pessimism about reform and quickness to see slaveholders as simply trapped in the system reflected his acceptance of culture and race as bases of political order. On the American construction of race, see Cheryl I. Harris, "Whiteness as Property," *Harvard Law Review*, vol. 106, no. 8, 1993, pp. 1707–1791; and Nell Irvin Painter, *The History of White People* (New York: W. W. Norton, 2010).

6. Du Bois, *Black Reconstruction* (New York: Russell and Russell, 1962), p. 182.

7. Lowe's exact words, spoken in Parliament, were more condescending: "I believe it will be absolutely necessary that you should prevail on our future masters to learn their letters." *Hansard*, 3rd series, vol. 188, col. 1549, July 15, 1867. I have rendered the quote as it was soon popularly received and has been remembered because, quite apart from its origin, it captures an essential social and ethical dynamic of democracy: having power over one another, we also have reason to care about one another's knowledge and experience of the world. Democrats cannot afford to be strangers to one another—not too radically or for too long, anyway.

8. See Jonathan Gould and David Pozen, "Structural Biases in Structural Constitutional Law," *New York University Law Review* (forthcoming at time of writing; available at https://papers.ssrn.com/sol3/papers.cfm ?abstract_id=3797051); and *McCulloch v. Maryland*, 17 U.S. 316 (1819).

9. I am well aware that this procedure would not do well with the current Supreme Court. Democratic movements have often had to overcome judicial resistance. Treating this as an insurmountable barrier would mean giving up at the start. See Akhil Reed Amar, "The Consent of the Governed: Constitutional Amendment Outside Article V," *Columbia Law Review*, vol. 94, 1994, pp. 457–508, on the case for an inherent democratic right to amend the constitution; and Sanford Levinson, *Our Undemocratic Constitution: Where the Constitution Goes Wrong (And How We the People Can Correct It)* (New York: Oxford University Press, 2006), pp. 171–177.

10. See Jesse Wegman, *Let the People Pick the President: The Case for Abolishing the Electoral College* (New York: St. Martin's Press, 2020), on making the case for legislative revision to award the majority of electoral college votes to the winner of the national popular vote; Jeremy Waldron, "Five to Four: Why Do Bare Majorities Rule on Courts," *Yale Law Journal*, vol. 123, no. 6, April 2014, pp. 1692–1730, on the cogency of supermajority requirements in judicial voting; Jed Handelsman Shugerman, "A Six-Three Rule: Reviving Consensus and Deference on the Supreme Court, *Georgia Law Review*, vol. 37, 2003, p. 893, on legislative strategies for judicial supermajority requirements; and Jonathan Gould, Kenneth Shepsle, and Matthew Stephenson, "Democratizing the Senate from Within," Harvard Public Law Working Paper No. 21-11, March 25, 2021, on ways to make the Senate more representative through adjustments to Senate voting rules (available at https://papers.ssrn.com/sol3/papers .cfm?abstract_id=3812526).

11. Simplification might also reduce the appetite for simplified myths, from goldbuggery to Bitcoin fetishism—displaced expressions of the desire to understand the world and to help shape it. On the structure and psychology of conspiracy theories, see David Singh Grewal, "Conspiracy Theories in a Networked World," *Critical Review*, vol. 28, no. 1, 2016, pp. 24–43.

12. See Quinn Slobodian, *The Globalists: The End of Empire and the Birth of Neoliberalism* (Cambridge, MA: Harvard University Press, 2018): "The foundational neoliberal insight is . . . that the market does not and cannot take care of itself" (p. 2). Market-led global economic governance was "a set of proposals to defend the world economy from a democracy that became global only in the twentieth century" (p. 4). This is a task of "statecraft and law" (p. 11) whose founders, such as Wilhelm Ropke, believed that "to diminish national sovereignty is most emphatically one

of the urgent needs of our time" (p. 11). The overall goal is "not a partial but a complete insulation of private capital rights" via "institutions of multitiered governance that are insulated from democratic decision making" (p. 12).

13. Roland Bénabou and Jean Tirole, "Belief in a Just World and Redistributive Politics," *Quarterly Journal of Economics*, vol. 121, no. 2, May 2006, 699–746.

14. Raj Chetty et al., "Mobility Report Cards: The Role of Colleges in International Mobility," National Bureau of Economic Research working paper, 2017 (available at https://www.nber.org/papers/w23618). For incisive discussions of meritocracy's distortions, which have influenced my discussion here, see Michael J. Sandel, *The Tryanny of Merit: What's Become of the Common Good?* (New York: Farrar, Straus and Giroux, 2020); and Daniel Markovits, *The Meritocracy Trap: How America's Foundational Myth Feeds Inequality, Dismantles the Middle Class, and Devours the Elite* (New York: Penguin, 2019).

15. See Kim Parker, "The Growing Partisan Divide in Views of Higher Education," Pew Research Center, Aug. 19, 2019 (available at https://www.pewresearch.org/social-trends/2019/08/19/the-growing -partisan-divide-in-views-of-higher-education-2/).

16. Jan-Werner Müller makes this observation about the Trump administration's appointees in *Democracy Rules* (Princeton, NJ: Princeton University Press, 2021), a book bristling with perceptive comments on the state of democracy.

17. Walt Whitman, "Song of Myself," in *Selected Poems*, ed. Justin Kaplan (New York: Library of America, 1996), p. 188.

18. See Martha C. Nussbaum, "Patriotism and Cosmopolitanism," *Boston Review*, Oct. 1, 1994 (available at https://bostonreview.net/martha -nussbaum-patriotism-and-cosmopolitanism); and George Kateb, "Patriotism and Other Mistakes," in *Patriotism and Other Mistakes* (New Haven: Yale University Press, 2006).

19. Martin Luther King Jr., "Beyond Vietnam—A Time to Break Silence," speech, Riverside Church, New York City, April 4, 1967.

20. Du Bois, *Black Reconstruction*, pp. 205 (The fight for antiracist enfranchisement and radical Reconstruction of the South that followed the Civil War "was a test of the nation's real belief in democratic institutions. And the fact that the ideal of abolition-democracy carried the nation as far it did in the matter of Negro suffrage must always be a source of intense gratification for those who believe in humanity and justice"); 264 (praising abolitionist congressman Thaddeus Stevens's unyielding support for "democracy, both in politics and in industry" and his pronouncement that "this is not a white man's government. . . . To say so is political blasphemy, for it violates the fundamental principles of

our gospel of liberty. This is Man's Government, the Government of all men alike"). See also Du Bois, "The Reconstruction of Freedom," in ed. Andrew G. Paschal, *A W. E. B. Du Bois Reader* (New York: Collier, 1971).

21. John Stuart Mill, *On Liberty and Other Essays*, ed. John Gray (New York: Oxford University Press, 1991), pp. 493–494. The pair actually wrote the book in 1861, but like some of Mill's other most iconoclastic writing, it appeared very late in his life.

22. George Orwell, "England, Your England" (available at https://orwell.ru/library/essays/lion/english/e_eye).

23. Pauli Murray, *Proud Shoes: The Story of an American Family* (New York: Harper, 1956), p. 271 ("It is little wonder").

24. Murray, *Proud Shoes*, pp. 275–276.

25. Wendell Berry, "The Unsettling of America," in *Essays*, vol. 1 (New York: Library of America, 2019), p. 232.

26. Samuel P. Huntington, *Political Order in Changing Societies* (New Haven, CT: Yale University Press, 1968), p. 262.

27. Langston Hughes, "In Explanation of Our Times," in *Selected Poems* (New York: Knopf, 1959), pp. 281–283, 282.

28. Walt Whitman, "Song of Myself," in *Selected Poems*, ed. Justin Kaplan (New York: Library of America, 1996), pp. 188 ("every atom"); 211 ("the sign of democracy"; "I will accept nothing"); 215 ("quivering me"). The final line alludes to Alfred Tennyson's 1842 poem "Ulysses": "Come, my friends/'Tis not too late to seek a newer world."

INDEX

the people *(continued)*
  See also popular sovereignty;
    rule of the people; sovereign
    people
personal freedom, 50–51,
  239–241
Philadelphia convention, 74–77
pin factory of Adam Smith,
  128–130
platform economy, 162–163
platforms (political), 195
Plato, 66–67
plurality, in democracy, 16
political democracy, 228–231, 236
political economy, 125, 167–168
political history
  and capitalism, 29–30
  democracy in twenty-first
    century, 41–42
  and government, 29–31
  politics as words, 33–37, 38, 40
  and politics in Hobbes's ideas,
    44–49
  and politics of force in the
    United States, 31–33
  and post-1989 world, 27–29
political institutions, colonization
  by capitalism, 161–166
political nihilism, 11–12, 13, 31,
  32–33, 42
political order, 46, 49, 51, 54–55,
  57
political parties
  and power, 197–198
  purpose and loyalty to, 194–196
  and questions, 193–194, 197,
    199
  in recent years (2016–2021),
    196–197, 198
  and voters, 194–199
politics (generally)
  and class, 24

and collective choices, 44–45
creations of, 217–218
demands on, 9
and democracy, 22, 44–45,
  48–49, 50, 220
and freedom, 50–51
and groups, 218–219
as ineffectual, 2–3, 5, 7, 11, 13
inevitability and life without,
  13, 22
and law, 50–52
and markets, 119–120, 128,
  135–136, 138–139, 141–143,
  152–157, 160–161, 165–166
as modern idea, 43–44, 45–47,
  55–56
need for, 55–56
and norms, 109, 114–118,
  216–217
in post-1989 world, 29
power in, 166, 168–169
and problems to solve, 9–11
role in democratic crises, 14–15
selfishness in, 33
and sovereignty, 52–54, 58
understandings of, 15
as words and talk, 33–37, 38, 40
politics in the United States
and capitalism, 159–161,
  166–167
consensus in, 104–105, 106,
  108, 109, 110
and democracy, 104–107, 109
distancing from and skepticism
  towards, 18–19
Hobbes and Rousseau on, 55
money and donations, 158, 161
new system needed, 225–226
norms in, 32
and politics of force, 31–33
and rich's influence, 159–161
types of people in, 203–204

JEDEDIAH PURDY teaches at Duke Law School and is a noted scholar of environmental, property, and constitutional law. His work has appeared in the *Atlantic*, the *New York Times*, and the *New Yorker*, among other outlets, and he is on the editorial board of *Dissent*. He lives with his family in North Carolina.